Learning under Neoliberalism

Higher Education in Critical Perspective: Practices and Policies

Series editors:
Susan Wright, Aarhus University
Penny Welch, Wolverhampton University

Around the globe, universities are being reformed to supply two crucial ingredients of a purported 'global knowledge economy': research and graduates. Higher education's aims, concepts, structures and practices are all in process of change. This series provides in-depth analyses of these changes and how those involved – managers, academics and students - are experimenting with critical pedagogies, reflecting upon the best organization of their own institutions, and engaging with public policy debates about higher education in the 21st Century.

Volume 1
Learning under Neoliberalism:
Ethnographies of Governance in Higher Education
Edited by Susan Brin Hyatt, Boone W. Shear and Susan Wright

Volume 2
Creating A New Public University and Reviving Democracy:
Action Research in Higher Education
Morten Levin and Davydd J. Greenwood

Volume 3
Death of the Public University?
Uncertain Futures for Higher Education in the Knowledge Economy
Edited by Susan Wright and Cris Shore

Learning under Neoliberalism

Ethnographies of Governance in Higher Education

◆ ◆ ◆

Edited by

Susan Brin Hyatt, Boone W. Shear and Susan Wright

berghahn

NEW YORK · OXFORD

www.berghahnbooks.com

First edition published in 2015 by

Berghahn Books

www.berghahnbooks.com

©2015, 2017 Susan Brin Hyatt, Boone W. Shear and Susan Wright
First paperback edition published in 2017

Library of Congress Cataloging-in-Publication Data

Learning under neoliberalism : ethnographies of governance in higher
education / edited by Susan Brin Hyatt, Boone W. Shear and Susan Wright.
    pages cm
    Includes bibliographical references and index.
    ISBN 978-1-78238-595-0 (hardback : alk. paper) — ISBN 978-1-78533-
    526-6 paperback — ISBN 978-1-78238-596-7 (ebook)
    1. Higher education and state—Cross-cultural studies. 2. Education,
Higher—Administration—Cross-cultural studies. 3. Universities and colleges—
Administration—Cross-cultural studies. 4. Educational anthropology.
5. Ethnology. 6. Neoliberalism. I. Shear, Boone W. II. Hyatt, Susan Brin,
1953– III. Wright, Susan, 1951–
    LC171.L43 2015
    378.1'01—dc23

                                                                2014029579

British Library Cataloguing in Publication Data

A catalogue record for this book is available from the British Library

ISBN: 978-1-78238-595-0 hardback
ISBN 978-1-78533-526-6 paperback
ISBN: 978-1-78238-596-7 ebook

Contents

◆◆◆

Acknowledgements

We are grateful to all of the contributors to this volume. Davydd Green-wood, in addition to providing our Afterword, reviewed the manuscript at several stages of its development and provided excellent feedback and suggestions. Sue Wright was our constant champion, encouraging our efforts and moving us forward. The Reading Together group, in which Art Keene played a critical role, at the University of Massachu-setts was, in many respects, the impetus for this project. Penny Welch, co-editor of LATISS, and the staff at Berghahn Books put up with delays and were consistently helpful and supportive. Boone wishes to thank his daughter Rose for being such a great kid.

Introduction: higher education, engaged anthropology and hegemonic struggle

BOONE W. SHEAR AND SUSAN BRIN HYATT

◆◆◆

Higher education in the global knowledge economy

On 22 August 2013, President Obama announced a new plan to further reform higher education in the United States (Obama 2013). Speaking from the campus of the State University of New York Buffalo, Obama set the stage for his intervention. He acknowledged some of the on-going social inequalities and hardships facing individuals and families, and decried the exorbitant costs of higher education that are leading to 'crushing' amounts of student debt and are pricing some students out of higher education altogether. As a solution to economic suffering and precariousness, Obama promised to increase access to higher education, make higher education more affordable, and ensure that student debt would be curbed and made more manageable. Obama was resolute, stating that, 'higher education is still the best ticket to upward mobility in America, and if we don't do something about keeping it within reach, it will create problems for economic mobility for generations to come' (Obama 2013).

As a way to safeguard this Shibboleth of education as a pathway to the American Dream, Obama charged Secretary of Education Arne Duncan – the architect of the Obama administration's education reform efforts that have further marketised primary and secondary education in the U.S.A. (Lipman 2011) – with the task of 'lead[ing] an effort to develop a new rating system for America's college's before the 2015 college year' (Obama 2013).[1] As Obama explained, colleges would need to be rated through 'metrics like, how much debt does the average student leave with? How easy is it to pay off? How many students graduate on time? How well do those graduates do in the workforce? Because the answers will help parents and students figure out how much value a college truly offers' (Obama 2013).

These new metrics, along with the ability of universities to engage in cost-saving innovations, would then presumably be used to rate schools so that student-consumers could make the best-informed, rational choices based on the instrumental, economic *value* of education offered by each institution. To further facilitate this transformation, these metrics would then be used to 'change how we allocate federal aid for colleges'. In sum, Obama laid out a framework that would further codify on-going processes of marketisation and surveillance at the university, bringing the heterogeneous and unruly U.S.A. higher education terrain into closer alignment with the more consolidated and centralised higher education systems of other OECD nations.

As we write this introduction, Obama's plans have yet to take final shape, let alone be implemented, but of particular importance, for us, is the ideological context from which these policy proposals emerge. For Obama, education reform is necessary for individual economic success because of a broader discursive framework shaping education and economic policy today, where 'greater and greater global competition in a knowledge-based economy' is understood as a key fact of our current lives. In a global knowledge economy, nations, regions and municipalities are positioned in direct competition with each other; economic success at every scale is dependent on the ability to commodify and own knowledge as well as on the availability of skilled workers who can both create products for and provide services to knowledge-based corporations.

This neoliberal fantasy of unbridled market competition via the marketisation of knowledge provides the ideological terrain from which much of the education reform efforts in the past few decades have emerged. As the chapters in this volume show, universities both bear the marks of neoliberal restructuring and are enlisted into participating in further restructurings through discursive and material transformations that are reshaping institutional objectives, influencing the nature of academic practice, and instilling new beliefs, affects and desires in students, faculty and administrators. It is precisely these dynamics – these implications of the university, its people and its practices in broader economic and cultural transformations – that we are interested in here.

The origin of this volume can be traced to a collaborative project in the Anthropology Department at the University of Massachusetts Amherst in 2007–2008. For the better part of two years faculty, graduate students and undergraduates met together to investigate, discuss and attempt to respond to the changing conditions at the university from which we research and write; learn and teach; and accommodate, reform and resist (see Shear and Zontine this volume). One of the outcomes of this project was a symposium that produced earlier versions of four of the chapters in this volume, all of which were originally published in *Learning and Teaching: The International Journal of Higher Education in the Social Sciences* (LATISS) along with John Clarke's chapter examining the modernization of U.K. universities. (The chapters by Hyatt, Lyon-Callo, Shear and Zontine and Clarke appeared in the 2010 (vol, 3, no. 3) special issue of LATISS and that by Davis in 2011 (vol. 4, no. 1). A pair of chapters previously published in LATISS, one by Cris Shore (2010 vol. 3, no. 1) and another by Susan Wright and Jakob Williams Ørberg in 2008 (vol. 1, no. 1), investigating university reforms in New Zealand and in Denmark respectively, further strengthen the comparative aspects of this volume. All of these chapters have been revised and updated. Finally, Davydd Greenwood takes measure of the authors' work in the Afterword and points a way forward through collaborative, participatory research. Greenwood, whose own writing on education and action research (see, for example, Greenwood 2002; 2007a; 2007b) has helped to inspire much of the work in this volume, also provided critical and helpful feedback on all of the chapters.

In this introduction, we aim to situate the university as an important location of hegemonic struggle. In reflecting on the dilemmas and challenges we have faced in each of our own university settings, we illustrate how universities – and the people who teach, learn and work at universities – are thoroughly implicated and embroiled in processes of economic and cultural production. We briefly describe the contours and manifold impacts of neoliberal restructuring of the university in relation to the broader political scene. Universities – as institutions that are often presented as vehicles to produce people, knowledge and products for social well-being and coherence – offer an unusually rich and important location for critical investigation and for the politicisation of cultural production.

We then argue that ethnography, with its emphasis on lived experience, can be a particularly effective tool with which to explore both the local manifestations of broader processes as well as to uncover areas of slippage, discontinuity and surprise between the global and the local, between structure and agency and between theory and practice. We use several examples to illustrate how ethnographic research and engaged teaching can uncover and mobilize the unexpected insights found in the interstitial spaces connecting people and cultural processes. We describe how each of the chapters in this volume relies on the use of ethnographic methods including participant-observation, qualitative interviews and reflexive analysis to help us think through how academic practices, working conditions and university objectives are structured through changing conditions that can be linked to dominant class interests. We suggest that by calling attention to and revealing the workings of these agendas – as well as by investigating the beliefs, desires and practices of those attempting to negotiate and respond to these same agendas, including students, faculty, administrators and other community members – we can become better equipped to understand and resist the conditions that we are in. Such reflexive analysis is essential if academics and students are to imagine new possibilities, institutions and practices and are to work for potential transformations, most particularly through engaged learning and teaching.

Some brief notes on neoliberalism

Before we proceed further, allow us to take a brief detour to consider the theoretical and political entanglements of our titular frame, *Learning Under Neoliberalism: Ethnographies of Governance in Higher Education*. Given the ubiquity of neoliberalism as a conceptual frame and signifier, as well as the increasing number of critiques of neoliberalism's textual ubiquity, we feel obliged to discuss how we understand and are treating neoliberalism in relation to the chapters in this volume.

As Ferguson (2010), Clarke (2008) and others have suggested, browsing through the scholarly literature might lead one to the conclusion that neoliberalism is everywhere, an agenda that is saturating our lives in myriad ways. Appearing at once as heterogeneous in its manifestations yet coherent as a project, neoliberalism can operate as a sort of master signifier that gathers together a motley mix of social processes and deleterious conditions in the social field; it purports to explain inequality, poverty and oppression in relation to historical change, social and economic restructuring, global economic and cultural flows, contemporary governance and policies associated with privatisation, marketisation and the withdrawal of the state from particular social welfare provisioning. All this can be accounted for and contained within a neoliberal imaginary. As Elyachar (2012: 76) succinctly put it, 'referring to neoliberalism has become a shorthand way for signalling all that is wrong in the ethnographic present'. Though sometimes conceptually and politically useful, an imagined coherence can also work to stunt theoretical investigation into the nature of neoliberalism(s), as well as leave little room for manoeuvre away from neoliberalism's reach (Elyachar 2012; Ferguson 2010; Gibson-Graham 1996).

In its everywhere taken-for-granted-ness, neoliberalism works to conceal as much as it reveals about the world (Clarke 2008). Scholars have been attempting to move away from analyses that present neoliberalism as a taken-for-granted and coherent worldview and have instead identified and mobilized multiple neoliberalism(s) using more conceptual precision and complexity. In fact, one of the contributions of this volume is to show how ethnography serves to highlight the ways in which similar constellations of ideas – not least about university reform – find very different expressions and outcomes in different national settings. Adopting a historical approach, some scholars argue that neoliberalism should be understood as processual and always unfolding (Canaan 2013), or as transitioning from one incarnation and context into new assemblages (Hyatt 2011). Others argue that neoliberalism is necessarily always in a hybrid form (Clarke 2008), is assembled differently in different locations (Ong 2006; 2007), and both constitutes and is constituted by local conditions, contingent encounters and social movements (Bockman 2012; Goldstein 2012).

Like the scholars above we, too, reject any notion of neoliberalism as an entirely coherent, cohesive project. We agree with Clarke (2008), Kingfisher and Maskovsky (2008) and others that it is precisely in the specificity of particular cultural arrangements and assemblages that we can find interesting contradictions, spaces where neoliberalism's reach might be averted and possibilities for new logics, practices and worlds to emerge.

This recent theoretical challenge to a presupposed neoliberal hegemony – and concomitant attention to heterogeneity and contingency – is indicative of a rapidly changing political and cultural terrain in which ethnographic work is taking place. On-going economic crises and deepening inequalities, dissolution of the Washington Consensus, social movements and protests in the Middle East, Occupy, Idle No More, 38 degrees, uprisings in Turkey, Chile and Brazil have reshaped public discourse, policy and politics and have created openings for both conservative retrenchment and radical change. Thatcher's statement that There Is No Alternative is no longer axiomatic. Though some states have turned to progressive and even radical reforms,[2] more have doubled-down on the logics of marketisation and privatisation associated with neoliberal restructuring, joining these processes with populist rhetoric and authoritarian measures to impose austerity and protect the interests of the elite. At the same time, visions and practices for new worlds – what we might describe as a 'politics of possibility' (Shear 2014; Cornwell 2011; Escobar 2004; Fórum Social Mundial; Gibson-Graham

2008b; Gibson, Cameron and Healy 2013; Holbrook 2013; Miller 2011; Molina 2013; Quinones Jr. et al. 2009) – appears to be spreading at the community and local levels, suffusing grassroots politics, and in some cases connecting across political contexts through social and informational networks.

As anthropologists study with communities and social movements, and study up (Nader 1969) and study 'through' (Shore and Wright 1997) and struggle against power (Lyon-Callo and Hyatt 2003; Greenwood 2007b; Shear and Lyon-Callo 2013), theoretical approaches and political commitments are forged anew; they are recast through negotiated relationships with research subjects/collaborators whose own interests, hopes and desires are themselves resituated by and responding to a changing cultural-political terrain. At a certain level then, the divergent theoretical understandings of and approaches involving 'neoliberalism' – or any other political framework – might be understood as *moral* commitments and *strategic* choices to emphasize particular problems and sets of relations that might produce particular epistemological and political effects. Indeed, we understand knowledge production – what scholars and students say and think, write and teach – not only to reflect reality (a necessarily partial and situated view of reality) but also to construct and constitute it (Burke and Shear 2014; Clifford and Marcus 1986; Gibson-Graham 2008a).

A central aim of this volume is to explore ethnographically how the practices of engaged scholars and teachers are being constrained, produced and reconfigured in relation to new discourses and rationalities associated with neoliberal governance – processes like marketisation, privatisation, responsibilising individuals, auditing and accountability, and entrepreneurialism – as well as how teaching about these transformations might create possibilities for new interventions. If, as engaged scholars, we intend our research, writing and teaching to produce possibilities for a more democratic, socially just, egalitarian future, we must remain vigilant; we must remain aware of and on guard against the processes that push and pull our identities and desires. We need investigations that can help us reflect on how our own practices as engaged scholars are being constrained and configured in relation to broader cultural-economic forces, in order to be able to locate possibilities for effective agency and intervention.

Our adherence to the moniker and concept of neoliberal governance, can be considered in part a strategic choice for two interrelated reasons. First, we find it important to draw attention to the relationship between global-capital, international and state policies, and university transformations – and most especially to those transformations that encourage or coerce individuals to invest themselves in university restructurings and reforms. We are interested, as are all of the scholars whose chapters appear in this volume, in investigating the way in which the university's practices and relevant social actors are recast by discourses that work to shape and manage the 'conduct of conduct' (Lemke 2001: 191 citing Foucault). Second, we wish to position the chapters in this volume in a shared political-theoretical space while at the same time providing enough room for each of the authors to be able to make their own commitments in relation to the different ways that they understand, experience, and care about the impacts of neoliberal restructuring at the university. Thus, we find it less important to define neoliberalism succinctly and more important to position 'neoliberalism' as a relatively open signifier that can help us think about governance and social reproduction across scale and space. We are not making the claim that neoliberalism is all that there is or that the term neoliberalism can adequately capture and explain all of the problematic transformations at the university. Rather, we are suggesting that in order to see these different cases through a comparative lens, deploying the notion of neoliberalism is a useful trope that allows us to situate individual instances in a larger context.

In a recent commentary, Maskovsky (2012) reminds us that the various crises at the university are not solely a product of neoliberalism; as he notes, new forms of right-wing populism, including the Tea Party movement in the U.S.A., have impelled the adoption of austerity measures that outflank an earlier era of neoliberal reforms. Like Maskovsky's example, the chapters in this volume examine the discursive articulations of neoliberalism with other forms of governance, power and oppression. As Shear and Zontine illustrate in their chapter, attributing too much explanatory power to any particular 'strong theory' can work to prescribe outcomes in advance and lead to political despair and/ or disengagement (and see Gibson-Graham 2006). We are, however, beginning from the position that neoliberal processes are powerfully reshaping university life across national contexts in myriad, problematic ways, and are implicating universities and the people in them in capitalist relations of production and interrelated forms of oppression.

Universities and social reproduction

Of course, universities have never been unencumbered by broad cultural-economic processes. Characterizing universities and academic life-gone-by as either spaces of free inquiry on the one hand, or as hotbeds of radical indoctrination on the other elides the always deep integration and entanglements of university practice with society writ-large. Certainly, one purpose of formal education in industrial societies has always been to produce people and products necessary for exploitation and economic growth (Barrow 1990; Bowles and Gintis 1976); this means producing workers with the requisite technical skills and also producing people who accept or invest themselves in the given social order (Althusser 1971; Sotiris 2013). Academics, students, and the teaching and learning that they do, are necessarily located in a compromised space, shaped in part by elite interests working through the state (Gramsci 2003; Shear 2008).

In short, the restructuring of universities today is not altogether novel and universities are always changing in relation to broader political-economic and cultural transformation (Rabo and Wright 2010). Nevertheless scholars, students, workers and activists are making the claim that contemporary restructuring is inordinately severe and profound, encompassing changes to university goals, governing structures, labour conditions, pedagogy, and curricula. These changes are not occurring evenly within and between nation states, but are structured through capital imperatives, international policies, differentially situated discursive regimes and local conditions − including historical differences in university systems − as well as in relation to the agency of administrators, academics, and students who negotiate, transform, and resist individually, collectively, and as part of broader social movements.

Outlining university reforms

Over the past few decades, university reform has been driven from two seemingly incongruous but in fact mutually reinforcing directions. First, higher education has been caught up in the broader neoliberal trend of privatisation. This trend has several dimensions found in various constellations in different countries. In some countries higher education, like other public services, has been *devalued* as a public good (exceptions include Denmark and Norway where higher education for domestic students is still free). Where social well-being has come to be understood, not as the obligation of government, but as the responsibility of individuals and the domain of the private sector, the percentage of public spending on higher education has generally decreased. Decreasing public funding has prompted universities in many locations to restructure internal budgets and seek out new sources of revenue, especially from international and domestic students and their families. Tuition and fees have skyrocketed in many locations, further structuring racialised class exclusions and generating a staggering amount of student debt. For example, in the U.S.A. student loan debt is now the largest form of unsecured debt, surpassing credit cards and auto loans (de Rugy 2013). Revenue from students is also extracted in the form of surplus value through poorly paid and unpaid labour. Student labour is interwoven into the university's hyper-exploitative growth industry – part-time and contingent labour (Bousquet 2008). In the United States, for example, non-tenured and non-tenure track instructors now account for about 75 per cent of college teachers. The American Association of University Professors has provided a graphic representation showing changing percentages of contingent labour in higher-education teaching over the past few decades in the United States (Curtis 2013).

Another identified area of potential revenue has been the private sector, itself. Industry-university partnerships, what Shore and McLauchlan (2012) researching in New Zealand identify as 'third stream' activities, are enacted through a variety of different arrangements including commercialization, technology transfer, corporate investment and public-private partnerships. Again the existence of business and corporate interests at the university is nothing novel, but both the sheer number of relationships as well as the degree of intimacy and shared intention is certainly worth noting (Washburn 2005).

> What is new is the extent to which university-business linkages have become *institutionalized* through the direct involvement of the universities themselves [Etkowitz 2003; Laredo 2007] in what appears to be conscious strategies to translate university knowledge into revenue through leasing academic and technological resources to business [Shore and McLaughlin 2012: 267].

For-profit higher education is posing both a challenge and an opportunity to more traditional higher education structures. In the United States for example, for-profit universities offering degrees through flexible, on-line programs have exploded in numbers (Lee 2012). At the same time, in response, pubic and non-profit private universities are also adopting on-line, profit models as increasingly important new sources of revenue. Public, not-for-profit and private enterprises are becoming intertwined in new and complex ways (as Davis shows in her chapter in this volume).[3]

The second direction of change is that even while universities have restructured in relation to public disinvestment and concomitant privatisation logics, the professed importance and *value* of higher education to the health and welfare of both the individual and society has never been greater. As Wright explains (2014: 297–298), the discursive production of the global knowledge economy has upped the stakes of higher education for individual, social, and national prosperity. As she writes

> ... through the 1990s [the work of the Organization for Economic Co-operation and Development (OECD)] promoted the idea that the future lay in a global economy operating on a new resource – 'knowledge'. This idea was taken up by other transnational organizations like the European Union (EU), the World Economic Forum (WEF), and the World Bank (WB). They argued that a future global knowledge economy was both inevitable and fast approaching. Each country's economic survival, they maintained, lay in its ability to generate a highly skilled workforce capable of developing new knowledge and transferring it quickly into innovative products and new ways of organising production. The OECD in particular developed policy guidance for its members (the thirty richest countries in the world) to make the reforms deemed necessary to survive this global competition. It measured and ranked their performance and galvanized national ministers into an emotionally charged competition for success and avoidance of the ignominy of failure. Universities were thrust centre stage in this vision of the future. They were to 'drive' their country's efforts to succeed in the global knowledge economy.

In the imaginary of the global knowledge economy, 'knowledge is treated as a raw material' (Rabo and Wright 2010: 2 citing Slaughter and Rhoades 2004: 17) for 'mining' and 'refining' (Rabo and Wright 2010). Indeed, the catchphrase of the Danish reforms was 'From idea to invoice': the reforms introduced tighter methods of steering and governing universities, so that they could be trusted with greater state investment, to produce ideas which could be harvested by the private sector and converted into innovative products. Thus, universities have come to be understood as primary sites for economic production itself, engines of economic growth that power the economy by creating knowledge-products for private sector growth as well as providing workers who have the abilities to succeed within and help grow private industry.

Internally, universities have restructured to more closely resemble for-profit corporations in structure and practices. In contrast to the decline in percentage of tenure-track faculty, the ranks of administrators and their salaries swelled. In the U.S.A. for example, 'employment of administrators jumped 60 per cent from 1993–2009, 10 times the growth rate for tenured faculty' (Hechinger 2012). Relations between administrators and faculty have become more hierarchical and university governance has become more centralized, leading to new identities and identifications *within* the university. As Shore (2010: 26) notes, [administrators] 'now claim to *be* the University, and relegate staff, alumni, and students to the role of "stakeholders"'.

Along with new administrative relations have come new managerial techniques intended to facilitate more revenue generation, commercialisation, rationalisation and standardisation of academic practices in line with university objectives. These include performance evaluations, point systems, and other accountability measures that have created new institutional forms and individual behaviours (Brenneis 2009; Canaan 2008; Strathern 2000; Wright 2012; Wright 2014). Indeed, these components of what Shore and Wright (1999; 2000) describe as audit culture can be understood precisely as technologies of governance that encourage individuals to understand themselves and act in new ways, in accordance with new university objectives.

While audit culture disciplines and reconfigures subjects inside the university, universities are implored to externalise the outcomes of internal audits through ranking systems (as well as through other forms of 'reputation management') (Wright 2012) in order to compete for prestige, corporate partnerships, government support, and in order to attract students. A growing, global market for students – particularly for students who can pay the full costs of tuition and fees – and the importance of higher education to national success more generally, has become a central plank in economic development initiatives in both the global north and global south. Universities in 'developed' countries are extending their reach across borders through international campuses and as part of global universities and regional development hubs (Looser 2012; Ross 2009). As Naidoo (2008) suggests the commodification of higher education is likely to continue to reproduce hierarchies and stratifications between nation states. 'Developing' nations who are enticed and pressured to participate in knowledge economy development are at a distinct disadvantage and can be positioned as high volume, profit-making sites and 'markets for mass dumping of low-quality knowledge' (Naidoo 2008: 94) for higher education enterprises in the global north.

Subject making, negotiation, resistance

Despite the engaged and critical approaches that as anthropologists and other academics we bring to our own research, it is sometimes difficult for us to gain a perspective on the ways that we, too, are enrolled in and produced through cultural processes in our own lives. Indeed, it is both fascinating and disheartening to see the ease with which some of our colleagues – both as individuals, and at the departmental level – have been brought into new relationships, assemblages, and strategies for capital accumulation by accepting, accommodating and sometimes eagerly embracing new initiatives and adopting concomitant subject positions of student consumers, academic entrepreneurs and revenue generators, and in general, increasingly calculating and competitive, individual rational actors in relation to teaching, publications, research opportunities, and so on.

Of course, complicity and participation in problematic processes cannot be fully accounted for by a lack of awareness of these changes. We do not mean to suggest that what is required here is simply a process of 'waking up' through consciousness-raising. Indeed, we find ourselves being pushed, pulled, and reshaped in conflicting ways, even as we engage in activist research, critical pedagogy, and collective struggles. It is important to keep in mind that identities and desires are not singular but are contradictory and complex. And subject formation is not always a clean, concatenated process, but takes place along multiple psychic registers. As Clarke, and Shear and Zontine, discuss in their chapters in this volume, we must be aware not only of new information produced through critical investigations. We must also be attuned to the complex, emotional and affective processes that are experienced and embodied through our lived experience, what Williams (1977) called the 'structures of feeling' that shape and delimit our political horizons.

We do not claim here that ethnographic investigation and critical, engaged teaching is a 'solution' to the problems associated with higher education reform, let alone neoliberal restructuring. We do want to suggest, however, that critical and reflexive investigation can be understood as a process of recognizing ourselves as cultural-political subjects, and exploring the ways in which we are caught up in 'webs of meaning' and relations of power of our own re-making. With this recognition, comes the possibility for transformation through engaging in new practices of thinking, teaching, and learning.

The profound impacts of neoliberal restructurings at the university, then, offer a particular moment of opportunity for teaching and learning. The ascension of the knowledge economy as discourse and performative practice has, perhaps, thrown universities – and the people in them – more fully into the centre of political struggle. This new configuration is reflected in the way in which recent student protests and movements

have been influenced by and helped to constitute broader social movements (Helepololei 2013; Juris 2012; Neary 2012; Schwartz-Weinstein
2013; Wilson 2012). The incorporation of students (and academics) into
these movements can be an important pedagogical process; students
can begin to recognize their own interests not as singular antagonisms,
but as connected in complex, contradictory ways with those of other
oppressed, exploited, and disaffected groups, communities and populations across space.

At the same time, we see teaching and learning at the university
itself as a space of radical possibility. The classroom is an opportunity
to help us – as teachers, students and workers – realise ourselves as
political subjects through theoretical investigation and discussion, but
also through projects that forge collaborative relationships and alliances
with community organizations and social movements. If, indeed, the
university has become a more integral, more central site of social and
economic and social reproduction, then learning and teaching about
these conditions opens onto a horizon in which faculty and students
can more clearly realize their everyday practices as part of a broader,
hegemonic struggle.

Ethnographising neoliberalism at the university

In the chapters that follow, the authors bring their particular understandings of neoliberalism to bear on their examinations of different
instantiations of neoliberal ideology, policies, and practices in a range
of national and academic settings. Four of the chapters are set in the
U.S.A. and three are from Denmark, New Zealand and the United Kingdom. Despite the differing national contexts, there are important conti-
nuities among the case studies represented here.

One of the themes that extends across the chapters is that of central-
isation. All of the chapters address the ways in which national policies
are severely limiting the autonomy of academic institutions. In some
respects, the U.S.A. has been the setting that has been most resistant
to centralised systems of oversight because of its size and complex in-
terweaving of private and public forms of funding and governance (see
Hyatt 2004: 25). Yet, political currents in the U.S.A. have also moved
towards an emphasis on greater standardisation. While the U.K. has
long had a National Curriculum that all schools have had to adhere to,
for example, in the U.S.A. 45 out of 50 states have only recently agreed
to adopt the so-called Common Core, which emphasizes language and
math skills.

At the post-secondary level, many of the private, elite institutions of higher learning in the U.S.A. have remained relatively insulated from many of the changes discussed by the contributors to this volume. It is perhaps telling that all of the U.S.A.-based authors – Hyatt, Lyon-Callo, Shear and Zontine, and Davis – are located in public universities; public sector institutions have experienced particularly significant economic disinvestment and have become targets for political scrutiny compared to private colleges and universities. For example, in 2011, the governor of Florida, Rick Scott, announced that Florida did not need any more anthropologists and that public resources would be better directed away from the social sciences and humanities and towards the STEM disciplines – Science, Technology, Engineering and Math – which he claimed would produce graduates better prepared for the current job market and which would also be more likely to generate economic development.[4]

Countries with more centralised management of education, like the U.K., Denmark and New Zealand, have long been subject to national policies that mandate how students and faculty are evaluated; the outcomes of these 'exercises' are tied to funding allocated by their central governments. In a desperate quest for new sources of revenue, universities in many countries are now seeking out private philanthropists as benefactors. British novelist Malcolm Bradbury, in his 1987 satirical novel *Cuts*, lampoons the unexpected consequences of this frantic pursuit. As a consequence of the draconian austerity measures being enacted by then Prime Minister Margaret Thatcher, Bradbury portrays a beleaguered university that ends up with professors bearing ironic and humorous honorifics like the 'Durex Chair of French Letters', Durex being the name of a British condom or 'French letter' manufacturer.

More seriously, Brian McKenna (2009) has addressed the ways in which corporate interests that fund higher education also acquire the power to suppress intellectual inquiry and debate. McKenna describes how public campuses in the state of Michigan, and even one private college also located in Michigan, have become beholden to Dow Chemical, a corporation headquartered in that state and known internationally for its disastrous impact on the environment and on people's health. McKenna (2009) documents several cases in which research that incriminated Dow in serious incidents of dioxin contamination was either censored or ignored.

The search for additional revenues has also led universities to recruit large numbers of overseas students who often come from elite families and who can afford to pay the full costs of tuition and fees. As Shore notes in his chapter in this volume, 'Catering for the overseas student market, which in 2006 numbered over 90,000 students, contributed an estimated $2 billion to New Zealand's economy in 2005'. This phenomenon is also apparent in other universities in Europe as well as in North America. While international students often are a great asset to campus life, their value for governments and administrators is that they are able to foot hefty bills for the cost of their courses. Concerns about overseas students' language proficiency in university-level classrooms have also necessitated the creation of entirely new tiers of language classes which, on many campuses, constitute yet another growing revenue stream.

These endeavours can, of course, also backfire. Shore (this volume) also describes how the Chinese press carried several stories portraying the quality of English language teaching in New Zealand as insufficient, thereby prompting several high-ranking government ministers and university administrators to undertake an emergency mission to China to try to repair this damage. As universities now see themselves as institutions that are global, rather than national, competition for international students has intensified. A new tack in this crusade has been for universities to open branches in distant places that glitter with the promise of affluent consumers, who are seeking the cultural capital of a degree from a prestigious western university without having to leave home. In this regard, the wealthy Gulf States have been particularly attractive destinations (Abi-Esper 2012).

New York University (NYU), an elite private institution undergoing a fluorescence of popularity at the moment, has been one of the most vigorous actors on that front and in 2010, NYU established 'NYU Abu Dhabi'. On one of its web pages, which promotes its identity as 'The Global Network University', its offerings are described as follows:

> No university has a greater global presence. NYU leads all universities in students studying abroad; over 40 percent of our undergraduates now study abroad, and each year the number increases. In September 2010, NYU opened NYU Abu Dhabi, an audacious step in higher education: the first comprehensive liberal arts and science campus to be operated abroad by a major American research university, offering a complete NYU education to undergraduates outside of New York City and from around the world and creating another 'portal campus' to gain access to this dynamic, global network university.[5]

Controversies around such issues as hiring practices and academic freedom in settings like the Gulf States (and China) have been neatly side-stepped, as universities engage in a new kind of neo-colonial undertaking, refashioning themselves as truly global institutions that are bringing Western educational values and experiences to waiting postulants in far-away places. As Shore (this volume) writes:

> What we see in New Zealand in thus a reflection of a more global process in which the traditional *idea* (or meaning) of the university is shifting: from being primarily an instrument of nation-building and the cultural reproduction of a certain notion of 'national culture' and 'education for citizenship', New Zealand universities are increasingly being conceived of as transnational corporations competing in the global market for the provision of commercial educational services (emphasis as in the original).

Whether this provisioning is taking place on the campus of the home university or through creating satellite campuses and programmes elsewhere, Shore has identified how internationalization is profoundly altering the priorities of academic institutions.

Western and OECD universities are also attracting investments from other countries, some of which come with clandestine agendas and expectations. As McKenna (2009: 41) writes, 'It is not just corporate donors ... that can constrain free inquiry, but for some universities, it is foreign governments'. A growing concern in many places is the proliferation of Confucius Institutes, Chinese language and culture centres entirely funded by the Chinese government and hosted by universities outside of China. Institutions that elect to become sites for Confucius Institutes do not have any purview over the curriculum or hiring of Institute instructors (Simcox 2009). Recently, the Canadian Association of University Teachers called on Canadian Universities to close Confucius Institutes based on claims of restrictions on what topics could be addressed in these classes as well as concerns about hiring practices (Ghoreishi 2014). In November 2013, McMaster University in Hamilton, Ontario announced its decision to close its Confucius Institute based on the fact that the Chinese government forbad Confucius Institute employees from participating in the Fulan Gong movement (Bradshaw and Freeze 2013).

Of course, these examples are not intended to suggest that universities were not also vulnerable to such ideological meddling prior to the neoliberal era. Indeed, during the Cold War years, many universities became sites for research that bolstered capitalist models for development and disparaged 'communist' or socialist alternatives. Rather, it is to call attention to the ways in which new conceptualisations of the role of universities in the world have also created new opportunities for the suppression of particular political perspectives.

As we have stated earlier in this introduction, we acknowledge the multiple contradictions associated with the notion of 'neoliberalism'. That one of the chapters, authored by Wright and Ørberg, needed substantial revision between the time of its initial publication (2008) and the present in order to account for changes in Danish Higher Education that they were unable to foresee illustrates the point that we are dealing with a shape-shifting and somewhat slippery phenomenon. We hope that in this introduction and in all of the chapters that follow, we have embodied the insight offered by Shore in his chapter, in which he writes: '... I argue that the new model of the entrepreneurial and corporate university has not so much *replaced* the traditional functions and meaning of the university as *added* a new layer of complexity to the university's already diverse and multifaceted roles in society' (emphasis as in the original). In his contribution to this volume, Shore meticulously periodises and analyses the chronology of changes in New Zealand's universities since the 1980s. He illustrates the fact that neoliberal ideas stretch across the political spectrum, noting that in the 1980s, it was a Labour government that initiated the first wave of neoliberal reforms. These changes were then carried forward and intensified by far more conservative governments in the 1990s. The trends that Shore identifies in his examination of higher education in New Zealand – the conscious internationalisation of the student body and concomitant marketing of New Zealand universities; the emergence of a more authoritarian regime of governance in universities; and the range of market-driven reforms that were instituted – all find echoes in the other case studies.

In their chapter on Denmark, Wright and Ørberg offer a vivid illustration of one of the ironies of neoliberal ideology and practice: that is, although the most ardent proponents of neoliberal policies claim to be promoting greater opportunities for 'freedom' and 'choice', the state has never been a more intrusive presence in the lives of its citizens than it is now (Hyatt 2004: 26). Wright and Ørberg describe the paradoxical ways in which efforts on the part of the Danish government to make universities more autonomous and 'self-owning' have actually resulted in a far more invasive and authoritarian systems of governance through emphasizing the notion that universities must be income-generating and open to a range of interested parties, including government, that are glossed as 'stakeholders' (a point also made by Shore). But, like Shore, Wright and Ørberg also leave the door open to concede that there are possibilities for resistance and refusal. As they write, 'We find a clear model for government steering of universities. But no rationality is ever completely coherent or closed; we also find other elements which confuse the model and point to possible ways that university leaders and academics may find room for manoeuvre'.

John Clarke illustrates the concrete effects of modernization and managerialism in British universities, presenting interrelated material, discursive, and affective transformations. Clarke describes higher education as a governable system, configured through logics and practices of competition. These logics provide direction to university operations and academic practice, which can then be more easily managed and assessed in relation to external, strategic objectives. Like Shore, and Wright and Ørberg, Clarke also looks for the fissures and contradictions in people's responses to these changes that might open up a space for, as he puts it, 'alternative ways of making communities'. Of particular importance here is Clarke's attention to how academics collectively understand and experience university restructuring as a loss of an imagined, romanticized academic community. This irreconcilable loss, Clarke suggests, results in a 'collective professional melancholia' which hinders effective political response to university restructuring, Like the other contributors, Clarke's analysis is also clearly rooted in the messiness of the everyday and commonplace, and he also sees in this messiness possibilities for resistance and for shaping a future that moves beyond a simple nostalgia for an unrealistically romanticised past.

All of the chapters in this collection were written by authors who reflect on the ways that academics and students are variously implicated in the machinations, changes, resistances and accommodations that we discuss. Clarke describes his chapter as 'a sort of participant ethnography, reflecting the experience of working in, and talking about the higher education sector in the U.K.'. Shore refers to 'personal observations' to denote the epistemological stance from which he derives much of his data. Shear and Zontine's analysis is, in part, a reflection of their own engaged research project. Lyon-Callo scrutinizes his own teaching and community engagement in relation to education reform and, Davis calls her chapter a form of autoethnography. As she notes, 'an autoethnographic approach can provide valuable insights into the tensions between the neoliberal environment and being an academic in such a setting'. Hyatt describes the outcome and insights garnered from an ethnographic methods course she taught. Thus, we see ourselves very much as located within the landscapes we describe, not outside of them.

In her chapter, Davis provides three examples that illustrate how neoliberal ideas have penetrated the public institution in which she taught. She provides a trenchant analysis of the ways in which the use of numerical measures to assess student achievement and establish standards for admission, while claiming to be 'objective', actually mask the ways in which such measures reinforce the privilege of some students at the expense of others. The claim that this is a meritocratic process serves the larger agenda of many institutions, which seek to raise their rankings based on these measures in order to attract a wealthier, more middle-class and often whiter student body as a way of boosting their national prestige and desirability (a theme also touched on by Hyatt). Davis' second example illustrates the fallacies inherent in neoliberalism's much-touted notion of the 'public-private partnership' by showing how her public institution became a host for an evening business degree program operated by an elite private institution whose main campus was located in another part of the city. That programme and its resources, however, were never made accessible for the full-time students at the public institution. As Davis puts it: 'The message that the students received was that they could partake in the *aspirations* of neoliberalism: they could hope to be admitted to the private university and might even envision themselves being business majors; but there was no provision for *accessibility* to the programme' (emphasis as in the original).

Most important, perhaps, and in ways echoed by Shear and Zontine in their chapter, Davis vividly illustrates how processes of measurement, accountability and access to funding streams are all used as ways to tamp down – or deflect entirely – possibilities for activist responses. She shows how many aspects of neoliberalism have given way to – or at least shaded into – far more authoritarian mechanisms of rule that foster self-policing through the use of fear as a tactic.

Like Clarke, Shear and Zontine suggest that simply critiquing and revealing the workings and impacts of deleterious processes may not always lead to political mobilization, and they urge us to pay attention to the relationship between discourse and affect. Shear and Zontine were PhD students in the Department of Anthropology at the University of Massachusetts when they wrote their original article. They reflect on a departmental reading group intended to investigate and respond to changing conditions at the university. They explore the ways in which the group's impulses towards activist responses were tempered by the enormity of the challenges they faced in trying to imagine 'undoing' neoliberal reforms at the university. 'The more we understood and em-

phasized our understandings of neoliberalism and university corporatisation, the harder it was to bring to mind realistic responses.' Shear
and Zontine find a way forward by drawing from Gibson-Graham's
mobilization of 'weak theory'. This is a way of avoiding the totalising
and often politically disabling effects of such 'strong' concepts as 'capitalism' and 'neoliberalism' by seeing the world as instead inherently
unstable and rife with contingencies and possibilities. 'By exploring
the unknown, rather than extending and exploring the known ... weak
theory can be strong politics – it opens up social options that would
be inaccessible to a theorist intent on eliminating surprise' (Gibson-
Graham 2006: 205n15; as cited by Shear and Zontine, this volume).

This emphasis on the role that global economic processes play in
contouring American public education is taken up by Vincent Lyon-
Callo in his discussion of how parents of primary and secondary school
pupils and university students alike imagine their future in the global
economy as bound up with the need to emphasize individual achievement over collective action. Lyon-Callo's work draws on his own participation in these debates in his home state of Michigan, a state with
an economy that has been decimated by the collapse of the U.S.A. car
industry. Lyon-Callo shows how in reaction to a newly urgent sense
of economic insecurity, parents and college students consistently embraced strategies that re-inscribed the values of competition and consumerism despite a lack of evidence that these tactics would effectively
counter the negative impacts of economic restructuring. He explains
how this reaction 'made sense' to the very same people who had been
most disadvantaged by economic restructuring. He argues for a kind of
dialogic teaching and ethnographic practice as a route towards fostering
alternative understandings among community members and university
students.

Lastly, Hyatt considers the implications of the changing role that
universities, particularly those located in cities, have come to play as
engines for local economic development. Hyatt arrived at many of her
insights through an ethnographic methods class she taught in 2003, in
which students carried out research projects in the primarily African-
American neighbourhood surrounding Temple University's main campus, located in North Central Philadelphia. Hyatt describes how her
students' engagement with local residents allowed them to see how
Temple's adoption of strategies for re-making and marketing the campus and its adjacent community in order to attract new constituencies
of upscale, predominantly white and middle-class students, affected the
local long-term resident population.

The resulting gentrification, a key feature of neoliberal economic development, threatened to accelerate long-term trends that had systematically displaced African-American community members. In the course of their project, the students and their professor discovered that actions taken by the university itself had helped to produce the very symptoms of decline that their new redevelopment projects purported to remedy. This circumstance is hardly unique; as we write this introduction, there is a dispute brewing in New York City between NYU and its neighbours in the adjacent community of Greenwich Village over the university's plans to construct four new high-rises. These plans have just been put on hold following a New York Supreme Court decision that the parcels of land the university planned to use were actually public parks (Anuta 2014).⁶

Taken together, the chapters in this volume present a rather grim picture of academic life in the late 20th and early 21st centuries. And yet, it is our intent to offer them as hopeful rather than pessimistic. As we show, our engagement with teaching critical thinking makes our classrooms into places where students begin to understand how their lives are imbricated in larger political movements and where social change can begin 'in place'. All of the chapters point to inconsistencies, cracks, contradictions, and possibilities in the various expressions of neoliberalisms that can be exploited in various ways and where the future is far from being a *fait accompli*.

One of the critical strategies for intervention and change, which the authors in this volume advocate, is to use our teaching as a site where we can encourage students, colleagues, and ourselves to examine how they and their communities are implicated in the larger processes we wish to understand and critique. Hyatt's class not only developed an understanding of how neoliberal models for economic development were affecting the residential community located in proximity to Temple's campus; they also engaged in a collective activist response. In addition to their ethnographic projects, students were required to submit shortened versions of their research written for a general audience. At the end of the course, one of the students, working with Hyatt and the CEO of the Community Development Corporation with which the class had partnered assembled the class research papers into a tabloid newspaper. The Community Development Corporation was able to raise sufficient funds to print 10,000 copies of the student-authored newspaper, so that every household within the study area received a free copy. The newspaper provoked debate and discussion within the community, and provided an alternative portrait of the neighbourhood, representing it as a heterogeneous site with a long-standing history of community activism, thereby countering the image of inexorable decline that the city and the university too often deployed as part of their redevelopment agendas. Although there was no follow-up action after the newspaper was published and distributed (and Hyatt left the university shortly thereafter) local residents at least felt vindicated that their voices were heard. One of the challenges of activism in academia is, of course, the short time frame of semesters or academic years, which constrain possibilities for sustained political action. As Greenwood (2007b: 251) writes, we need to explore further 'how to make AR [Action Research] an available teaching and research strategy that is both sustainable as a pedagogical activity and that engages universities in internal organizational change processes...'

Davis and Lyon-Callo also address strategies they use to encourage students to examine the ways in which their own lives and aspirations are compromised by the very same policies that have destroyed local economies in their communities. Lyon-Callo stresses the point that, though his students often reject the possibilities for collective action as a strategy for changing or resisting these policies, they begin reflecting on the fact that the shifts they have witnessed in their own lives were not inevitable or pre-ordained; they were the result of policy decisions, taken at specific moments in time by actors who can be identified. Lyon-Callo describes an exercise he did in which students were asked to interview four people they knew whose lives had been affected by the economic downturn in Michigan. Students then used this data to generate proposals for collaborative projects that could potentially be undertaken in cooperation with community members and local organisations. As Lyon-Callo notes, 'Producing proposals in this one class did not in itself transform the local community but it did begin to transform how the students thought of both anthropology and the possibilities of collective actions'. In a similar vein, Davis describes teaching strategies in which she used the contradictions facing the viability of a Global Black Studies programme at her university as a 'teachable moment'. She used a number of the documents related to the controversy as class readings and had students situate the local conflict within a much broader plane of political imperatives. Davis also describes how her students in another class engaged in semester-long ethnographic studies of how 'neoliberal policy and ideology were translated in a particular space. Students documented such manifestations as community surveillance of the burgeoning immigrant population and the shift from a manufacturing to a service economy that kept certain residents in perpetually low-wage jobs'.

Whereas Davis, Hyatt and Lyon-Callo show important pedagogical possibilities in the classroom, Shear and Zontine suggest that alternative modes of learning and teaching among students and faculty – even something as seemingly innocuous as a departmental reading group – can cut through the discursive dominance of neoliberal capitalism, 'indeed, the group's social practices and academic work were done collectively and without regard for – and in defiance of – productivity markers, intellectual property, and entrepreneurial investment.' These new practices can offer a different set of subjective conditions from which to think and act in the world.

It used to be that academic settings stood in stark contradistinction to other kinds of 20th century workplaces. The classic image of files of undifferentiated workers, entering drone-like through the portals of their workplaces, first stopping to punch their timecards in a desultory fashion and then submitting to the indignities of surveillance by their supervisors and managers, was once the quintessential – if stereotypical – view of life on the factory shop floor. Those of us who worked in more professional settings were exempt from this kind of oversight.

Now, though we would be foolish to underestimate the privileges still accorded to those academics who enjoy secure employment (a shrinking percentage, admittedly), nevertheless many aspects of our lives are becoming more like the lives of the old industrial working class – more insecure, more closely surveilled, more highly disciplined – just at the same moment that the industrial working class is disappearing from our contemporary economic landscapes. The ways in which these chapters point us towards new possibilities for political action is a vision that is intended to spur us into thinking more creatively about the new kinds of alliances we might need to forge in order to counter the oppressive trends of the present moment, not only within universities but in society more broadly. Such tactics will surely involve us making common cause with other constituencies outside of academia, constituencies – like undocumented immigrants, women on state benefits, and the unemployed, to name just a few examples – who have been far more bruised and battered by the depredations of neoliberalism and its curious doppelganger, the law-and-order state, than we have been. Indeed, organizers, activists, community groups, and social movements have much to teach us about effective forms of resistance, cultural struggle and ways of imagining and enacting new social and economic worlds.

It remains for all of us to take up the challenge of working both inside and outside of academia to create visions for new political possibilities that reach beyond the limits and constraints that the audit culture and the new managerialism have set for us, beyond the symbolic and material constraints of capitalist production, authoritarianism, and multiple forms of oppression. This collection is a modest nod in that direction.

Notes

1. See Lipman 2004 and Johnson 2008 for excellent ethnographic works investigating neoliberal restructuring and primary/secondary education in the United States.
2. See, for example, Iceland's response to corporate finance capital http://leaksource.wordpress.com/2013/03/10/icelands-revolution-against-globalist-banksters/, or Bolivia's recently policy towards abandoned factories and worker cooperatives, http://www.socialistproject.ca/bullet/888.php, as two of many examples.
3. A department chair of a social science program at a major public university reported to us that without the revenue generated from for-profit extended education programs, her department and possibly others at the university would simply collapse. She went on to explain how the possibility of new tenure-track faculty lines were becoming more dependent on whether or not a department was able to generate revenue through on-line courses of extended education.
4. While the American Anthropological Association issued a very tepid response to Governor Scott's pronouncements (http://www.aaanet.org/issues/policy-advocacy/upload/letter-to-gov-scott.pdf), the post-graduate students at the University of South Florida mounted a much more robust reaction (http://anthropology.usf.edu/thisisanthropology/).
5. 'The Global Network University', http://www.nyu.edu/global/the-global-network-university.html.
6. See also Gregory 2013 on Columbia University's plans to expand in another part of New York City and Etienne's 2012 account of the relationship between the University of Pennsylvania and its neighbours in West Philadelphia, to name some additional examples.

References

Abi-Esper, Nicole (2012) 'American Universities in the Gulf, *Arab American Institute,* < http://www.aaiusa.org/blog/entry/american-universities-in-the-gulf/ > (accessed 16 January 2014).
Anuta, Joe (2014) 'NYU Expansion hits bump', *Crain's New York Business,* 12 January, < http://www.crainsnewyork.com/article/20140112/REAL_ESTATE/301129979/nyu-expansion-hits-bump > (accessed 18 January 2014).
Althusser, Louis (1995) 'Ideology and Ideological State Apparatuses: Notes Towards an Investigation', *Lenin and Philosophy and Other Essays,* Monthly Review

Press, < http://www.marxists.org/reference/archive/althusser/1970/ideology .htm > (accessed 15 January 2014).

Barrow, Clyde W. (1990) *Universities and the Corporate State: Corporate Liberalism and the Reconstruction of Higher Education, 1894-1928*, Madison: University of Wisconsin Press.

Bockman, Johanna (2012) 'The Political Projects of Neoliberalism', *Social Anthropology/Anthropologie Sociale*, 20 (3): 310–317.

Bowles, Samuel and Gintis, Herbert (1976) *Schooling in Capitalist America: Education Reform and the Contradictions of Economic Life*, New York: Basic Books.

Bousquet, Marc (2008) *How the University Works: Higher Education and the Low Wage Nation*, New York: New York University Press.

Bradshaw, James and Freeze, Colin (2013) 'McMaster Closing Confucius Institute Over Hiring Issues', *Globe and Mail*, 7 February.

Brenneis, Don (2009) 'Anthropology in and of the Academy: Globalization, Assessment, and Our Field's Future', *Social Anthropology*, 17 (3): 261–275.

Burke, Brian and Shear, Boone (2014) 'Engaged Scholarship for Non-Capitalist Political Ecologies', *Journal of Political Ecology*, 21.

Canaan, Joyce E. (2008) 'A funny thing happened on the way to the (European Social) Forum: or how new forms of accountability are transforming academics' identities and possible responses', in Joyce E. Canaan and Wesley Shumar (eds), *Structure and Agency in the Neoliberal University*, New York: Routledge, 256–277.

Canaan, Joyce E. (2013) 'Resisting the English Neoliberalising University: What Critical Pedagogy Can Offer', *JCEPS: The Journal for Critical Education Policy Studies* 11(2): 16–56.

Clarke, John (2008) 'Living With/In and Without Neo-liberalism', *Focaal – European Journal of Anthropology*, 51: 135–147.

Clifford, James and Marcus, George (1986) *Writing Culture: The Poetics and Politics of Ethnography*, Berkeley: University of California Press.

Cornwell, Janelle (2011) 'Subjects of Scale/Spaces of Possibility: Producing Cooperative Space in Theory and Enterprise' Open Access Dissertations, Paper 436. Accessible at Scholarworks@UmassAmherst, < http://scholarworks.umass.edu/ etds/ >

Curtis, John W. (2013) 'Trends in Instructional Staff Employment Status, 1975-2011'. Washington, DC: AAUP Research Office, 20 March, < http://www.aaup .org/sites/default/files/files/AAUP_Report_InstrStaff-75-11_apr2013.pdf > (accessed 16 January 2014).

de Rugy, Veronique (2013) 'Student Loan Debt Increases by 281 percent over 10 Years. Mercatus Center George Mason University, < http://mercatus.org/publi cation/student-loan-debt-increases-281-percent--over-ten-years > (accessed 14 January 2014).

Elyachar, Julia (2012) 'Before (And After) Neoliberalism: Tacit Knowledge, Secrets of the Trade, and Public Sector in Egypt' *Cultural Anthropology*, 27 (1): 76–96.

Escobar, Arturo (2004) 'Beyond the Third World: Imperial Globality, Global Coloniality, and Anti-Globalization Social Movements' *Third World Quarterly*, 25 (10): 207–230.

Etienne, Harley F. (2012) *Pushing Back the Gates: Neighborhood Perspectives on University-Drive Revitalization in West Philadelphia*, Philadelphia: Temple University Press.

Etkowitz, H. (2003) 'Research Groups as "Quasi Firms": The Invention of the Entrepreneurial University', *Research Policy*, 32 (1): 109–121.

Ferguson, James (2010) 'The Uses of Neoliberalism', *Antipode* 41 (1): 166–184.

Fórum Social Mundial website, < http://www.forumsocialmundial.org.br/index.php > (accessed 8 January 2014).

Ghoreishi, Omid (2014) 'Canada's Association of University Teachers Calls on Universities to Close Confucius Institutes', *Epoch Times*, 1 January.

Gibson-Graham, J.K., Cameron, Jenny and Healy, Stephen (2013) *Take Back the Economy. An Ethical Guide for Transforming Our Communities*, Minneapolis: University of Minnesota Press.

Gibson-Graham, J.K. (1996) *The End of Capitalism (As We Knew It). A Feminist Critique of Political Economy*. Minneapolis: University of Minnesota Press.

Gibson-Graham, J.K. (2006) *A Postcapitalist Politics*, Minneapolis: University of Minnesota Press.

Gibson-Graham, J.K. (2008a) 'Diverse Economies: Performative Practices for Other Worlds', *Progress in Human Geography*, 32 (5): 613–632.

Gibson-Graham, J.K. (2008b) '"Place-Based Globalism": A New Imaginary of Revolution', *Rethinking Marxism*, 20 (4): 659–664.

Goldstein, Daniel (2012) 'Decolonizing "actually existing neoliberalism"', *Social Anthropology/Anthropologie Sociale*, 20 (3): 304–309.

Gramsci, Antonio (2003) 'The Intellectuals', In *Selections from the Prison Notebooks*, (trans.) Q. Hoare and G. Nowell Smith (eds), New York: International Publishers, 3–23.

Greenwood, Davydd J. (2002). 'Action Research: Unfilled Promises and Unmet Challenges', *Concepts and Transformations* 7(2): 117–139.

Greenwood, Davydd J. (2007a) 'Pragmatic Action Research', *International Journal of Action Research* 3(1 + 2): 131–148.

Greenwood, Davydd J. (2007b) 'Teaching/learning action research requires fundamental reforms in public higher education', *Action Research* 5(3): 249–264.

Gregory, Steven (2012) 'The Radiant University: Space, Redevelopment and the Public Good', *City and Society* 25(1): 47–69.

Hechinger, John (2012) 'The Troubling Dean-to-Professor Ratio', *Business Week*. 21 November, < http://www.businessweek.com/articles/2012-11-21/the-troubling-dean-to-professor-ratio > (accessed 15 January 2014).

Helepololei, Justin Allen Keoki (2013) 'Notes on a Common Insurrection: Violence and Transversal Solidarity in Occupied Barcelona', *Affinities*, 7(1): 48–67.

Holbrook, Robert Saleem (2013) The Jackson Plan: Lessons from Jackson, Mississippi, < http://sfbayview.com/2013/the-jackson-plan-lessons-from-jackson-mississippi/ > (accessed 30 January 2014).

Hyatt, Susan Brin (2004) 'Keeping the Bureaucratic Peace', *Anthropology Today* 20 (3): 25–27.

Hyatt, Susan Brin (2011) 'What was Neoliberalism and What Comes Next? The Transformation of Citizenship in the Law-and-Order State' in Cris Shore, Susan

Wright and Davide Pero (eds) *Policy Worlds: Anthropology and the Analysis of Contemporary Power.* Oxford: Berghahn Books, 105–124.

Johnson, Amanda Walker (2008) *Objectifying Measures: the Dominance of High-Stakes Testing and the Politics of Schooling,* Philadelphia: Temple University Press.

Juris, Jeffrey (2012) 'Reflections on #Occupy Everywhere: Social Media, Public Space, and Emerging Logics of Aggregation', *American Ethnologist,* 39 (2): 259–279.

Kingfisher, Catherine and Maskovsky, Jeff (2008) 'Introduction: The Limits of Neoliberalism', *Critique of Anthropology,* 28 (2): 115–126.

Laredo, P. (2007) 'Revisiting the Third Mission of Universities: Toward a Renewed Categorization of University Activities?', *Higher Education Policy,* 20 (4): 441–456.

Lee, Suevon (2012) 'For-Profit Higher Education: The Industry, By the Numbers' *Huffington Post,* < http://www.huffingtonpost.com/2012/08/09/for-profit-higher-education_1761369.html > (accessed 8 January 2014).

Lemke, Thomas (2001) 'The Birth of Bio-politics: Michel Foucault's Lecture at the College de France on Neo-liberal Governmentality' *Economy and Society,* 30 (2): 190–207.

Lipman, Pauline (2004) *High Stakes Education: Inequality, Globalization, and Urban School Reform,* New York: Routledge.

Lipman, Pauline (2011) 'Neoliberal Education Restructuring: Dangers and Opportunities in the Present Crisis', *Monthly Review,* 63 (3): 114–127, < http://monthlyreview.org/2011/07/01/neoliberal-education-restructuring > (accessed 7 July 2014).

Looser, Tom (2012) 'The Global University', *Cultural Anthropology,* 27 (1): 97–117.

Lyon-Callo, Vincent and Hyatt, Susan Brin (2003) 'The Neoliberal State and the Depoliticization of Poverty: Activist Anthropology and the "Ethnography From Below"', *Urban Anthropology and the Studies of Cultural Systems and World Economic Development,* 32 (2): 175–204.

Maskovsky, Jeff (2012) 'Beyond Neoliberalism: Academia and Activism in a Nonhegemonic Moment', *American Quarterly,* 64 (4): 819–822.

McKenna, Brian (2009) 'Dow Chemical's Knowledge Factories: Action Anthropology Against Michigan's Company Town Culture', *Anthropology in Action,* 16 (2): 39–50.

Miller, Ethan (2011) 'Occupy! Connect! Create! Imagining Life Beyond "The Economy"' in Amber Hickey (ed.) *A Guidebook of Alternative Nows,* Los Angeles: Journal of Aesthetics and Protest Press, 21–34.

Molina, Marta (2013) 'The Zapatista's First School Opens For Session. Waging Non-Violence: People-Powered News & Analysis' 12 August, < http://wagingnonviolence.org/feature/the-zapatistas-first-escuelita-for-freedom-begins-today/ > (accessed 8 January 2014).

Nader, Laura (1969) 'Up the Anthropologist: Perspectives Gained from Studying Up', in Del Hymes (ed.) *Reinventing Anthropology,* New York: Random House, 284–311.

Naidoo, Rajani (2008) 'Entrenching International Inequality: The Impact of Global Commodification of Higher Education on Developing Countries' in Joyce E.

Canaan and Wesley Shumar (eds) *Structure and Agency in the Neoliberal University*, New York: Routledge, 84–100.

Neary, Mike (2012) 'Teaching Politically: Policy, Pedagogy, and the New European University', < http://www.edu-factory.org/wp/teaching-politically/ > (accessed 8 January 2014).

Obama, Barack (2013) 'Remarks by the President on College Affordability – Buffalo, NY' Washington, DC: The White House, Office of the Press Secretary, 22 August, < http://www.whitehouse.gov/the-press-office/2013/08/22/remarks-president-college-affordability-buffalo-ny > (accessed 16 January 2014).

Ong, Aihwa (2006) *Neoliberalism as Exception: Mutations in Citizenship an Soveriegnty*. Durham, NC: Duke University Press.

Ong, Aihwa (2007) 'Neoliberalism as a Mobile Technology', *Transactions of the Institute of British Geographers.* 32 (1): 3–8.

Quinones Jr., Benjamin, Fretel, Alfonso Cotera, Poirier, Yvon, Kawano, Emily, Johnson, Pierre and Delille, Tara (2009) 'A Non-Patriarchal Economy is Possible: Looking at Solidarity Economy from Different Cultural Facets' in Marcus Arruda (ed.) *Alliance for a Responsible, Plural, and Solidarity-based Economy (ALOE)*, Rio de Janeiro: Workgroup: 'Visions of a Responsible, Plural, Solidarity-Based Economy', < http://aloe.socioeco.org/IMG/pdf/Non-patriarchal_economy_is_possible.pdf > (accessed 17 January 2014).

Ross, Andrew (2009) 'The Rise of the Global University', in Andres Ross (ed.) *Nice Work If You Can Get It: Life and Labor in Precarious Times,* New York and London: New York University Press, 189–206.

Schwartz-Weinstein, Zach (2013) 'Not Your Academy: Occupation and the Futures of Student Struggles', in *Is This What Democracy Looks Like?* Social Text Collective, < http://socialtextjournal.org/periscope_article/is-this-what-democracy-looks-like/ > (accessed 8 January 2014).

Shear, Boone (2008) 'Gramsci, Intellectuals, and Academic Practice Today' *Rethinking Marxism*, 20 (1): 53–65.

Shear, Boone (2014) 'Making the Green Economy: Politics, Desire and Economic Possibility', *Journal of Political Ecology,* 21: 193–209.

Shear, Boone and Lyon-Callo, Vin (2013) 'Kalamazoo's Promise: Exploring the Violence of Economic Development', *City and Society,* 25 (1): 70–91.

Shore, Cris (2010) 'Beyond the Multiversity: Neoliberalism and the Rise of the Schizophrenic University', *Social Anthropology/Anthropology Sociale*, 18 (1): 15–29.

Shore, Cris and McLauchlan, Laura (2012) '"Third Mission" Activities, Commercialisation and Academic Entrepreneurs', *Social Anthropology*, 20 (3): 267–286.

Shore, Cris and Wright, Susan (1997) 'Policy: A New Field of Anthropology,' in Cris Shore and Susan Wright, (eds.) *Anthropology of Policy: Critical Perspectives on Governance and Power,* London and New York: Routledge.

Shore, Cris and Wright, Susan (1999) 'Audit culture and Anthropology: neo-liberalism in British higher education', *Journal of the Royal Anthropological Institute,* 5 (4): 557–575.

Shore, Cris and Wright, Susan (2000) 'Coercive Accountability: The Rise of Audit Culture in Higher Education' in Marilyn Strathern (ed.) *Audit Cultures.*

Anthropological Studies in Accountability, Ethics, and the Academy, London: Routledge.

Simcox, Robin (2009) 'Funding with Strings Attached', *The Guardian*, 31 March, < http://www.theguardian.com/commentisfree/2009/mar/31/university-funding-china-iran > (accessed 18 January 2014).

Slaughter, Sheila and Rhoades, Gary (2004) *Academic Capitalism and the New Economy: Markets, State, and Higher Education*, Baltimore, MD: The John Hopkins University Press.

Sotiris, Panagiotis (2013) 'Higher Education and Class: Production or Reproduction?' *The Journal for Critical Education Policy Studies*, 11 (1): 95–143.

Strathern, Marilyn (ed.) (2000) *Audit Cultures. Anthropological Studies in Accountability, Ethics and the Academy*, London: Routledge.

Washburn, Jennifer (2005) *University Inc.: The Corporate Corruption of Higher Education*, New York: Basic Books.

Williams, Raymond (1977) *Marxism and Literature*, Oxford and New York: Oxford University Press.

Wilson, William Moss (2012) 'Just Don't Call Her Che', *New York Times*, 28 January, < http://www.nytimes.com/2012/01/29/opinion/sunday/student-protests-rile-chile.html?pagewanted = all&_r = 0 > (accessed 8 January 2014).

Wright, Susan (2012) 'Ranking Universities within a Globalised World of Competition States: to What Purpose, and with What Purpose for Students?' in Hanne Leth Andersen and Jens Christian Jacobsen (eds) *Quality in Higher Education in 21ˢᵗ Century*, Frederiksberg: Samfundslitteratur, 79–100.

Wright, Susan (2014) 'Knowledge that Counts: Points Systems and the Governance of Danish Universities' in Dorothy Smith and Allison Griffith (eds) *Under New Public Management: Institutional Ethnographies of Changing Front-line Work*, Toronto: University of Toronto Press.

Wright, Susan and Annika Rabo (2010) 'Introduction: Anthropologies of University Reform', *Social Anthropology/Anthropologie Sociale*, 18 (1): 1–14.

CHAPTER 1

'After neoliberalism'? The reform of New Zealand's university system

CRIS SHORE

◆◆◆

Introduction: neoliberalisation and the New Zealand experiment

The title of this chapter should be read either as irony or as a statement of extreme optimism[1]. If neoliberalism describes a phase of economic and social history then we are clearly not out of the woods yet, despite the claims of the former Labour Party leader and Prime Minister Helen Clark that the New Zealand era of neoliberalism is now over (Clark 2002: 463). In fact the word 'neoliberalism' is itself misleading and problematic as it tends to encourage an idea of something universalising and monolithic; a singular phase through which a great many advanced industrial nation-states have passed – or will soon be passing. Like Peck and Tickell (2002: 463) and Larner and Walters (2004) I prefer to use 'neoliberal' less as a noun than as a verb, i.e., 'to neoliberalise' or, to use the more passive tense, 'to be subject to' the discipline of neoliberal reforms. 'Neoliberalisation' generally refers to a multi-faceted and continually changing set of processes, which assume different forms in different countries. This is also the sense in which geographers like Peck and Tickell use the concept of 'neoliberalisation', to refer to a set of processes that may have lasting effects on the structure and organisation of the economy, systems of management, and the constitution of individuals as persons. It is by studying those effects in their minutiae that we can track the contours of much larger and more diffuse 'macro' processes of globalisation and capitalist modernity.

This chapter explores these themes in the context of the attempts by successive governments to reform New Zealand's university system since the 1980s. The reform of New Zealand's tertiary education sector provides an important site for studying the trajectory of those processes that we have come to associate with neoliberalisation. During the 1980s, New Zealand earned the dubious accolade of having been the prototype for the development of many of the free-market ideals and practices of neoliberalism. As John Gray has shown, the neo-liberal experiment in New Zealand was one of the most ambitious attempts at constructing the free market as a social institution to be implemented anywhere this century (Gray 1999). The model which became known as the 'New Zealand Experiment' was hailed by the World Bank, *The Economist*, and the Organisation for Economic Co-operation and Development (OECD) as an example for the rest of the world to follow (Kelsey 1997: 62). The radical restructuring of tertiary education during the 1980s was to make New Zealand 'arguably a paradigm case of neo-liberal governance' (Robertson and Dale 2002: 463). The government rushed to embrace the new neoliberal doctrines of 'New Institutional Economics', 'Public Choice Theory' and 'Agency Theory' with all the fervour of a convert. The curiously powerful and unprecedented influence of neoliberal theory stemmed largely from the New Zealand Treasury's drive to restructure the public-sector 'under the influence of a small group of 'new-breed' reformers noted for their sensitivity to market liberalism doctrine espoused by the Chicago School and by think-tank institutes such as the Centre for Independent Studies and Institute of Economic Affairs' (Althaus 1997: 138; see also Olssen 2002: 62; Olssen and Peters 2005). As historian Jamie Belich (2001: 412) wrote, the 'notorious shortage of checks and balances' in New Zealand's political system meant that what for the rest of the world was a 'fad', in New Zealand became a 'fetish'.

Somewhat perversely, New Zealand's neoliberal experiment was spearheaded by a radical Labour government during the early 1980s, but was carried forward after 1990 by a more conservative and traditionally interventionist National government. The 1980s Labour-led administration was the same government which, under David Lange, held fast to an anti-nuclear policy, a position that made New Zealand something of a pariah as far as the U.S.A. White House and Pentagon were concerned. Lange's powerful finance minister, Roger Douglas, became enchanted by the economic theories of the Chicago School. In New Zealand, Douglas's brand of monetarism became known as 'Rogernomics'. Like 'Thatcherism' in Britain and 'Reaganism' in the United States, this sought to 'roll back the frontiers of the state' through the deregulation of labour markets, the privatisation of state assets and a radical agenda of tight fiscal restraint. This inevitably resulted in the familiar pattern of rising unemployment, misery and privation in the traditionally more 'protected' sectors of the economy. However, most New Zealanders would probably agree that, the pain of restructuring and the insecurities of 'flexibilisation' notwithstanding, the reforms of the 1980s did open up the country's economy and society in some quite beneficial ways. Prior to the 1980s, as Belich (2001: 463) observes, New Zealand had been a somewhat homogenous, conformist, masculist, egalitarian, monocultural and colonial society subject to heavy formal and informal regulation, with a closed rural economy that was far too dependent on the U.K. market. By the end of the 1990s, the country had become, for better and for worse, one of the least regulated societies in the world, economically even more than socially.

New Zealand as a case–study

From a European regional or global perspective, New Zealand offers up a number of significant points for international comparison. First, like other comparable OECD states such as Denmark, Norway, Finland and Austria, New Zealand is a country with a relatively small population (4.4 million), but highly educated and with a high standard of living. In terms of its GDP, New Zealand stands roughly in the lower-middle half of OECD rankings per capita (i.e. it was positioned 20th out of the 30 OECD countries in 2006 and 21st in 2012). Second, New Zealand is a country with eight universities, two of which were former agricultural colleges and at least two of which aspire to be 'World Class' as defined by *The Times Higher Education Supplement* and *Shanghai Jiao Tong University* academic measures. Third, alongside these universities there are a number of other tertiary education institutes, private providers and government-funded 'Crown Research Institutes' financed from the public purse, all of which compete for funding with the universities.

New Zealand's traditional economic strength has been its farming and agriculture sector: the country boasts arguably the largest and the most efficient dairy industry in the world. This has long been the largest foreign export earner, although recently the dairy industry has been overtaken by tourism. What the government terms 'export education' has also become a significant earner (Ministry of Education 2006). Catering for the overseas student market, which in 2006 numbered over 90,000 students, contributed an estimated $2 billion to New Zealand's economy in 2005.[2] As Dr Michael Cullen, the former Labour Finance Minister (and Minister for Higher Education), pointed out,

> ... international education is our fourth largest export industry. It has a vital role to play in fostering linkages into the world and helping us to lift our own education and research standards. Attracting the

best is therefore a critical part of our economic transformation agenda (Cullen 2006a).

Much of this growth was due to Asian students, particularly from China, seeking professional qualifications from English speaking universities and lured to New Zealand by promises of what private-sector providers describe as a 'relaxing' but 'educative experience' in 'a pristine natural environment' (International Partners for Study Abroad 2006). This also helps explain why the New Zealand government has been such an enthusiastic advocate for the inclusion of 'higher educational services' in the various World Trade Organization talks. As one influential UNESCO briefing document on education and 'GATS' put it:

> Trade in higher education is a million dollar business. The demand for higher education, on the one side, is growing, while on the other side, trans-border education (e.g., private or for-profit higher foreign university campuses, IT Academies, twinning arrangements with other universities, corporate universities, virtual universities, open universities, e-universities etc.) is increasing. The capacity of the public sector has not kept up with this demand. This coupled with the recent developments of ICTs and the ensuing growth in online learning has resulted in the creation of this very lucrative market (UNESCO 2006).

Many of the neoliberal reforms of higher education currently underway in Europe and elsewhere (Brenneis, Shore and Wright 2005), have already been extensively trialled in New Zealand. These include, *inter alia*, the ending of government grants for students and the introduction of fees and student loans; a shift towards a 'user pays' philosophy of higher education and attempts to instil a more competitive ethos among university staff and students; and a much stronger emphasis on the commercial exploitation of academic research and on the development of closer ties between the universities and industry. The University of Auckland now boasts over 620 pending or granted patents and has created its own private company – 'UniServices' – whose mission is to promote the 'commercialisation of intellectual property' and to manage the University's growing number of private financial contracts. In 2003 alone UniServices filed 43 patents, a figure which it claims is equal to that of Cambridge and other leading European universities (UniServices 2003: 1). As its 2009 *Profile* proudly declares: 'We have 200 fields of patented technology, run 120 licensing deals and, as noted elsewhere in this profile, the market value of companies based on University technology is $850 million' (UniServices 2009: 10).

Other major neoliberalising innovations and competitiveness strategies include the reorganisation of the structure of university governance in accordance with corporate business models, the development of an 'exporting education' industry, the promotion of entrepreneurialism and the introduction of new calculative disciplinary practices through the use of auditing technologies, 'benchmarking' exercises, annual performance reviews, research assessment exercises and other calibrated measures of performance (Strathern 2000). This emphasis on economic competitiveness and free-market economics has also gone hand-in-hand with a new conception of the student as an economically rational responsibilised and self-interested subject (i.e. consumer and customer) for whom tertiary education represents a private investment rather than a public good or right.

What we see in New Zealand is thus a reflection of a more global process in which the traditional *idea* (or meaning) of the university is shifting: from being primarily an instrument of nation-building and the cultural reproduction of a certain notion of 'national culture' and 'education for citizenship', New Zealand universities are increasingly being conceived of as transnational corporations competing in the global market for the provision of commercial educational services. While these trends are hardly novel or surprising, their effects on the culture of academia and on evaluations of what counts as proper 'knowledge' merits closer attention. As Lyotard noted over a decade-and-a-half ago in his essay on *The Postmodern Condition:*

> The question (overt or implied) now asked by the professionalist student, the State, or institutions of higher education is no longer 'is it true'? but 'What use is it?' … This creates the prospect for a vast market for competence in operational skills (Lyotard 1994:51).

Of course, it is difficult for any 'reasonable' person to argue against the common-sense principle that knowledge ought to be 'useful', particularly when that knowledge production is funded by taxpayers. But the issue now is not so much 'useful for whom' so much as *how is academic 'usefulness' to be evaluated or defined* in a world increasingly driven by the logic of free markets and laissez-faire individualism?

Effects of neoliberalisation on tertiary education in New Zealand

Following the well-marked footsteps of Larner and Le Heron (2005), we can identify three distinct phases in the history of the neoliberalisation of New Zealand's universities. First, the period between 1984 and 1989 was marked by the state's rapid withdrawal from areas of production whilst still trying to maintain its traditional welfarist and social justice aspirations. Second, the period between 1989 and 1996 was a more aggressive and punitive phase in which marketisation was extended, but coupled with the development of neo-conservative and more authoritarian social programmes. The third phase (1997 to 2013) continued many of these earlier trends and was characterised by an emphasis on internationalisation, forging commercial partnerships and developing external links with industry and government. However, what complicates this heuristic schema is the fact that these different phases and their often contradictory agendas have not so much *replaced* or substituted one another, but rather, have been 'added on' to each other in a cumulative, sedimentary fashion. This layering of different policy agendas helps explain the complexity and highly textured nature of modern university life. In the following pages, I illustrate some of the more striking effects of this accumulation of competences and roles on institutional practices and everyday behaviour within New Zealand's universities.

Phase 1: 1984 – 1989

While much of industry and the state sector were being radically 'marketised', universities remained relatively untouched by these processes. The New Zealand Treasury's post-1987 'briefing' advocated the separation of university functions into three areas: teaching, research and more general functions. Teaching would henceforward be funded by a declining government subsidy and increased student fees, while research was to be financed by competitive tendering for state funds and private contracts. The university sector remained relatively un-differentiated. Although universities generally catered for their own region, it did not particularly matter which university a student attended – unless one wanted to study dentistry, medicine or engineering – because each university taught a full suite of arts and science courses, and most universities were not ranked or differentiated by research-ranking exercises or competitive league tables. Tertiary education continued to be understood as a 'public good' or service to be funded by the state, rather than an individual economic investment. This paradigm was about to be overturned, though, by the Hawke Report (1988) and the response to its recommendations in the government's subsequent 'White Paper' which laid the ground for a radical restructuring of tertiary education according to an explicit market model. Elsewhere too, the corporatisation of the public sector was underway and greatly increased the power of managers, accountants and auditors over more traditional notions of professional autonomy and reliance on sectoral expertise.

Phase 2: 1989 – 1996

As in Britain, the radical rethinking of tertiary education was foreshadowed by government-sponsored reports (most notably the 1988 Hawke Report). The 1989 Education Amendment Act and 1990 Public Finance Act marked the beginning of a period of quite profound transformation. Over the next decade, New Zealand's universities were to experience a variant of the commercialisation process that had reformed the rest of the state sector, with the introduction of new management practices of audits and benchmarking. Foremost among the developments during this period were:

1. The introduction of new competitive funding regimes, with a corresponding emphasis on expanding student numbers, and the adoption of Hawke's recommendation that universities should generate their own funds and become more commercial. This was accompanied by the introduction of a controversial student loan scheme and the adoption of the principle that the universities, rather than the government, should set student fee levels.
2. A shift in the role of the universities from 'elite' institutions to 'mass' educators. This 'massification' was driven partly by the new financial pressures, but it was also influenced by OECD reports that showed New Zealand's low position in the tertiary participation league table compared with other OECD members. Since the increase in student numbers was not matched by a corresponding increase in staff, the result was a rapid increase in teaching loads for staff.
3. A reorganisation of university governance and accountability. Councils were to become smaller bodies with reduced representation of 'internal stakeholders' (i.e. students and staff), responsible for appointing their 'chief executive officers' (or vice-chancellors) on fixed-term contracts. The new CEO/VC rather than Council would assume the role as legal employer for all statutory staff. Henceforth, accountability was to be of a contractual kind with 'more extensive use of charters, audit procedures and performance appraisals to regulate universities and to tighten controls' (Olssen 2002: 63–4). Hawke had also proposed abolishing the University Grants Committee which would have meant that the contract between universities and the state would

in future be directly with the Ministry of Education. That prospect generated such fear about the loss of institutional autonomy that two universities (Auckland and Canterbury) initiated legal proceedings against the government (Butterworth and Tarling 1994; Olssen 2002).

4. The shift towards 'EFTS-based funding' (i.e., government funding for all the universities' costs for teaching, research and overheads based on calculations of the number of their 'Equivalent Full-Time Students'). Universities would no longer be funded by five-year grants but according to the number of students they recruited, the rationale being that competition for students would necessarily improve efficiency. The universities responded by expanding provision, not only via new courses, but by setting up satellite campuses, strategic alliances, and various capital works projects.

5. This increasingly competitive, market-driven environment promoted the view of students not only as 'consumers' and 'customers', but as 'units of economic resource' for Departments and Faculties. This inevitably led to pressure on the universities to maximise recruitment by enlarging class sizes and introducing more popular programmes. Henceforward, a university's success and financial vigour was largely calculated in terms of retaining 'bums on seats'.

This period also witnessed the rise of quantitative indicators that would allow comparability across departments, faculties, universities and countries. There was a new emphasis on formal student evaluations, driven by concerns over quality and by demands from university managers. During the mid-1990s, a system of annual staff performance appraisals (or 'APRs') was introduced. There were also the beginnings of formal benchmarking of departments and formal workload calculation models. In short, the technologies of New Public Management became more diffuse and widespread. As Larner and Le Heron summed it up:

> Overall, what happened during this second period was the recoding of diverse elements of the university into calculable and comparative terms ... and the introduction of a new generation of indirect governing techniques (Larner and Le Heron 2005: 850).

Effects of Phase 2's new competitive regime: some ethnographic illustrations

The general effect of Phase 2's increasingly competitive environment on the identity, ethos and institutional self-understanding of New Zealand's universities can be summarised in four points.

Changes to professional relationships: Among academics, these tended to become more competitive and less cooperative. The new funding system fuelled fierce competition not only between universities but also between (and within) Faculties. Departments became more 'siloed and defensive' (Larner and Le Heron 2005: 850) as departments fought each other for control over courses. To give an example, as Head of the Anthropology Department I became involved in an unusual dispute with the Music Department during 2005–06. Internal university reorganisation a few years earlier had resulted in the transfer of Music out of the Arts Faculty and into a newly created National Institute for Artistic and Creative Industries (or 'NICAI'), whose new Dean had acquired a reputation for her tough managerial style and the numerous high-profile redundancies and sackings during her tenure. Previously, staff had taught across the Departments and shared 'EFTS' income. But relations inevitably became more competitive and strained when the Music Department was relocated into the new NICAI faculty. The Head of Music, recently recruited from Britain and under pressure to generate more teaching revenue, identified the highly popular (*ergo*, lucrative) 'Popular Music' (PopMus) course as an obvious cash-cow. However, for historical reasons including his Department's preference for classical music and performance-based classes, these courses had always been taught by ethnomusicologists from the Anthropology Department. Having failed to persuade the University authorities that these courses belonged to Music, he adopted an alternative approach, and tried to recruit the Anthropology staff member who taught the large Stage 1 'PopMus' courses, by offering fast-track promotion to a Senior Lectureship. As was subsequently pointed out to me, this 'poaching' was not only ill-advised and un-collegial, it was also technically 'illegal' insofar as it breached a number of University rules and standard employment practices. However, given the market model of Departmental funding it was also quite rational and understandable. The dispute eventually resulted in an agreement on the 'boundaries' (academic and territorial) between ethnomusicology and music proper, but not without involving detailed mediation between the Heads of Department, their respective Deans and the Pro-Vice-Chancellor for Academic Affairs.

The introduction of a new 'rationality of accountancy': Another effect of these changes was the introduction of greater 'cost-consciousness' into academia. Hitherto, Departments had had little control over their budgets as most items of expenditure (i.e., staff salaries and operational funds) were determined elsewhere. This is still largely the case in terms of salaries, but now Departments are expected to function as 'cost-centres' and manage their own 'discretionary' budgets and 'operational' funds. Heads of Department are regularly sent on training courses to learn about budgetary planning, handling temporary contracts and the importance of maintaining financial health by meeting the annual 'EFTs target'. Until the recent introduction of the research assessment model known as the Performance Based Research Fund (PBRF), all aspects of a department's income were based on the number of EFTs it attracted to its degree programmes and to each course. Thus each department is in competition for students with others in the same subject across the country and with cognate disciplines in the same university. As a result, strategic academic planning and staffing decisions have invariably been conducted in terms of a Department's economic opportunity costs and calculations of which areas of the teaching programme are likely to bring in the greatest 'EFTS' revenue. Departments that refuse to play this competitive game (or that play it poorly) either lose income from falling student revenue, or find themselves 'punished' by faculty managers (who ultimately control Departmental budgets) through the withholding of extra resources.

A new politics of audit and accountability: A key aspect of the reforms has been the widespread introduction of the principles and techniques of financial auditing into the governance of universities. These include 'benchmarking' and new systems for 'performance appraisal' that are designed to render all aspects of university work 'commensurable' (and thus numerically measurable) for the managerialist aim of producing competitive league-tables of 'excellence' (Brenneis, Shore and Wright 2005). Academics are increasingly required to specify and quantify their 'outputs' and 'learning outcomes' and what is increasingly a 'skills-based' model of knowledge. One effect of all this has been to create a new 'politics of performativity' within universities (Shore and Selwyn 1998). 'Productivity' is typically measured in terms of student numbers (i.e. the popularity of courses and the income each generates), although the introduction of the PBRF has added further 'performance indicators' so that research productivity and impact can now also be measured and ranked nationally and internationally (more on this below).

Greater internationalisation: New Zealand's universities, which had traditionally been orientated towards the United Kingdom, started to recruit staff and students from more diverse overseas sources. This period also saw the rise of new transnational university consortiums such as APRU (Asia-Pacific Rim Universities), the Australian 'G8' grouping of elite institutions and 'Universitas 21'. New Zealand's universities now habitually 'benchmark' themselves against the universities in these consortia – particularly those of Australia's 'G8'. The benchmarking mentality is used in contradictory ways by university managers (who typically stress the need for greater productivity) and staff (who see the data as evidence of chronic under-resourcing). For example, in 2005 the *Times Higher Education Supplement* (THES) ranked the University of Auckland 53rd among the world's leading universities. The following year Auckland had climbed to 48th position. University academics and managers were understandably pleased by this international recognition of their institution's standing and used these statistics repeatedly in their publicity and promotional literature. However, university managers seldom drew attention to statistical comparisons that challenge their policy priorities. For example, university managers' predilection for commercialisation of research and the higher-income earning faculties of Engineering, Medicine and Science meant that they have paid little attention to the much higher international status of Auckland University's Humanities and Social Sciences which were ranked 30th in the 2014 QS World University Rankings. At the same time, the complaint often voiced by academics is that New Zealand's universities receive only 60 per cent of the funding of their Australian counterparts, although this comparison was frequently used more as a boast than a lament.

Phase 3: 1996 – 2008

In the third phase, the earlier initiatives continued, but were complicated by an emphasis on 'partnering' and a new government narrative of the 'knowledge society' and 'global knowledge economy'. This brought with it a new institutional self-understanding, the core elements of which were evident in other OECD countries during the early 1990s (see Kelsey 1997; Larner and Le Heron 2005). Bill Readings, writing more than a decade ago, summed it up thus:

> The contemporary university is busily transforming itself from an ideological arm of the state into a bureaucratically organized and relatively autonomous consumer-oriented corporation. The sign of this transformation is the way in which appeals to the notion of 'excellence' drop from the lips of university administrators at every turn. To understand the contemporary university, we must ask what excellence means (or doesn't) (Readings 1996: 457).

While Readings's critique of the discourse of 'excellence' has undoubtedly stood the test of time, he was wrong to pose the 'consumer-oriented corporation' against the 'ideological arm of the state'. For New Zealand at least, these two agendas appear to have been successfully combined. Turning universities into 'consumer-oriented corporations' is exactly what the government-backed ideologies of commercialism and entrepreneurship have sought to achieve. According to the New Zealand Ministry of Education, universities are now expected to be prime movers in delivering the government's 'economic transformation agenda' (Tertiary Education Committee 2006). As former Treasury Minister Michael Cullen summed it up, the mission of university education would be to 'equip the country with the kind of 21st Century skills needed to drive economic transformation ... and provide a bridge between the world of learning and the world of work' (Cullen 2006b).

The defeat of the Labour-led government in 2008 and the election of a new administration led by National Party leader John Key brought an intensification of that policy, but with a far stronger emphasis on promoting science, technology, engineering and medicine (the so-called STEM subjects) and commercialisation of university knowledge. For New Zealand's Ministry of Education, tertiary education and research must play an increasingly central role in providing wealth, opportunity and employment, driving the economy and strengthening the country's status as a knowledge society. As the 2008 Tertiary Education Commission *Briefing* for the new government proclaimed:

> For New Zealand to participate effectively in the global environment, it needs to develop networks of world class firms, research institutions and tertiary education organizations that collaborate for the benefits of New Zealand's economic and social development (Tertiary Education Commission 2008).

Ministry of Education documents also continually stress the need to strengthen New Zealand's research performance and international linkages in order to promote 'the uptake overseas of New Zealand's educational intellectual property' (Ministry of Education 2007: 33).

Thus, after 1996 New Zealand's universities were increasingly positioned (and positioning themselves) as transnational commercial enterprises located in a competitive global knowledge economy. In this knowledge-economy narrative, 'universities are represented as a new agent of national development – a key means of fostering international competitiveness and social cohesion in a global and turbulent world' (Larner and Le Heron 2005: 852). Tertiary education institutions were thus encouraged to seek new 'partnerships', particularly with business and the private sector (but also with government agencies) because they were now continually under pressure to find new income streams. At the same time, they were increasingly shaped by the need to 'manage risk', but in a world where new kinds of risk have emerged that were previously unimaginable. We see this particularly in the way Heads of Department are advised to handle student complaints and 'problem staff' and in the increasingly prescriptive work of University Ethics Approval Committees. The University's primary concern in each of these areas has little to do with health and safety or teaching or research quality per se, but a great deal to do with insurance indemnity and avoiding legal liability. One of the most popular 'HoD Training Workshops' that is put on every year at the University of Auckland is aptly titled 'Avoiding Lawyers' Bills'.

For the university, a key area of 'risk' is in terms of the reputation of the institution and the impact that negative publicity can have on recruitment and market share. For example, in 2005 the Chinese press carried a number of stories about the poor quality of language tuition in some of New Zealand's private tertiary education institutions. The result was a dramatic decline the following year in the number of Chinese students coming to New Zealand. A high level delegation of ministers and vice-chancellors was subsequently dispatched to China to try and ameliorate the damage and restore the reputation of New Zealand's tertiary education sector.

What this means at the level of everyday life: some ethnographic illustrations

Let us turn briefly to consider some of the implications of these developments for students and academics.

Neoliberal spaces and the formation of new academic subjectivities

One of the most obvious consequences of the introduction of this market model into the New Zealand university system is that academics are being compelled to behave in more entrepreneurial, individualistic and competitive ways. Continuous surveillance and monitoring of individuals and their performance also has a profound effect on people's subjectivities and behaviour, as Foucault (1977) demonstrated in his study of 'panopticism' and the history of the modern prison. The introduction of competitive and often punitive teaching and research assessment exercises in the U.K. and elsewhere has also introduced forms of 'pan-opticism' into tertiary education (Shore and Roberts 1995; Perryman 2006). While these exercises are typically justified in the name of promoting 'transparency', 'accountability' and 'efficiency', they also work as disciplinary technologies and fuel what, to echo Beck (1997), can be termed a 'political economy of insecurity'. The internalisation of external norms of audit and control work to induce an ethic of self-discipline and 'continuous self-improvement', which, in turn, often leads to stress and burn-out. As with the spread of 'audit culture' in the British universities (Shore and Wright 1999; Shore and Wright 2004; Shore 2008), Auckland University's academics are made increasingly conscious that their activities and output are being monitored and measured by anonymous Ministry officials and accountants in the administrative offices of the Vice-Chancellor's building (or 'Vice House' as it is colloquially termed).

In order to complete their degrees, students have been forced to accumulate large amounts of personal debt, thus encouraging an often reckless habit of borrowing and consumption against expectations of future income (albeit for the now more virtuous goals of investing in oneself and 'self-improvement'). Government loan schemes have encouraged this, but these loans are far from 'interest free'. As one post-doctoral student summed it up with irony, student loans are 'a means of getting young people to finance their own unemployment in a period marked by the sustained loss of jobs and dissolution of the traditional apprentice scheme' (cited in Larner and Le Heron 2005: 860n3). When these loans were first introduced, they were extremely low, and some students, acting with the kind of calculating financial acumen the government has elsewhere sought to encourage, took advantage by buying cars and even properties. But being exposed to financial risk has made many students wary about the 'market value' of the degrees they read, which has tended to encourage a more cautious and instrumental outlook on university education in general; a view more attuned to the idea of education as a private investment rather than a social or intellectual good. In my experience, some students have come to regard themselves, at least partially, as consumers and 'customers', although this is not necessarily an unhealthy development if it encourages expectations of quality teaching and provision from the universities.

The rise of new regimes of audit and accountability

In 2003, New Zealand introduced its first research assessment exercise, the Performance-Based Research Fund. Modelled on the Hong Kong and U.K. Research Assessment Exercise (RAE), the idea was to allocate a portion of the government's block grant to Higher Education institutions according to research performance, the quality of which would be measured and judged by national panels of experts appointed from the ranks of New Zealand scholars (Boston 2005; Curtis and Matthewman 2005). The portion of the block grant was to be 5 per cent in the first year, increasing incrementally to 20 per cent of overall government funding by year 5. Initially, university staff broadly welcomed this as until 2003 funding had followed students which meant that all higher education institutions received the same amount of funding irrespective of whether they did any research or not. A report by the New Zealand Vice-Chancellors' Committee in 2006 clearly showed that most of the increased investment in tertiary education after 2000 had been channelled into the non-university tertiary sector and into 'tertiary-type B education', i.e., 'programmes based on practical, technical or occupational skills for direct entry into the labour market' (NZVCC 2006: 12). New Zealand's universities were being further penalised by 'a funding model which does not recognise adequately the statutory obligations of universities to teach in a research-rich environment' (NZVCC 2006: 1).

New Zealand's university vice-chancellors and academics thus welcomed a change in the funding system that would produce a more strategic approach to research-led education. However, unlike the U.K.'s RAE scores which measured overall departmental performance, the Performance-Based Research Fund (as its name suggests) reflected the performance of each *individual* staff member. Since this personal rating was deemed 'private' and 'confidential', however, the university staff unions were able to negotiate a deal which meant that nobody – apart from the individual concerned and officials at the Tertiary Education Council – was entitled to know the score. After the first PBRF round, university managers were imploring Heads of Department to take all necessary measures to improve departmental research ratings by focusing resources on those staff who were borderline and who might, just possibly, advance a grade. The problem was that unless staff voluntarily declared their scores, there was no way for the Head of Department to know (apart from guessing) on whom they should concentrate attention and resources in order to advance a grade.

Effects of the PBRF

When the 2003 PBRF scores were announced, the results showed that Auckland was by far the leading research university in the country, much to the surprise and annoyance of its principal rival, the University of Otago. Yet instead of bringing about stability or closure on the issue of international research standing, it soon became apparent that this was only the first salvo in what was to become an on-going process of performance appraisal and improvement, and further rounds would be held in 2006 and 2012. Following its 2003 ranking, the University of Auckland embarked on an aggressive advertising campaign to market itself as New Zealand's 'premier' research institution. Large advertisements resembling motorway signs were placed across the country proclaiming Auckland as New Zealand's 'No. 1 University'. In the run-up to the 2006 PBRF round this competitive gaming and strategic repositioning intensified as New Zealand's universities jockeyed for a larger share of the PBRF pie and to claim the mantle as New Zealand's 'leading' research-led university. That title was eventually claimed by both Otago and Auckland universities, and later by Victoria University in Wellington thanks to clever gaming of the system. Yet after the release of the results each university contrived to spin its own interpretation of the final scores.

The highly individualistic nature of the PBRF scores inevitably impacted on collegiality. Many academics who professed to have scored an 'A' rating used this to argue for special privileges such as a reduction in teaching loads or exemption from administrative duties. When the Faculty failed to meet these demands, some colleagues complained bitterly about the injustice of it all 'given how much money I am bringing in' and 'how much my research score is earning for this University', as it was sometimes put to me as a Head of Department. The new institutional self-understanding of universities as commercial enterprises has clearly impacted on the self-understanding of some staff. Those new to academia, by contrast, were not entered into the PBRF and were therefore labelled as 'non-research active'. Many found this bureaucratic classification upsetting and offensive (the system was later revised to include the category of 'New and Emerging' researcher). At the same time, Auckland's research success and financial reward led to the channelling of PBRF income into a central fund that was subsequently used for 'strategic hiring' of highly research-active staff from other universities in New Zealand. In short, it became a *de facto* transfer fund used to poach key players from rival universities.

Perhaps the most noticeable effect was simply the amount of angst and anger that this system engendered. Much of this was due to the new computerised 'Research Information Management System ('RIMS'), which was supposed to simplify the process of entering and checking one's personal data but perversely ended up making it much more complicated, time-consuming and stressful.

Contestation over the meaning of 'the University'

During 2005, while these PBRF pressures were building, university employees throughout the country were also engaged in a major industrial action. A year after taking up my post, and as a member of the Association of University Staff (AUS), I joined what colleagues informed me was the first university staff strike in over a decade. The cause of the dispute was only partly over wages and conditions. University pay scales in New Zealand have failed to keep up with inflation and are some 20 to 30 per cent lower than comparable jobs in Australia, as I was frequently informed. This is another consequence of increasingly competitive 'benchmarking' exercises: staff unions have learned to play the 'benchmarking and ranking' game as well. But the strike was also focussed on that familiar trade unionist talisman of 'collective' bargaining. Pedestrians in Auckland were thus confronted with the bizarre sight of hundreds of university staff, many dressed in full academic regalia, shouting in unison the ritual chant: 'what do we want? MECA!' When do we want it? Now!' 'MECA' in this instance was the acronym for 'Multi-Employer Contract Agreement' which the union was insisting on, rather than the 'divide-and-rule' tactics of each university negotiating its own local rates.

At roughly the same time (June 2005), the Vice-Chancellor circulated the new *University of Auckland's Draft Strategy Plan 2005–12*. For many staff, this document epitomised the new managerialist regime being introduced through the reform process. Its opening pages declare that the University's 'strategic goals', are to 'establish the University of Auckland as New Zealand's premier research university'. It also committed the university to achieving a PBRF ratio of 20 per cent A's and 50 per cent B's by 2006 and to increasing graduate completion rates to 800 MAs and 500 PhDs per year. Virtually every staff member that I spoke to thought these goals were hopelessly unrealistic. These and other criticisms were taken up in a formal letter of complaint to the University Chancellor signed by twenty-three Professors on the University Senate (Kelsey and Wills 2005). One of the key aspects of the Plan that staff objected to was its 'narrow and instrumentalist' view of the university, its teaching and its research. As the letter observed, the draft Plan was written entirely from the perspective of the Administration *being* the University. What it completely failed to recognise was that staff and students are what collectively *constitute* 'the University', not its governors or central management team. The letter reminded the VC that, according to the 1961 University of Auckland Act (section 3.2):

> The University shall consist of the Council, the professors emeriti, the professors, lecturers, junior lecturers, Registrar and librarian of the University for the time being in office, the graduates and undergraduates of the University, the graduates of the University of New Zealand whose names are for the time being on the register of the Court of Convocation of the University of Auckland, and such other persons and classes of persons as the Council may from time to time determine.

In short, without its staff and students, 'the University' as a meaningful body ceases to exist. The letter continues:

> In this document, however the staff are treated as an individualized proletarian workforce that is subordinate to an organizational hierarchy of managers. This relationship is expressed in disciplinary language: staff are people 'of whom the University must demand excellence' (Draft Strategic Plan 2005: 12:11); whose 'reward systems' are to be based on competition and reflect their individual value to the organization (2005: 14:20); and who are to be 'led and coached' by managers to pursue the University's strategic objectives (2005: 14.29) (Kelsey and Wills 2005: 2).

This relegation of academics to the role of adjuncts of the university was not the result of an error or oversight. The same dualism can be seen in the University of Auckland's Charter which lists the 'staff' as just one among some twenty 'stakeholder' groups (including industry, employers, business organisations, accrediting bodies, schools, government agencies, Crown Research Institutes and Maori and Pacific Island communities) whom 'the University' identifies as people to be consulted (University of Auckland 2003: 15). This is a key example of how the new neoliberal governance regime has redefined the idea of the university: from a corporate body composed primarily of teachers, students and alumni, 'the university' has come to mean a collection of stakeholders to be managed by administrators according to the principles of financial accountancy and New Public Management.

The Plan's narrow and instrumentalist conception of research was also singled out for criticism by the signatories to the letter.

> Our research is treated as a commercial venture whose value is to be judged in terms of research income and scores on the deeply flawed

PBRF ranking, while students are treated as a source of revenue. Constant references to competition, flexibility and individual merit clearly signal a desire to replace collective employment salaries and conditions with discretionary, individualized and differential 'rewards' for achieving these' (Kelsey and Wills 2005: 2).

The letter warned that the overall effect of this strategy would be to alienate rather than unite academics and general staff. It also noted the lack of recognition of the contribution of senior staff to the overall administration and governance of the University as 'staff and managers' are typically referred to as two discrete entities. This critique of the University's concept of 'governance' is important. As one long-time member of the University of Auckland Senate wrote in November 2006:

It is worth noting that many of the World's great universities have been in existence for many hundreds of years and their collective governance using a Senate or similar structure to oversee the policy of the university has ensured that they have survived mad governments, civil wars and deluded vice-chancellors much longer than any commercial corporation. We should go back to the historical model of collective governance before we risk destroying the institutions we all used to love.[3]

Another major criticism of the Plan was the absence of any stated 'objectives' reflecting the University's role as a public institution and part of a *national* university system that is supposed to play a vital role in the 'public good' and the social and political (as well as economic) well-being of the nation. According to the 1989 Education Act (section 162(4)(a)), the university has a statutory obligation to accept the role as 'critic and conscience' of society and to respect the Treaty of Waitangi (whose principles include the protection of Maori language, tribal right to self-regulation, the right of redress for past breaches and the state's duty to consult with Maori). These social considerations find little space within the dominant managerial discourse of the university as a revenue-generating enterprise. Finally, criticisms were also raised regarding the Plan's assumption that the aspiration to become the only truly world-class university in New Zealand is best achieved by a corporatised model of the University, led by a de facto 'Chief Executive' who decides policy (accountable only to a Board of Directors) and Division Managers (DVCs, Deans and Librarian) whose role is to cajole and induce an intrinsically reluctant, menial workforce to do what is required by 'the University'. That quest for international standing centres on the dubious science of international rankings, which are treated as valid measures of 'quality' despite the serious questions and controversies over their integrity and methodology (see Marginson and van der Wende 2007).

To sum up, the draft 'Strategic Plan', in the opinion of the Association of University Staff, a large number of professors on Senate and a larger component of the academic staff thus:

1. equated 'the university' with its administration (the mouthpiece for which is the Vice-Chancellor and his management team)
2. reinforced a centralised, corporate model of control that gave virtually no consideration to the idea of collegial governance
3. placed the principles of competition and commercialisation of research over those of collaboration with academic colleagues in other New Zealand universities and the pursuit of knowledge as a legitimate end in itself
4. ignored all the other public good functions of the university and
5. fetishised dubious international rankings of supposed research quality.

These criticisms eventually resulted in some minor amendments of the plan which, complaints and criticisms notwithstanding, was approved at the next meeting of Council in August 2005. However, what is more analytically significant is the new idea of the university reflected in the plan and the new rationality of governance that it epitomised: namely, a vision of the modern university as a centralised transnational business corporation modelled according to the logic of free market economics and New Public Management, where research excellence is to be encouraged primarily to improve global rankings, increase revenue and 'market share' and promote the overseas up-take and commercialisation of New Zealand's educational intellectual property.

Conclusions: whither New Zealand's universities?

The account above gives some indication of the historical trajectory that New Zealand universities have followed over the past three decades as successive governments have tried to re-conceptualise and reform the university in order to meet the challenges of the supposed emerging 'global knowledge economy'. As I have sought to illustrate, different eras produced new and complex policy formations with sometimes overlapping but often contradictory agendas. Despite their formal independence from government, universities have always served national policy objectives. In the past that entailed nation-building, 'education for citizenship' and cultural reproduction of a canon of knowledge which was generally conceptualised in a national vein. Today, instead, following successive waves of neoliberalisation and the apparent re-discovery of the economic and commercial importance of university knowledge (Peters 2001), government ministers and officials require New Zealand's tertiary education institutions to play an increasingly prominent role in creating 'an investment system which supports the Government's social and economic goals, and in particular the economic transformation agenda'.[4] This entails not only developing closer relations with business and harnessing research more aggressively to commercial interests, but also producing the skills base for students to compete more effectively in the global knowledge economy. Yet at the same time, the universities are expected to meet a plethora of other government goals, including 'nation-building', 'Treaty obligations', 'international research excellence' and social integration of New Zealand's increasingly heterogeneous population. New Zealand universities are thus awkwardly positioned between two competing policy visions: as champions of wealth creation and innovation that will drive the economy forward into the 'knowledge society' and a new era of internationalisation as research becomes increasingly aligned with industry; and as repositories of 'culture' and bastions for forging national identity, citizenship, social cohesion and other TEC and Government-defined 'strategic priorities' – including the role of 'critic and conscience' of society (Tertiary Education Committee 2006: 6). No wonder academics in New Zealand are often left feeling bewildered and demoralised.[5]

For many academics in New Zealand there is a sense of déjà vu in all this. During the 1990s, the government launched a 'Green Paper' on the future of tertiary education in which a number of radical ideas were mooted, including the reorganisation of universities into competitive corporate entities governed by Crown-appointed boards, the exposure of universities to the full force of market forces and a 'relaxing' of the traditional role of academics as the 'critics and conscience of society' (Pockley 1998). What provoked particular controversy then was the 'proposal to transform the management of universities from self-governing councils, with strong academic representation, into companies ruled by boards appointed by government to ensure compliance with "national goals"' (Pockley 1998: 320). That proposal epitomises the way university governance has been progressively 'neoliberalised' and how such reforms, once enacted, quickly become normalised.

What we are also witnessing in New Zealand, as elsewhere, is an increasing internationalisation of universities through strategic investment in technologies for the creation of a 'Virtual University' system and the development of mass, online open courses (MOOCS'). These trends were already evident in 2001 when Rupert Murdoch, the Australia-born media baron, sought to link his *New International* company with the 18-member university network *Universitas 21* in a move designed to capture the major share of the rapidly growing global market for online higher education (Fitzsimons 2002: 389). In that year, the Universitas 21 network was incorporated as a company in London. Murdoch's idea was to offer custom-designed higher education programmes over the Internet aimed at college graduates who are already working, so that they can be awarded Universitas 21 degrees. With over 500,000 students and 44,000 academics, Universitas 21 would seem to be well positioned to capture a large slice of the global market. According to the former Vice-Chancellor of Melbourne University, distance-learning through e-education consortiums is the way of the future and may replace individual campus brands (Fitzsimons 2002: 389) We can already see how these changes are affecting the constitution of subjects who work and study in universities. As New Zealand academic John Freeman-Moir (2005) observes, the question that academics are increasingly asking themselves today is not so much 'what use is university knowledge', but 'do I still work in a university?'

◆

Cris Shore is Professor of Social Anthropology at the University of Auckland, New Zealand.His research interests include the anthropology of institutions, policy and power, particularly in the context of the European Union. With Susan Wright, he has made a pioneering contribution to the study of 'audit culture' and its effects. He is author of thirteen books including Building Europe: the Cultural Politics of European Integration (Routledge 2000), Corruption: Anthropological Perspectives (with D. Haller, eds, Pluto Press, 2005) and Policy Worlds (with S. Wright and D. Peró eds, Berghahn 2011). He is currently working on a Royal Society of New Zealand project exploring the 'Crown' and constitutional reform in New Zealand and other Commonwealth countries.

Notes

This chapter originally appeared in *Learning and Teaching: The International Journal of Higher Education in the Social Sciences* Spring 2010, 3(1): 1–31.

1. An earlier version of this chapter was published as a Working Paper in University Reform at the Danish School of Education in 2007 http://www.dpu.dk/site.aspx?p = 9165. I would like to thank colleagues at DPU and the anonymous reviewers for LATISS for their helpful comments.
2. This represents a significant drop from the peak of 121,000 in 2003 when record numbers of Chinese students were attending New Zealand's tertiary education institutions (Cullen 2006a).
3. Unsigned letter posted on the Internet by a 'long-time member of the University Senate, who has witnessed the changes as they evolved over the years' (November 2006), http://www.geocities.com/hoodwinkedatauckland/GovernanceMatters.pdf (accessed 28 November 2006).
4. 'Tertiary Education Reforms: Overview Cabinet Paper', released 27 July 2006 (cited in NZVCC 2006: 1).
5. See Collini (2003; 2009) for a comparative analysis of somewhat similar conditions confronting academics in the U.K.

References

Althaus, C. (1997) 'The application of agency theory to public sector management', in G. Davis, B. Sullivan and A. Yeatman (eds) *The New Contractualism*, Melbourne: MacMillan Education, 137–153.

Beck, U. (1997) *The Reinvention of Politics: Rethinking Modernity in the Global Social Order*, Cambridge: Polity Press.

Belich, J. (2001) *Paradise Reforged: A History of the New Zealanders from the 1880s to the Year 2000*, Auckland: Allen Lane/Penguin Press.

Boston, J. (2005) 'Performance-Based Research Fund – implication for research in the social sciences and social policy', *Social Policy Journal of New Zealand*, 24 (March): 55–84.

Brenneis, D, Shore, C. and Wright, S. (eds) (2005) 'Getting the measure of academia: universities and the politics of accountability', *Anthropology in Action* (Special Issue on University Reform in Cross-Cultural Perspective), 12, no. 1: 1–10.

Butterworth, R. and Tarling, N. (1994) *A Shakeup Anyway: Government and the universities in New Zealand a decade after the reform*, Auckland: Auckland University Press.

Clark, H. (2002) 'Implementing a progressive agenda after fifteen years of neo-liberalism: the New Zealand experience', presentation to London School of Economics, 21 February.

Collini, S. (2003) 'HiEdBiz', *London Review of Books*, 25, no. 21: 3–9.

Collini, S. (2009) 'Impact on humanities', *Times Literary Supplement*, 13 November.

Cullen, M. (2006a) 'International education. The way forward', speech to Education New Zealand's Annual International Education Conference, Sky City Convention Centre, Auckland.

Cullen, M. (2006b) 'Ministerial Foreword, 2007/12: Developing the Second Tertiary Education Strategy', *2007/12 Developing the Second Tertiary Education Strategy*, Ministry of Education, Wellington: 1.

Curtis, B. and Matthewman, S. (2005) 'The managed university: the PBRF, its impacts and staff attitudes', *New Zealand Journal of Employment Relations*, 30, no. 2: 1–18.

Fitzsimons, P. (2002) 'Documents and Debates: virtual geography and the "academic" question of the university', *Journal of Education Policy*, 17, no. 3 (June): 385–391.

Foucault, M. (1977) *Discipline and Punish: The Birth of the Prison*, Harmondsworth: Penguin.

Freeman-Moir, J. (2005) 'Do we still work in a university?' Keynote address to AUS AGM, Canterbury University. Christchurch, 28 October, < http://aus-canter bury.blogspot.com/2005/10/john-freeman-moirs-keynote-address.html > (accessed 3 January 2006).

Gray, J. (1999) *False Dawn: The Delusions of Global Capitalism*, London: Granta Books.

Hawke, G. R. (ed.) (1988) *Report on Post Compulsory Education and Training in New Zealand*, Wellington: Government Printer.

International Partners for Study Abroad (IPSA) (2006), 'Learn English in Auckland, New Zealand', < http://www.studyabroadinternational.com/New_Zealand/ Auckland/New_Zealand_Aucklan.html > (accessed 6 September 2006).

Kelsey, J. (1997) *The New Zealand Experiment: A World Model for Structural Adjustment?*, Auckland: Auckland University Press.

Kelsey, J. and Wills, P. (2005) *Submission on University's Strategic Plan. Letter to the Chancellor Signed by 23 Members of Senate*, Auckland: University of Auckland.

Larner, W. and Le Heron, R. (2005) 'Neoliberalising spaces and subjectivities: reinventing New Zealand universities', *Organization*, 12, no. 6: 843–862.

Larner, W. and Walters, W. (2004) *Global Governmentality: Governing international spaces*. London: Routledge.

Lyotard, J.-F. (1994) *The Postmodern Condition: A Report on Knowledge*. Minneapolis: University of Minnesota Press.

Marginson, S. and van der Wende, M. (2007) 'To rank or to be ranked: the impact of global rankings in higher education', *Journal of Studies in International Education*, 11, nos. 3–4: 306–329.

Ministry of Education (2006) *Export Education in New Zealand: A Strategic Approach to Developing the Sector. An Overview* (updated 28 June 2006), Wellington.

Ministry of Education (2007) *The International Education Agenda 2007–2012*, Wellington, New Zealand: Ministry of Education International Division, < http:// www.minedu.govt.nz/ ~ /media/MinEdu/Files/EducationSectors/Internation alEducation/PolicyStrategy/11950%20ie%20agenda%20final%20download% 20100807.pdf > (accessed 16 March 2009).

New Zealand Vice-Chancellors' Committee (NZVCC) (2006) *An Investment Approach to Public Support of New Zealand's Universities. Submission on behalf of the New Zealand Vice-Chancellors' Committee.*

Olssen, M. (2002) 'The restructuring of tertiary education in New Zealand: governmentality, neo-liberalism, democracy', *McGill Journal of Education*, 37, no. 1: 57–78.

Olssen, M. and Peters, M. (2005) 'Neoliberalism, higher education and the knowledge economy: from the free market to knowledge capitalism', *Journal of Education Policy*, 20, no. 3: 313–345.

Peck, J. and Tickell, A.I. (2002) 'The urbanization of neoliberalism: theoretical debates neoliberalizing space.' *Antipode*, 34, no. 3: 380–404.

Perryman, J. (2006) 'Panoptic performativity and school inspection regimes: disciplinary mechanisms and life under special measures', *Journal of Education Policy*, 2: 147–61.

Peters, M. (2001) 'National education policy constructions of the "knowledge economy": towards a critique', *Journal of Educational Enquiry*, 2, no. 1: 1–22.

Pockley, P. (1998) 'New Zealand universities face privatization bid', *Nature*, 392, no. 6674: 320.

Readings, B. (1996) *The University in Ruins*, Cambridge, MA.: Harvard University Press.

Robertson, S. and Dale, R. (2002) 'Local states of emergency: the contradictions of neo-liberal governance in education in New Zealand', *British Journal of Sociology of Education*, 23, no. 3: 463–482.

Shore, C. (2008) 'Audit culture and illiberal government: universities and the politics of accountability', *Anthropological Theory*, 8: 278–298.

Shore, C. and Roberts, S. (1995) 'The panopticon paradigm of higher education: quality assessment as "disciplinary technology"', *Higher Education Review*, 27, no. 3: 8–17.

Shore, C. and Selwyn, T. (1998) 'Managing "cultural change": the marketization and bureaucratization of higher education', in D. Jary and M. Parker (eds) *Dilemmas of Mass Higher Education: Issues for a post-Dearing HE System*, Stafford: University of Staffordshire Press, 153–172.

Shore, C. and Wright, S. (1999) 'Audit culture and Anthropology: neo-liberalism in British higher education', *Journal of the Royal Anthropological Institute*, 5, no. 4: 557–575.

Shore, C. and Wright, S. (2004) 'Whose accountability? Governmentality and the auditing of universities', *Parallax*, 10, no. 2: 101–117.

Strathern, M. (ed.) (2000) *Audit Cultures. Anthropological Studies in Accountability, Ethics and the Academy*, EASA, London: Routledge.

Tertiary Education Committee (2006) 2007/12: *Developing the Second Tertiary Education Strategy* (Draft discussion document released 29 August 2006), Wellington: Ministry of Education.

Tertiary Education Commission (2008) *Briefing to the Incoming Minister* (November), Wellington: Ministry of Education, < http://www.tec.govt.nz/upload/downloads/bim-2008-oia.pdf >

UniServices (2003) *Annual Performance Review*, Auckland: University of Auckland < http://www.uniservices.co.nz/uploadedfiles/uniservices/2003uniservices_apr.pdf > (accessed 22 December 2006).

UniServices (2009) *The Innovation Advantage: UniServices Profile*, Auckland: University of Auckland, < http://www.uniservices.co.nz/uploadedfiles/uniservices/UniServices per cent20Profile.pdf > (accessed 2 April 2009).

United Nations Educational, Scientific and Cultural Organization (UNESCO) (2006) *Trade in Higher Education and GATS* (Briefing paper on GATS), < http://www .unesco.org/education/studyingabroad/highlights/global_forum/gats_he/ba sic_gats_he.shtml > (accessed 22 December 2006).

University of Auckland (2003) *The University of Auckland Charter 2003,* < http:// www.auckland.ac.nz/uoa/the-university/official-publications/charter-2003 > (accessed 22 December 2006).

CHAPTER 2

Using ethnographic methods to understand universities and neoliberal development in North Central Philadelphia

SUSAN BRIN HYATT

◆◆◆

Ethnographic fieldwork and neoliberalism

Walking along Old Elvet, a street in Durham, England, home to one of the most elite universities in the U.K., I pass by a building that, back in the mid-1990s, when I first visited Durham, was home to the Anthropology Department. It now houses a very elegant branch of the Swedish bank, Handelsbanken. Across the street, the building known as Old Shire Hall, which used to be the location for the university's administrative offices, is now empty and on the market. A real estate site (http://www.gva .co.uk/property/4239/) touts the 'unique conversion opportunity' that Old Shire Hall provides, noting its proximity to Durham's castle and cathedral, as well as to its expanding shopping district.

Around the U.S.A. and around the world, universities are realizing that, in many cases, they sit on prime real estate located in proximity to gentrifying neighborhoods. Eager to exploit these resources for economic gain, they are selling off buildings to acquisitive speculators and investors.

On the other hand, in their voracious need for land in order to modernize science labs, libraries, residence halls, gyms and other facilities, universities are also annexing surrounding properties at sometimes astounding rates, displacing more modest working-class communities and their residents by asserting that these communities are 'blighted.' As Steven Gregory (2013: 49) writes of Columbia University's plans to expand its campus into the surrounding New York city neighbourhood, Manhattanville, 'Columbia and its supporters represented Manhattanville as an obsolete, former manufacturing district that was no longer capable of contributing to the city's economy'.

Universities wield a mighty sword in the context of many contemporary cities, with their emphasis on gentrifying downtowns and reliance on income from tourists, suburban visitors and other out-of-towners. In some cases, universities are, themselves, tourist destinations; in other instances, especially in the case of elite universities, they hold the promise of attracting affluent students, faculty members and their families to help bolster struggling urban economies.

But, what of the modest neighborhoods that often throng such campuses? The paragraph below was written by one of my students, Monica Miller who, in the spring of 2003, was an undergraduate member of my Ethnographic Methods class. Along with the other students in the class, Monica's work was part of a larger mission aimed at creating an ethnographic portrait of the African-American neighbourhood adjacent to Temple University's main campus in North Central Philadelphia. As Monica writes,

> The expression 'Not in My Backyard' or NIMBY refers to the fact that residents of middle-and upper-class neighborhoods often engage in protest against stores and other enterprises they do not want to locate in their pristine communities. But, in the case of inner city neighborhoods, when it comes to commercial facilities such as supermarkets, residents are often left asking the question, 'Why not in my backyard?' The answers to this question often given by corporations or other outsiders are that inner city neighborhoods do not provide enough business or that residents lack consumer loyalty, or that insurance costs are too high. What my research has uncovered, however, is that ... supermarkets are part of an industry that is increasingly competitive, resulting in a move towards larger and larger stores.... It is not the residents of the neighborhood who are to blame for the lack of supermarkets but the corporate strategies of the industry that work against the interests of urban neighborhoods (Miller 2004: 13).

Monica's insights above and in her longer research paper on the history of the neighbourhood's struggle to attract a supermarket to their underserved community demonstrated that she had learned a great deal through first-hand experience about the back-story that both explains the unequal distribution of resources across Philadelphia's fractured neighbourhood landscapes and that challenges the 'naturalisation' of this inequality.

One of my goals in teaching courses on Ethnographic Methods is to help students understand in concrete terms the real and immediate effects of such abstract and contradictory concepts as 'neoliberalism' and 'globalisation'. For those of us who teach in urban universities, conducting fieldwork projects in the neighbourhoods proximate to our campuses is one way to introduce students to the local impact of neoliberal models for economic development which have served to intensify pre-existing inequalities. Like those policies associated with neoliberalism more broadly, the neoliberal development model is a market-driven strategy that targets particular spaces for private investment and business ventures aimed at attracting upscale consumers. In cities across the U.S.A., the outcome has most often been a commodification of particular neighbourhoods by promoting investments that cater to the tastes of particular constituencies, including students, suburbanites and tourists.

In Spring 2003, the students in my Ethnographic Methods class at Temple University examined the history of local uneven development, including new plans to make the neighbourhood a destination and more desirable residential location for students and faculty. We began carrying out ethnographic research in the neighbourhood surrounding Temple's main campus. Although it was not my initial intent when we launched the class, we ended up learning a great deal about how our institution was heavily implicated in a new era of development plans that were severely compromising the viability of the neighbourhood for local residents. Our fieldwork was undertaken collaboratively with a local community development corporation, whose dynamic leader, Paula Peebles, worked very closely with the students and me to facilitate the semester-long project we called, 'The Death and Rebirth of North Central Philadelphia'.

As we were beginning our research, we realised that there was a long history of this community and its relationship with Temple that we did not know and needed to find out. Not only was Ms Peebles able and willing to share her knowledge of the neighbourhood with us; we also discovered that she had also been a key activist in many of the struggles that had shaped community-university relations through the years. I had first met Paula through a local community education programme in the autumn of 2002 and approached her about teaming up with me to teach the Spring 2003 ethnographic methods class. We established an immediate rapport based on our shared understanding of and appreciation for the challenges and rewards of community organising. We agreed that in return for the cooperation of Paula and her organisation, the Renaissance Community Development Corporation (RCDC), it was important that the class produce some kind of product that, in addition to serving as an outlet to showcase the students' research, would also be of direct use to the neighbourhood in their struggles to resist the changes being promoted by Temple in concert with city agencies and private developers.

In the interests of creating a document that would be relatively inexpensive, accessible and easily distributed, we decided to publish a neighbourhood newspaper that would be made up of articles written by the students based on their research. Initially, we planned to have a four-page insert which would be included in one of the local Black weekly newspapers: by the time the project was completed, we had produced and distributed 10,000 issues of our own tabloid-size 24-page neighbourhood newspaper throughout the 60 or so city blocks that made up the RCDC's service area.

In this article, my goal is to illustrate the insights that the students and I gleaned through this project about the multiple and often negative effects of current models for urban development and about the complex ways in which universities, in their new role as real-estate investors, are entangled in these larger social, economic and political agendas. As Ruben (2000: 213) put it: 'universities located in metropolitan areas have become major players in the new finance-dominated economy'. In learning about the history of the neighbourhood and its relationship to our own institution, it was clear that while university growth had been encroaching on the community for some time, what rendered this contemporary phase of the university's expansion particularly 'neoliberal' in character was its reliance on private real estate developers to create upscale housing and retail establishments aimed at attracting white, middle-class student-consumers to the neighbourhood. As we got to know the local residents and to understand the history of their struggles, we came to see that this new phase of development came into direct conflict with many of their own long-held hopes and dreams for the future of their community and that it had the potential – even the likelihood – of displacing ever larger numbers of residents from their streets and homes.

From commuter campus to 'Temple Town'

Like many other urban campuses in the U.S.A., Temple University is located in what has now become a predominantly African-American community. There is a long history of conflict between Temple University and its neighbours. Sally Harrison, a faculty member in the Temple architecture programme, describes Temple's relationship with its neighbours as follows:

> At North Philadelphia's centre is situated Temple University, an institution with its own identity and critical mass, itself a community of

over 30,000 and the largest landowner in North Philadelphia. In its context of physical and social disjuncture the university maintains an uneasy peace with its neighbours, having experienced growth in a kind of converse relationship to the decline of the surrounding community: one which it had originally been founded to serve. Although a major employer of the area's residents, the current North Philadelphia population is not economically critical to the function of the university. Unlike the historic relationship between factory and local neighbourhood, neither the skilled essential labour force nor its consumer market is drawn from the neighbourhood. The two worlds coexist, adjacent but unconnected (Harrison 1998: 6).

While Harrison's description is, in many ways, quite apt, through our own ethnographic work we came to question her claim that the university and the neighbourhood were fundamentally unconnected. While it is certainly fair to say that the decline of the neighbourhood was one consequence of the departure of the small manufacturing firms that had once been an integral part of the local landscape, we discovered that through the years, the neighbourhood had also been thwarted by the university, itself, which had made use of public policy initiatives, such as the favouring of so-called 'public-private partnerships' and the use of eminent domain (compulsory purchase) to seize local homes and business in the interests of championing campus expansion and neighbourhood gentrification.

Temple had begun its life in the 1880s as a privately funded night school for local students interested in church ministry; it soon expanded its offerings beyond theology to provide a broader range of courses for working-class students who commuted to the campus from around the city (Strom 2005: 116). In the 1950s, the university launched the first of its many ambitious programmes to expand its facilities with the goal of transforming itself into a more residential campus (Bear 1990: 40). Philadelphia's City Council enabled this expansion by altering local zoning regulations thereby allowing the university (and other major institutions, like hospitals), to displace local residents by seizing private homes and businesses for 'urban renewal'.

Media representations and public perceptions of Black neighbourhoods like North Central Philadelphia reinforced the notion that such communities were both uniformly poor (and uniformly Black), when, in fact, our historical research and qualitative interviews provided evidence to the contrary. A long-time resident of North Philadelphia, for example, Black businessman Floyd Alston, was featured in a 2003 article in the *Philadelphia Business Journal,* reminiscing about the illustrious past of Cecil B. Moore Avenue, a major thoroughfare that had once marked the southern boundary of the campus. As the article stated, '… Alston recalled the area around Cecil B. Moore as a thriving, stable, middle-class neighbourhood. Residents on the block where he grew up included an internist [family doctor], school teacher, postal workers, dentist, a grocery store owner, tailor, three numbers writers [bookmakers] and a man who sold booze' (Kostelni 2003). Like many others, Alston attributed the decline of the neighbourhood to the race riots sparked by a conflict between community residents and the police that erupted along Cecil B. Moore Avenue (then known as Columbia Avenue) in 1964 (Kostelni 2003; Clark 2005). The riots hastened both middle-class Black and white flight from the community.

Neighbourhood commercial strips in other cities and other Philadelphia neighbourhoods, however, suffered a similar decline even though they were not the sites of such riots. Goode and Schneider (1994: 30) note that 1970s suburbanisation hit Philadelphia particularly hard. As more affluent (and largely white) city residents flocked to newly built suburbs, the locus of political power also shifted away from cities, emboldening the federal government to adopt policies that favoured suburban counties over metropolitan areas. The withdrawal of federal funding for cities was particularly devastating for Philadelphia: in 1979, federal revenues amounted to 25.8 per cent of the city's tax base; in 1988, they were only 7.5 per cent (Goode and Schneider 1994: 30). Similarly, Kristin Koptiuch argues that the decline of North Central Philadelphia was due not to the riots but, rather, 'to bankers' redlining, realty disinvestment, middle-class black exodus, and federal cutbacks that Republican administrations have used since 1980 to starve the cities and undermine the traditional power base of Democrats' (1991: 90).

During the 1950s and 1960s urban renewal legislation allowed municipalities to use the power of eminent domain to seize blocks deemed to be 'blighted', designating them for 'redevelopment': however, neither of these terms – 'blight' or 'redevelopment' – was ever very clearly defined (see Mullins 2003, 2006 and Gregory 2013 for similar examples from Indianapolis and New York respectively). More often than not, urban renewal clearances resulted in the displacement of residents in primarily African-American communities, many of whom were actually not poor but were working- and middle-class (see Teaford 2000). An article in the New York Times from 1961 (and which therefore predates the riots) described Temple's use of urban renewal as follows:

> Temple University reports from Philadelphia that, although working in
> an area that 'is one of the worst slums in the city,' the renewal success
> in the first forty acres allocated to the university by the City Plan-
> ning Commission has encouraged the institution to ask for another
> ninety-seven acres to be certified for its use. … Eventually, the North
> Philadelphia slum area will house a modern university with 40,000
> students (Hechinger 1961).

By the mid-1960s, Temple's forced acquisition of properties on blocks surrounding the campus had generated an angry and organised response among residents of North Philadelphia. They formed an organisation called CURE – Citizens' Urban Renewal Exchange (Bear 1990: 40; Moore 2004: 8). Through actions coordinated by CURE, Temple entered into an agreement with its remaining neighbours in 1970. The resulting accord acknowledged that an estimated 7,000 neighbourhood residents had already been displaced over 20 years of Temple's expansion and agreed that Temple would not build beyond an agreed-upon boundary without involving neighbourhood residents in the discussion (Bear 1990: 40–41; Moore 2005: 8).

The next flashpoint in community-university relations occurred in 1984 and centred on a plan hatched by Temple's ambitious President Liacouras in concert with a major telecommunications company, Bell Telephone of Pennsylvania. Against all odds, Liacouras persuaded Bell's executives to locate their new state-of-the-art computer centre on land adjacent to the campus. Liacouras's vision was that the Bell building would anchor a proposed '11-acre area to the east of the urban campus that Temple is attempting to develop as an industrial park for high-technology concerns' (New York Times 1985). Despite the lingering suspicions left from the urban renewal era, neither Liacouras nor Bell Telephone consulted in any meaningful way with the community before announcing their plans. The response from the neighbourhood was predictably angry. Bear describes the reaction from one leading community activist:

> 'You see, our major concern then', community activist Paula Brown
> Taylor [later Paula Peebles] says now, 'was massive displacement.
> And we'd already gone through that. The rallying cry was "no more"'.
> On the streets and in the churches, a lot of people, for the very first
> time, were having their political consciousness raised by activists hard
> at work (Bear 1990: 56).

The Bell facility was constructed and opened in 1986: by the time I arrived on Temple's campus just ten years later, the building was vacant. In 1997, Temple purchased the building from Bell (which had itself been dissolved) and in 2006, it spent $16 million to convert it into a technology centre for student use (Carlson 2006). According to an article published in the *New York Times* in 1985, 'the four-story Bell structure ... is expected to employ 200–250 workers. ...' (New York Times 1985). A description of the original Bell facility in another article celebrating its conversion to the technology centre suggests, however, that the opportunities for neighbourhood employment had always been limited if not non-existent:

> Not long ago, this building was home to aisle upon aisle of main-frame computers providing vital operations for Bell Atlantic. Only a few dozen people came here each day to tend to the humming main-frames. ... (Carlson 2006).

Furthermore, the original plans for the anticipated 11-acre technology park never materialised.

The 1990s were punctuated by two major clashes between Temple and its neighbours. One was a controversy generated by a proposal to permanently close 13th Street to vehicular traffic, thereby separating campus space from the surrounding neighbourhood by creating a pedestrianised precinct. This plan was successfully opposed by neighbourhood residents who had already been inconvenienced through two years of campus construction projects with their resulting street closures and 13th Street was eventually re-opened to traffic.

The second was Temple's plan to erect a huge sports and entertainment complex on the Western edge of the campus. Originally called 'The Apollo of Temple', the facility was later re-named The Liacouras Center following the retirement of President Peter Liacouras from Temple in 2000. In addition to the basketball stadium as the centrepiece of the development, the plans for the Liacouras Center also included 'a 12-screen movie theatre, stores and a restaurant with live jazz' (Pulley 1995). The building opened in 1998, housing the basketball arena, a few fast food outlets on the ground floor facing the street, and a Barnes and Noble bookstore catering to Temple students.

When the plans for the Liacouras Center were announced, the Philadelphia City Council insisted that, in return for permission to build the facility, Temple would have to contribute $5 million towards improving housing for neighbourhood residents. In 2002, an article in the *Philadelphia Inquirer* noted that none of the planned housing renovations ever occurred and Temple had only contributed $1.5 million of its own funds, which were 'frittered away' by competing community groups:

according to one local activist, State Senator Shirley Kitchen, '"The plan was that we would all fight each other, and turn on each other and go on and forget like it never existed".... The housing "didn't happen and it's not going to happen"' (Burton 2002).

Beyond the community's disappointment over the failure of the agreement to create new affordable housing for community residents, the location was also of symbolic import. First of all, the new Liacouras Center was built on the west side of Broad Street: since Broad Street had long constituted the western boundary of the campus, this represented something of a further incursion into what had long been perceived as non-university community space. Second, the arena was located at the corner of Cecil B. Moore Avenue and Broad Street, an intersection that had once been known as 'Jump Street' and which in an earlier era was at the heart of the Black arts district.

The expansion of Temple University into this area was a blow to local residents. As Sally Harrison notes, in describing the community suspicion that threatened to compromise the launch of her own 'Urban Initiatives' collaborative architectural project,

> ... [U]ndeflected from its own goals, the university continued in its historic role as an institutional real-estate developer. At the Urban Initiatives Project's outset, the university announced its plans for the construction of a huge sports arena which would expand the campus into the community's domain, dislocating some residents but, more importantly, appropriating the threshold to the neighbourhood's iconic street of jazz heritage (Harrison 1998: 17).

Harrison goes on to describe her students' research in which neighbourhood residents were asked to generate cognitive maps of the community. She recalls one older resident's map: 'Poignantly, his memories of Cecil B. Moore Avenue, once the locus of jazz-oriented night life that gave it the name "Jump Street" reveal a powerful sense of the loss of place-identity endured by the community' (Harrison 1998: 20–21).

The construction of the Liacouras Center definitively preempted the long-cherished desire of local residents to see the Jump Street entertainment district revived, however unrealistic or fanciful those hopes may have been. Furthermore, the original name, The Apollo of Temple, intended to be a humorous play on the 'Temple of Apollo', at least had some linguistic resonance with the historic Black arts venue in Harlem, The Apollo Theatre. Renaming the facility 'The Liacouras Center' marked the space as now decisively belonging to the university, rather than to the community.

The construction of the Liacouras Center was a key victory in President Liacouras's long-standing desire to see the neighbourhood around the campus turned into what he called 'Temple Town', a campus-identified space 'where students, professors, alumni, and community members will gather for entertainment, socializing, and business' (Blum 1995). The explicit 're-branding' and marketing of the surrounding neighbourhood as 'Temple Town' made the residents – and us – wonder what place they would have in this new order.

When I launched our collaborative project in North Philadelphia in 2003, very little of this background was known to the students in the class or to me. I had arrived on campus just as the Liacouras Center was being built but after most of the protests were over. I followed some of the controversy over the proposed closing of 13th Street but did not realise at the time that this conflict took place in the context of a long history of clashes between the neighbourhood and the university. Nonetheless, the students and I set out to explore the community that lay just beyond the academic buildings and parking lots that had hitherto circumscribed our views of North Philadelphia. As we began our work, we had no idea that the neighbourhood stood on the threshold of another series of changes that would, again, create major upheavals for local residents.

Off of the campus and into the streets: exploring 'The death and rebirth of North Central Philadelphia'

We began our research in January 2003. From the very beginning, Paula Peebles was involved in the organisation of the course. Despite her own hectic schedule, she provided lively and engaging lectures for all of us on the history of the neighbourhood and on the struggles and successes of her organisation. Students then chose topics for their research projects including housing, health, the local Black press, community economic development, childcare, and youth among others. For each topic, Paula generously provided the students with lists of names of people to interview and agencies to visit, drawing from her own extensive personal and professional networks. Paula also greatly eased the students' entrée into the community by notifying prospective interviewees about the research and requesting their cooperation.

In carrying out their interviews, students were instructed to ask each of their informants the following two questions:

> Do you believe that at some point, North Central Philadelphia *did* die?
> *When* do you think this happened and *why* do you think it happened?

Is North Central Philadelphia now in a process of rebirth? If so, when do you think this rebirth began? Which individuals or organizations do you think have been most active in bringing about this rebirth? Why?

Over the course of the semester, the students conducted about 40 qualitative interviews. In addition, there were several community events that spring, which commanded our attention. We attended the RCDC's annual general meeting and participated in other activities, including a prayer vigil and discussion prompted by the tragic shooting of a neighbourhood store clerk by a local youth and a ground-breaking for a new mixed-income housing development to replace Richard Allen Homes, Philadelphia's oldest public housing complex (see Hyatt 2003). Several students attended other events located in churches, community centres, health clinics and other spaces. The proximity of these activities to our campus proved to be a boon and our collective focus on one community meant that there was a dynamic synergy as students shared information and data. From the beginning, the students were told that in addition to their academic research papers, their work would also contribute to the creation of a neighbourhood newspaper. Along with their formal papers, they were also required to submit shorter pieces written in the style of a newspaper article. As the semester progressed, Paula and I began to think about how to construct the paper and about what impact we hoped it would have. By that point in the semester, we were all beginning to see the outline of an alternative story in contradistinction to the dominant narrative of how, through its development projects, the university was 'saving' the community from an 'inevitable' spiral of decline. We saw, instead, a vital neighbourhood that had long been beset upon and that had a history of fighting back.

Race and neighbourhood heterogeneity

When we started out, many of us, including me, had uncritically accepted the media images of North Central Philadelphia as a largely poor, Black 'ghetto'. By the end of the semester, however, several of the students remarked that although they had driven through the neighbourhood every time they came to campus, they had never really 'seen' it. Through our interviews and archival research, the students and I discovered that although the neighbourhood was overwhelmingly African-American, it was not uniformly poor: rather, it was characterised by tremendous class heterogeneity. In fact, many of the residents we interviewed lived in Yorktown, 'a suburban-style development built in the heart of the city to be marketed to middle-class African-Americans' (Clark 2005). In the early 1960s, when Yorktown was established, there were few options for homeownership for African-American families in Philadelphia. When they were first built, the homes sold for $10,000 to $14,000: by 2005, they were valued at $120,000 (Clark 2005).[1]

The housing in the neighbourhood spanned a range from the subsidised public housing that lined 11th Street, the eastern boundary of the campus, to the Jefferson Manor townhouses, now managed by RCDC, to the Jefferson Garden rental apartments, also managed by RDDC, to the tidy single-family owner-occupied homes that comprised Yorktown. We discovered that our questions about the death and re-birth of North Central Philadelphia elicited very different responses from different constituencies. The residents of public housing, whose communities were undergoing some rehabilitation through various federal initiatives, felt that the community was on its way back after a difficult period. The owner-occupiers living in the Yorktown homes, however, resented the question because they were sensitive to the ways in which their community was generally lumped into totalising images of North Philadelphia as an impoverished 'ghetto'. In fact, their area had actually long been home to working and middle-class families, who were homeowners and whose social ties to one another were deep and abiding. When student Dorothy Summers posed the question about the death and rebirth of North Central to one Yorktown community activist, she recorded the following response:

> What death are you talking about? Where does the death come in because we were here all along. … Death to me makes me think of a barren, blighted empty street where no one lives (Summers 2004: 6–7).

Her experiences interviewing working and middle-class African-Americans in the neighbourhood led Dorothy to a sophisticated critique of the work of sociologist William Julius Wilson, who has argued that in the post-Civil Rights era, working and middle-class Blacks abandoned inner city 'ghettos', leaving the only most impoverished residents behind (see Wilson 1987, 1996). As Dorothy concluded, in the article she wrote for our newspaper, 'While it is true that middle-class people of all races have continued to move out of Philadelphia, this perspective fails to acknowledge the class diversity that remains in urban communities, even in the post-Civil Rights era' (Summers 2004: 6). Dorothy and the other students also found reasons to criticise Wilson's claims about the extreme isolation of low-income inner-city African-Americans; in our interviews with public housing tenant-activists, for example, we heard sophisticated analyses of grassroots campaigns that had brought local people into contact with city, state and even federal bureaucracies.

When we realised that we had enough material to produce our own newspaper, Paula raised most of the funds we needed to support this endeavour by selling display ads to her local business contacts. I raised some additional funds from Temple, but not much: because of Paula's long history of activism in the community, university administrators were not pleased by our collaboration and generally did not support the project. During the summer of 2004, we devoted ourselves to getting the newspaper finished. With some of the funds that Paula had raised, we hired one of our most outstanding students, Monica Miller, to oversee the process. Fortunately for us, Monica had just graduated and did not yet have a full-time job. The Renaissance Community Development Corporation donated the use of a desk, computer, and telephone in their offices and we set up shop. Monica figured out how to use one of the early desktop publishing programmes and we began editing the articles that the students had submitted. Even a year after the class had ended, many of the students were still in town and were willing to further edit their contributions. We found a unionised print shop across the river in Camden, New Jersey that agreed to print 10,000 copies of the newspaper for a price we could afford and we hired a local newspaper distributor to deliver the newspapers door-to-door throughout the study area.

The publication was very well-received by neighbourhood residents and built on the question of whether the neighbourhood's had undergone a death and rebirth. The cover photo showed a newly constructed mixed-income housing development that was replacing one of the public housing communities, rising up in the shadows of a long-abandoned clothing factory. It was an apt image for the current moment in urban redevelopment: residential and retail developments were rapidly replacing old factories across the cityscape. What we also needed to grapple with was the question of how Temple, as a major local institution, was part and parcel of many of these neighbourhood changes.

Universities and neoliberal development

Of course, Temple's history of rather fraught relations with its neighbours is hardly unique. Many other urban campuses in the U.S.A. share these experiences. In a recent article, Gregory (2013) describes the strategies that Columbia University in New York City has used to seize control of a local planning process in order to accommodate a massive expansion of that campus. More recently, New York University has also been featured in the news as its plans for new construction impinge on the historic Greenwich Village neighbourhood. Across the Schuylkill River on the west side of Philadelphia, about five miles from Temple's campus, is the University of Pennsylvania, popularly known as 'Penn'. Where Temple is a public university, Penn is a wealthy, elite, private institution whose founding dates back to 1750. Although each of these universities has quite different histories and each has been engaged in somewhat different strategies for local economic development (see Strom 2005), there are also important points of convergence between them (and other universities). Penn's urban revitalisation projects, undertaken during the late 1990s and into the 2000s under the presidency of Judith Rodin (1994 to 2004), are widely regarded as a national example of how universities and communities can work collaboratively to rebuild an impoverished neighbourhood. As one journalist put it, '[Rodin] has been widely lauded as the arbiter of modern, enlightened community-university relations' (Schuerman 2007).

Rodin's rather triumphalist account of the rebirth of the neighbourhood around Penn's campus, now known as 'University City', (clearly the model for Liacouras's notion of 'Temple Town') is certainly informed by her awareness of Penn's history of having assumed a rather imperious stance towards its neighbours and she acknowledges the legitimacy of the fears of gentrification and displacement expressed by local residents (Rodin 2007: 94–95). Nonetheless, her book avoids grappling with fundamental questions about the nature of contemporary neoliberal development more broadly: including the increasing corporatisation and privatisation of public and university spaces that now inevitably accompanies these ventures.

A recent book by Harley Etienne (2013) presents a far more mixed view of the impact of Penn's expansion on local residents. While some of them appreciated the new amenities nearby, others resented the extent to which Penn was less than transparent with its residential neighbours. Universities, like Penn and Temple, often wield great local political clout with local government by virtue of the fact that, in the absence of manufacturing and other industry, they have become large regional employers (Rodin 2007: 14). As Rodin writes:

> In every one of the twenty largest cities in the United States, an institution of higher education or an academic medical center is among the top ten private employers.... Thirty-five per cent of the people who

work for private employers in these cities are employed by universities and their medical centers (2007: 14).

This statistic, impressive as it seems, masks the highly polarised and stratified nature of the employment generated by these institutions (see also Ruben 2000). On one hand, there are the skilled, well-remunerated jobs held by doctors, engineers, lawyers, and some professors (particularly those in well-funded professional schools like business, medicine, and law). On the other hand, the out-sourcing of the management of university facilities has meant that the vast majority of campus jobs likely to be held by local residents are low-end, minimum wage service sector jobs. Where the people who used to hold these jobs – in areas such as security, food service, building maintenance, landscaping and the like – were once university employees, with access to university benefits, these functions are now taken on by hourly paid workers who are hired through sub-contracted non-local firms (see Ruben 2000). Therefore, local residents no longer work directly *for* the local university or medical centre: they work *at* the university *for* the fast-food franchises that increasingly colonise dining halls and campus centres; for national janitorial and security contractors; for Barnes and Noble, a national bookstore chain that has taken over the management of many campus bookstores; and for national and international food service providers.

At Temple, in addition to the privatised food service, bookstore, security and janitorial services and other amenities, the Liacouras Center is also managed by a private corporation, Global Spectrum, a subsidiary of cable television giant, Comcast-Spectator. According to the section on company background from Global Spectrum's Web site,

> Global Spectrum provides innovative management, marketing, operations and event booking services for public assembly facilities, including arenas, civic and convention centers, stadiums, ice facilities, equestrian centers and theatres. The most professional and experienced senior management staff in the industry leads Global Spectrum. In addition to providing full scope-of-services for existing facilities that decide to 'privatize', [sic] Global Spectrum also provides pre-opening design and construction consulting services for the development phase of facilities under construction (http://www.global-spectrum .com/default.asp?lnopt = -1).

It is perplexing to note the quotation marks around the word 'privatize' in the text above! Indeed, privatisation and corporatisation are key tenets of neoliberalism and their deep incursion into academic settings in the present era is unprecedented. In fact, on Global Spectrum's Web site, the section devoted to listing the university facilities they manage shows university logos (including the trademark Temple 'T') alongside the Global Spectrum logo.

Likewise, one of Temple's new student housing developments, University Village, is managed by a company called American Campus Communities, headquartered in Austin, Texas. American Campus Communities advertises itself as:

> ... one of the nation's largest developers, owners and managers of high-quality student housing communities. We led the industry to a new plateau in 2004 when we became the first publicly traded student housing.... Since 1996, we've developed more than $1.5 billion in properties for our own account and our university clients, and we have acquired in excess of $2 billion in student housing assets. Also, we've become a national leader in third-party development and management of on-campus student housing, having been awarded the development of 46 on-campus projects (in addition to our 11 projects developed off campus) (http://www.studenthousing.com/company/).

National and multi-national corporations like Global Spectrum and American Campus Communities, have, of course, absolutely no connection to North Philadelphia or its history as a hub for Philadelphia's Black entertainment district and as an important locus of political mobilisation during the Civil Rights movement. They have no real connection to the university, either. They are the mechanisms through which universities, like Temple and Penn, and other corporatised institutions, maximise their profits and minimise their expenses, especially labour costs, since the jobs provided by sub-contractors usually pay minimum wage and rarely include benefits like health care, vacation days, sick leave or pensions. Nor do they offer any access to the university resources or to those privileges that used to be greatly valued by lower-waged university employees: use of campus facilities like libraries and gyms, tuition remission for courses and fee reductions offered to university employees' children.

One of the motivations that inspired Temple's President Liacouras to create 'Temple Town' was his desire to attract suburban, more affluent students to Temple's inner city campus. As an article in the *Philadelphia Inquirer* explained,

> Faced with declining enrollment, frustrated that fewer Philadelphia public school students are prepared to handle college, and worried

that technology will make it easier for universities with online offerings to steal away students, Temple president Peter J. Liacouras
has launched a vast overhaul so the university can lure more students from Philadelphia's suburbs. The push includes a new marketing campaign, tougher admissions standards, an end to remediation
for students unprepared for college, more recruiting at suburban high
schools, investments in distance learning, and construction projects
that could total $800 million. ... Temple's strategy is threefold: market-
ing, convenience, and the complete college experience that resident
life affords (O'Neill 1998).

Neighbourhood residents remain particularly sensitive to the suggestion that attracting 'suburban' and 'better qualified' students means diminishing the presence of minority students on campus. A 1998 article
in *The Chronicle of Higher Education* articulated this concern:

Temple has long maintained an uneasy relationship with the mostly
black community that surrounds its campus here, and the new plans
have prompted some locals to wonder whether Temple's president,
Peter J. Liacouras, is trying to 'bleach' the undergraduate population,
which is 25 per cent black. In a strategic plan approved by the Board
of Trustees last year, Mr Liacouras wrote that, 'weak students' from
the city could be driving away 'good' students from the suburbs. In
another section, he noted that undergraduate enrollment of white men
had plummeted. Roughly 8,460 white students are enrolled for this
fall, a decline of 31 per cent since 1990 (Gose 1998).

By the later 1980s, with the decline of the neighbourhood and in light
of some well-publicised crimes against students, more affluent parents,
both white and Black, had become reluctant to send their children to
study at urban universities like Temple. The new housing, the splashy
Licaouras Center and other amenities were intended to replace the appearance of a 'scary' African-American neighbourhood with a commercial district that would appeal to the aesthetic of white, millennial
suburbanites and their parents, for whom corporate logos and national
chains represent a comfortable and familiar milieu. These are the factors that make up the new corporatised environment of contemporary
university settings (see also Shear and Zontine's discussion of corporatisation, this volume).

Even with the development of new student apartment complexes,
like University Village, the demand for housing on and adjacent to the
campus has become voracious largely as a result of Temple's transformation from a commuter school to a residential campus. The lat-

est instalment in this story is that students are now seeking housing in Yorktown. As the owners of the Yorktown homes have aged, and since homeownership opportunities for African-Americans have now expanded dramatically from the time when the development was first built, real estate speculators are now buying up the homes as investment properties and renting them to students. When I was back in Philadelphia during the summer of 2008, and visited several of the Yorktown residents who had participated in the original Death and Rebirth project, many told me that they increasingly had to put up with their student-neighbours drinking, taking up parking spaces and generally disrupting the peace and cohesion of the Yorktown community. When the community was built, a city code was enacted stipulating that Yorktown homes should be inhabited only by single families but getting the city to enforce this code has been a challenge. According to resident Pam Pendleton-Smith, what people in Yorktown are concerned about is not so much gentrification as transiency. As she told me, 'As long as there has been a Yorktown community, there have also been Temple students living among us. We didn't even know that they were there a lot of the time. They didn't become a problem until 2000'. At that time, a Temple employee bought up three Yorktown houses, renovated them, and rented them to groups of Temple students (see also Zook 2008).

Adding to these anxieties among Yorktown residents, in the autumn of 2007, Temple's then-president, Ann Weaver Hart, announced The Temple University Employee Home Ownership Program, a plan modelled on a similar University of Pennsylvania programme but far more modest in its resources. Although this program was suspended for a time during the 2008 financial crisis, it is now back in operation. The university now provides a low-interest loan of up to $5,000, coupled with other public subsidies, to encourage Temple faculty, staff and students to buy houses within a certain radius of the campus (see http://www.temple.edu/hr/departments/benefits/homeownership.htm). The programme was publicly announced without any consultation with neighbourhood organisations or locally elected officials, further exacerbating the community's fears that Temple intended to displace them, once and for all.

Through working on the Death and Rebirth project, the students and I discovered a neighbourhood on our doorstep that was far more complex than media representations had ever suggested. We heard stories about the jazz clubs on Jump Street, about the memorable concerts that people had attended at the famous Uptown Theater on Broad Street, now long shuttered but once a first-class venue which had hosted such stars as Ray Charles, Stevie Wonder and the Jackson Five. We saw the multiple ways in which our institution, Temple University, was part of a complex history of both neighbourhood enrichment and, perhaps more to the point, neighbourhood disruption. We also began to question some of our assumptions, many of which reflected popular media representations (e.g., Smith 2006) about the contested and often opposing perceptions of what the past 'death' and current 'rebirth' meant for the campus and for various constituencies in the neighbourhood. The newspaper we produced provided an alternative narrative to the story of the deteriorating Black 'ghetto' by recognising and celebrating the community's many successes and by documenting its many struggles.

The students we teach in the U.S.A. have grown very accustomed to the presence of corporate interests in academic settings. They come to the university after years in state-sector schools, which are festooned with Coke machines and logos of other corporate sponsors, as schools struggle for adequate funding in this era of anti-tax sentiment and declining municipal revenues. Through our collective witnessing, the 'Death and Rebirth' project provided the students with an alternative perspective on the consequences of corporatisation and gentrification. We also came to see that this project of 'reclaiming' neighbourhoods from 'blight' – what Neil Smith (1996) has called 'urban revanchism' – is also an agenda with racialising effects as Black urban spaces become glossed as impoverished 'slums' and 'ghettos' in order to justify such interventions.[2]

In her stimulating article, 'Imagining justice: challenging the privatization of public life', Nancy Jurik makes the pertinent and critical recommendation that, 'We need to recognize and examine our own embeddedness in the new privatisation. We must consider how much such trends are colonizing our research, teaching and service agendas' (2004: 9). Although this was not my intention when we began the 'Death and Rebirth' project, awareness of the penetration of corporate interests into the university and, consequently, the neighbourhood where we were carrying out our work, heightened our understanding of both the solidity and the fragility of the community that we had came to know and appreciate. For those of us who seek to be activist-scholars, Jurik recommends that we combine 'teaching, research and activism' (2004: 10). As she writes, 'To accomplish what we get paid for and still actively promote social justice, we have to identify methods for making our teaching, research, and/or administrative activities complement scholarly activism' (2004: 10).

Part of our charge as activist-scholars is to make our students aware of the multiple landscapes that have characterised both our university environments and surrounding neighbourhoods during various historical periods and to show them how current neoliberal redevelopment projects heighten and exacerbate long-standing inequalities along axes of race and class. Though this raised political awareness does not – indeed cannot – guarantee any particular outcome, helping students to understand themselves and the institutions they inhabit as intrinsically political in nature is a first step toward encouraging their possible engagement in future efforts aimed at social change. Local fieldwork projects, especially those undertaken in close collaboration with community partners, have the potential to achieve that goal.

Acknowledgments

First and foremost, my deepest debt of gratitude is to Ms Paula Peebles, activist, community leader and teaching partner extraordinaire: this project would not have been possible without her. I am also greatly indebted to Monica Miller, who did such an admirable job, keeping Paula and me on track, contributing her excellent research skills, and making sure that the publication actually got finished, printed and distributed. The staff of the Renaissance Community Development Corporation provided a wonderful space for us to use as our 'Death and Rebirth' headquarters. I am appreciative of all of the students who participated in the 2003 class: for this paper, I have drawn particularly on the excellent research of Marcus Moore, Monica Miller and Dorothy Summers.

Some of these ideas were initially presented at a symposium entitled, 'Neoliberalism and Academic Practice', which was held at the University of Massachusetts in Amherst in April 2008. I thank Boone Shear for inviting me to participate in that event and for co-editing this book with me. I began thinking about writing specifically about the collaboration between community organisations and researchers during my year as a Boyer Scholar, 2006–07. I thank the Center for Service and Learning at IUPUI for that support and for providing such a collegial group of scholars. Members of the Millennium Black Studies Seminar at IUPUI also provided wonderful comments on an earlier draft of this article, as did Philadelphia community leader and activist Yumy Odom. Thanks are also due to Dana-Ain Davis, to Sue Wright, to Tina Morton and to Davydd Greenwood for his careful reading of this chapter and helpful suggestions. Any remaining deficiencies are reflections of my inability to integrate all of their excellent suggestions.

———————————————◆———————————————

Susan Brin Hyatt is Professor of Anthropology and Founding Director of the MA in Applied Anthropology at Indiana University-Purdue University Indianapolis (IUPUI). She is a former community organiser who worked on the South side of Chicago in the 1980s. Her research focuses on grassroots movements, social policy and poverty in the U.S.A. and the U.K. She is the co-editor of the forthcoming Routledge Companion to Contemporary Anthropology, with Simon Coleman and Ann Kingsolver, 2017.

Notes

This chapter originally appeared in *Learning and Teaching: The International Journal of Higher Education in the Social Sciences* Winter 2010, 3(3): 6–31.

1. According to Temple student Stephen Zook (2008), several families were displaced from North Central Philadelphia to facilitate the building of Yorktown. He writes, 'In order to create this oasis, the city took the 153-acre section by eminent domain, and sent several thousand people packing'.
2. Another example of engaged research that encourages students to examine the history of a neighbourhood that was displaced by the construction of an urban campus is Paul Mullins's urban archaeology project at Indiana University-Purdue University Indianapolis (see Mullins 2003, 2006, 2008).

References

Bear, Larry Alan (1990) *The Glass House Revolution: Inner-City War for Interdependence,* Seattle: University of Washington Press.

Blum, Debra (1995) 'The Apollo of Temple? Delphi-nitely', *Chronicle of Higher Education,* 17 March.

Burton, Cynthia (2002) 'How a blight plan in N. Philadelphia fell apart', *Philadelphia Inquirer,* 30 March.

Carlson, Scott (2006) 'A bigger and better complex', *Chronicle of Higher Education,* 14 April.

Clark, Vernon (2005) 'Experiment now cherished home', *Philadelphia Inquirer,* 21 October.

Etienne, Harley (2013) *Pushing Back the Gates: Neighborhood Perspectives on University-Driven Revitalization in West Philadelphia,* Philadelphia: Temple University Press.

Goode, Judith and Schneider, Jo Anne (1994) *Reshaping Ethnic and Racial Relations in Philadelphia,* Philadelphia: Temple University Press.

Gose, Ben (1998) 'Temple U. raises standards to woo suburban students', *Chronicle of Higher Education,* 11 December.

Gregory, Steven (2013) 'The Radiant University: Space, Urban Redevelopment, and the Public Good,' *City and Society* 25(1): 47–69.

Harrison, Sally (1998) 'Between tower and street', *Journal of Urban Design* 3, no. 1: 5–38.

Hechinger, Fred M. (1961) 'Campus vs. slums: urban universities join battle for neighborhood renewal', *New York Times,* 1 October.

Hyatt, Susan B. (2003) 'Report from the field: the death and rebirth of North Philadelphia', *North American Dialogue,* 6, no. 1: 12–16.

Jurik, Nancy C. (2004) 'Imagining justice: challenging the privatization of public life', *Social Problems,* 51, no. 1: 1–15.

Koptiuch, Kristin (1991) 'Third Worlding at home', *Social Text,* 28: 87–99.

Kostelni, Natalie (2003) 'Plans afoot to rehab Cecil B. Moore Ave.', *The Philadelphia Business Journal,* 5 September.

Miller, Monica (2004) 'Why not in my backyard? A community's campaign for supermarkets', in *The Death and Rebirth of North Central Philadelphia,* Camden, NJ: Renaissance Community Development Corporation, 12–13.

Moore, Marcus (2004) 'In the shadow of an ivory tower: race and space in North Central', in *The Death and Rebirth of North Central Philadelphia,* Camden, NJ: Renaissance Community Development Corporation, 7–8.

Mullins, Paul R. (2003) 'Engagement and the color line: race, renewal and public archaeology in the urban Midwest', *Urban Anthropology,* 31, no. 2: 205–229.

Mullins, Paul R. (2006) 'Racializing the commonplace landscape: an archaeology of urban renewal across the color line', *World Archaeology,* 38, no. 1: 60–71.

Mullins, Paul R. (2008) 'Marketing in a multicultural neighborhood: an archaeology of corner stores in the Midwest', *Historical Archaeology,* 42, no. 1: 88–96.

New York Times (1985) 'Around the Nation: Bell Computer Center Planned in Philadelphia', *New York Times,* 27 March.

O'Neill, James M. (1998) 'Temple raises the bar in attempt to attract students from suburbs', *Philadelphia Inquirer,* 9 February.

Pulley, Brett (1995) 'Temple U.'s dispute with Philadelphia stalls a giant sports complex', *The New York Times,* 5 July.

Rodin, Judith (2007) *The University and Urban Renewal: Out of the Ivory Tower and Into the Streets,* Philadelphia: University of Pennsylvania Press.

Ruben, Matthew (2000) 'Penn and Inc.: Incorporating the University of Pennsylvania', in G. White (ed.) *Campus, Inc.: Corporate Power and the Ivory Tower,* Amherst, NY: Prometheus Press, 194–217.

Schuerman, Matthew (2007) 'Can't we all just get along?', *The New York Observer,* 31 July.

Smith, Jesse (2006) 'Development: here comes the neighborhood: can Temple do for North Philly what Penn did for West Philly?', *Philadelphia Weekly,* 6 September.

Smith, Neil (1996) *The New Urban Frontier: Gentrification and the Revanchist City,* New York: Routledge.

Strom, Elizabeth (2005) 'The political strategies behind university-based development: two Philadelphia cases', in D. Perry and W. Wiewel (eds) *The University as Urban Developer: Case Studies and Analysis,* Armonk, NY: M.E. Sharpe, 116–130.

Summers, Dorothy (2004) 'A community of neighborhoods: the diversity of housing in North Central', in *The Death and Rebirth of North Central Philadelphia,* Camden, NJ: Renaissance Community Development Corporation, 6–7.

Teaford, Jon C. (2000) 'Urban renewal and its aftermath', *Housing Policy Debate*, 11, no. 2: 443–465.

Wilson, William Julius (1987) *The Truly Disadvantaged: The Inner City, the Underclass and Public Policy*, Chicago: University of Chicago Press.

Wilson, William Julius (1996) *When Work Disappears: The World of the New Urban Poor*, New York: Alfred A. Knopf.

Zook, Stephen (2008) 'Yorktown: the neighborhood, its history and rebirth', *The Temple News*, 19 May.

CHAPTER 3

To market, to market to buy a . . . middle-class life? Insecurity, anxiety and neoliberal education in Michigan

VINCENT LYON-CALLO

◆◆◆

Introduction

On a beautiful spring evening in 2007, I attended a meeting of the family council at my son's elementary school in Okemos, Michigan. A suburban community located near state government offices and Michigan State University, Okemos is the wealthiest city in the region. It boasts an ethnically diverse public school system that is widely regarded as one of the best in the state. The family council was one of several forums held throughout the community, ostensibly to provide information regarding an upcoming vote on a proposed bond to fund about six million dollars worth of computer technology. Meetings featured presentations by parents, the president of the school board, and representatives from the office of the superintendent (the chief administrator for the school district). Those supporting the bond organised a campaign representing it as an economic development tool. The new technology was represented as enhancing the quality of both the schools and the community.

Both community and individual level investments in education are frequently represented as an antidote to increased insecurities facing members of the middle class. I draw upon my interactions with both universities and K-12 schools to explore how such practices continue to make sense to students, parents, and policymakers despite the lack of evidence showing that such strategies are sufficient to overcome increasing inequalities and declining economic security for much of the U.S. population. I suggest possibilities for alternative practices challenging impacts of increasingly corporatised and individualised education upon subjects of the new economy.

This particular meeting began with a PowerPoint slide with Margaret Mead's famous saying, 'Never doubt that a small group of dedicated citizens can change the world; indeed, it's the only thing that ever has'. But, what was it about the world that needed to be changed? The presentation continued with an overview of the dismal state of Michigan's economy and the impacts on school funding of what was being referred to in Michigan at the time as 'a one-state recession'. The 2008 recession hit Michigan earlier and more severely than other states. Michigan was the only state to see house prices fall in 2006. Official unemployment in the state has been consistently two to two and a half times the national average, with official unemployment in March of 2010 leading the nation at 14.1 per cent. Over 3,000,000 manufacturing jobs were lost in Michigan in the first eight years of the twenty-first century, even before the bankruptcies that hit the automobile industry in 2009. Demand for food assistance, homeless shelters, and housing assistance were at all-time highs (Michigan Catholic Conference 2008) with one in every seven citizens receiving food stamps in the state in 2008.

As a result, everyone in the room was quite familiar with the state of Michigan's economy. But, then a slide appeared with a picture of Thomas Friedman's *The World is Flat* along with accompanying statistics about the declining standards of living for middle-class Americans, including data on outsourced jobs, how children today can expect to have virtually no stability in employment, and how a college education is no longer a guarantee of a middle-class life. That was represented as 'the new reality' that we needed to help students negotiate. In subsequent discussions with community members, that message proved to resonate quite well with their experiences. Most people expressed that the world had irreversibly changed in significant ways, and that the new globalised economy had produced a situation with little hope for a stable life for many people.

But, how did leaders of the school district suggest we work together to 'change the world' and respond to this 'new reality'? The answer was to pass the proposed bond proposal so that already relatively privileged students could be educated with cutting edge technology. That way, they could excel academically even in the context of global competition, and would thus have the best chance to avoid future economic instability.

This meeting became the impetus for a several year effort to build a collaborative ethnographic project working with school administrators, school board members, parents, and community members to try to facilitate a rethinking of how we approach the issues together in the context of the increasingly complex economic and emotional strains confronting the middle class in the United States. As Wacquant (2009), building upon earlier insights from Pierre Bourdieu (1998), notes in his book, *Punishing the Poor,* neoliberal restructurings destabilised waged labour while producing economic and emotional insecurities up and down the social scale. Many people who once thought of themselves as moderately well-off worry that their children will not be able to achieve middle-class status. A 2008 Pew Research Center report reaffirms this anxiety, noting that new stresses are challenging that very segment of the population who have seen their incomes decline in real terms since 1999. For the first time in over a half century, a majority of Americans described as middle-class did not feel they were doing better than they had five years earlier (Pew Research Center 2008).

I found that middle-class residents of Michigan were responding to this newfound insecurity through focusing their energies on educational aspirations, favouring individualised privilege over collective efforts to transform the systemic conditions producing increasing inequities. A perceived declining quality of public education combined with understood budgetary constraints at state and federal levels are being accepted as justifications for transforming public schools in a market driven, neoliberal manner.

Clearly, the early twenty-first century has been a challenging time for the middle class in the United States. The economic difficulties that have affected 'rust belt' states like Michigan for several years have now begun to be felt throughout the nation. The policies and practices of privatisation, marketisation and deregulation, justified in the name of individual 'freedom' and 'responsibility', have led to declining real wages for most workers along with growing levels of economic inequality (see, for example, Bernstein, McNichol, and Nichols 2008). Escalating costs for food, combined with plummeting real estate market with record levels of mortgage foreclosures and tightening of the availability of credit (which was maintaining the illusion of middle-class status for millions throughout the past decade), brought the consequences of decades of restructurings into sharper focus for many people.

Despite this new state of economic anxiety, collective movements aimed at addressing the class processes that have produced increased insecurities for working people have certainly not yet become widespread. But, as I have argued elsewhere (Lyon-Callo 2008), it is an oversimplification to suggest that these social actors are not actively responding to the impacts of neoliberal globalisation or that collective movements would emerge if only ordinary citizens were enlightened to what was 'really happening'. On the contrary, the people I encounter are often thoughtfully responding to conditions, but only in ways that make discursive sense to them. It is indicative of existing discursive and systemic conditions that class-based, collective movements are not particularly popular ways of responding. Therefore, it is essential to focus our ethnographic and analytic attention on the concrete practices through which social subjects respond to increasing social, emotional, and economic insecurities. The increasingly popular angst about economic insecurities, mistrust of large corporations and finance capital, and a loss of faith in either major political party have not yet resulted in movements aimed at transforming the class processes producing the insecurities such as those that were attempted at various points in the twentieth century. Why has that not occurred?

To address that question, I both analyse public policies around education and educational practices and draw upon my observations, interactions, and discussions with two groups of people: fellow parents in my children's school and students at my university. For the first group, I attended public meetings, paid careful attention to the campaign around the school bond issue, and engaged in dialogue with fellow community members about these issues to attempt to gain a fuller understanding of subject positions and practices. With the second group, I mostly entered into group and individual discussions with undergraduate students. Before discussing those particular cases, however, let me first turn to a discussion of the role of education in social and economic restructuring.

Neoliberal restructurings and the production of corporatised schooling and universities in the U.S.A.

Schools and universities are sources of knowledge production, which both help to craft material and ideological relations and are themselves a product of those conditions. Educational institutions reflect, reinforce, and produce particular ways of thinking and being. Education has historically played a particularly important role in both the popular imaginary about and the actual possibilities for upward mobility in the U.S.A. A correlation between educational achievement and lifetime earnings supports this connection. Similar correlations also exist between unionised workplaces and earnings, race and earnings, and class background and lifetime earnings, suggesting that it might not be so clear-cut to assume that an individualised focus on education remains the sole answer to upward class mobility. Whether accurate or not, a number of stories about the importance of education for attaining middle-class status have become taken-for-granted truths about life in the U.S.A. For example, the development of excellent public schools and universities producing both a highly educated population and cutting edge research and innovations within universities has often been credited with helping to produce the dominant economic position of the U.S.A. globally during the last half of the twentieth century. Furthermore, a tale of upward mobility through educational opportunities for all has been promoted as a strength of U.S. meritocracy.

Many of these beliefs constitute national myths about class mobility through American history. The funding formula for public (that is, state sector) schooling in the United States is most often based on local property tax revenue, a formula guaranteed to reproduce inequalities. We also know that the history of racial apartheid in the U.S.A. through the nineteenth and twentieth centuries did not provide anything resembling equal opportunities. As the work of Gary Orfield (Orfield and Lee 2006) and Jonathan Kozol (2005) show, even in the post-Civil Rights era, schools in the U.S.A. are becoming more segregated and more unequal as residential housing patterns continue to be characterised by patterns of racial and class segregation. In fact, a 2010 report by the U.S. Department of Education documents how economic segregation in schools increased during the first decade of the twenty-first century (U.S. Department of Education 2010). And, of course, analyses of how schools reproduce inequalities in the U.S.A. are not new. The works of Willis (1977) and Bowles and Gintis (1977) documented decades ago how schooling operated to both reinforce existing social class positions and produce class processes. Nonetheless, as inequalities throughout the nation have increased and economic well-being has become much less stable for many people, a faith in the belief that individual investments in education are key to individual and national success remains powerful.

Despite the public's professed belief in the importance of education, however, three decades of altered tax policies lowering the rate of taxation upon both individuals and corporations in the U.S.A., declining real wages for many working people across the nation despite increased rates of productivity, and a continued federal budgetary focus on military related spending has produced a perceived economic crisis accompanied by altered funding for education. Many administrators of K-12 schools and universities have responded by embracing market driven, neoliberal restructuring efforts. At the college and university level, the move towards market-driven, top-down, corporatised administrative efforts has been well documented. In one of the earliest works describing the corporatised public university, Aronowitz (2001) argued that transformations, where training and outcome-based assessments have been promoted and embraced, have actually impaired learning. Giroux (2007) offers a similar analysis, arguing that the neoliberal, corporatised university is exacerbating existing inequities, as education moves towards a narrowly defined notion of job training. Bousquet (2008) states that universities are crafting partnerships with private industry that increasingly exploit the labour of students through unpaid or low-paid labour undertaken under the guise of augmenting students' educational training with practical experiences. Students latch onto what they perceive as opportunities to gain experiences that might put them at a competitive advantage for prospective future employment. Not only are public colleges and universities serving as publicly funded training programmes for private capital, they are doing so in the name of enhancing the practicality of higher education.

Saltman (2007) makes an important intervention placing the corporatisation of schools and universities within a framework of the larger neoliberal march towards privatisation, deregulation, and market driven practices. He suggests that this is part of a larger class-based dynamic against participatory democracy and for corporate control. Saltman (2007) argues that a crisis (natural or man-made) is often a ready excuse for converting public schools to private ones through charter schools or voucher programmes or for adopting other market based strategies. Saltman's most important contribution to this debate is his analysis of how so many of these efforts in the U.S.A. and across the globe are being driven by private foundations and well connected educational leaders. In a public talk he gave at my university in April of 2009, Saltman criticised the ways in which both the Bill and Melinda Gates Foundation and Department of Education leader Arne Duncan promote the neoliberal approach of treating education like a business. He argued that the 'venture philanthropy' of wealthy donors, like Bill Gates and George Soros, 'pushes privatization and deregulation, increasing the centrality of business terms to describe schooling, like "competition", "choice" and "failure". "Grants" become "investments", "donors" become "investors" and a "grant list" becomes an "investment portfolio"' (Holderbaum 2009). Finally, he suggested that even though the economic recession of 2009 had led to some popular questioning of the neoliberal tenets of deregulation and unfettered markets, administrators of schools and universities were still embracing neoliberal policies and practices.

Russom builds upon Saltman's work by critiquing the efforts of the Department of Education in the first year of the Presidency of Barack

Obama (Russom 2010). Russom suggests that the market-driven, neoliberal restructuring of public schooling policies of the Bush administration have been expanded with the Obama administration. Governmental support promoted standardised test-driven education and public funding for largely non-union private charter schools, spurring educational reform through market-based competition. Ravitch offers a similar critique of recent directions in educational policies and practices in her most recent book. She argues that testing and competition between schools, combined with insufficient funding, has produced declining educational results. Like Saltman, she criticises the dominant position that private foundations have taken in promoting educational reforms. Such practices are not only producing worse education but the reliance on private foundations is fundamentally antithetical to democracy (Ravitch 2010).

The question that remains, however, is why these phenomena are occurring at this particular historical moment? How did it come to make sense to corporatise higher education, impose privatisation schemes and apply market principles to public schools and universities? Why did these measures occur in the absence of an effective alternative movement existing to challenge those moves? The processes unfolding within education today are the continuation of policies and practices that dismantled economic and emotional security for millions of other working people in other sectors years earlier. To understand what is happening in education, we need to analyse both the policies and the consent to, or resistance against, those policies within that broader social context.

While national policies like 'No Child Left Behind' or the impacts of private foundations upon educational policies are very important components of what has occurred, it is also important to explore ethnographically how these decisions are made, supported, or challenged at local levels. Through such an analysis of these debates as they played out in Michigan, I suggest that another important component is to analyse how increasingly insecure middle-class citizens are caught in a set of contradictions. They 'know' that individual pursuit of education is the only chance to secure an increasingly elusive place within the middle class. Yet, they also know that the quality of education is problematic and uneven and feel there is little they can do to change those conditions. When coupled with increasing debt and declining job prospects and within the context of popular discourses against public services and governmental programmes, it may appear to be common sense for well-meaning, concerned, increasingly insecure citizens to support efforts to neoliberalise education. To demonstrate that point, let me return to the issue of schooling in Michigan.

Educating against the impacts of globalisation?

Michigan provides for an interesting case study not only because of its extreme economic distress, but also because it funds education differently from the other U.S. states. In what was described as an effort to produce both economic development and more equitable school funding, Michigan voters adopted Proposal A in 1994. Funding schools through local property taxes was replaced by a new formula where the state funds local school districts from money generated by a state sales tax, a state-wide property tax, and a tax on cigarettes. Each school district receives a payment per pupil from the state based upon school enrolment. However, rather than per pupil payments to each district being equal, the state pays different amounts to different districts. Those districts that had taxed themselves at a higher rate prior to 1994, usually the wealthiest school districts, receive the highest payment. The funds coming from the state to local school districts are to pay for all instructional costs. Local communities are forbidden to tax themselves in order to pay for any routine operating expenses such as teacher salaries or supplies, but they can do so to support the cost of infrastructure development.

What is perhaps most significant about Proposal A for my argument is how it represents one of the earliest state-wide models of a market driven educational reform. The basic structure of the funding model, combined with the adoption of 'schools of choice' where students in a region can choose which school they attend, encourages competition for students between school districts. Districts are financially encouraged to lure students from other districts into their own district in order to receive more funding.

Of course, some school districts started at a disadvantaged point in this so-called 'free' market. The per-pupil allocation from the state leaves in place existing inequalities. Michigan's citizens, already living with some of the most racially and class segregated schooling and housing in the nation (Landauer 2006; Orfield and Lee 2006), voted to implement a funding system that, by design, largely maintained separate but unequal schooling. When Proposal A was passed, a basic funding amount for each school district was established based upon the amount of funding a district had been receiving under the local property tax system. At that time, funding for school districts differed by more than

$8,000 per pupil from the highest funded to lowest. Instead of establishing equally funded school districts, there was a stipulation that lower funded school districts would receive bigger annual funding increases. In practice, a combination of lean budgets and a political climate favouring privatisation and smaller government resulted in the funding gap between the highest and lowest funded school districts only being reduced by slightly over $1,500 during the first twelve years of Proposal A. Wealthier school districts continue to receive much larger allocations from the state per pupil. For example, my school district of Okemos, the wealthiest school district in Ingham County in terms of per capita income, received over one thousand dollars per student more than the neighbouring lower-income city of Lansing. There is also clearly a racial component to this funding mechanism. In a state where 41 per cent of African-American children lived in poverty in 2006, compared to 18 per cent of white children, the state provides significantly more funds to those districts with predominately white children.

This legislation has recently come under a great deal of criticism within the state. A 2009 editorial in *The Lansing State Journal*, entitled 'Use a special session to fix Proposal A' describes quite well the intent of the legislation and articulates the most popular criticisms. 'Proposal A was supposed to incentivise education improvements by tying aid to pupils. If you gained students, you gained cash; if you lost them, you lost the aid.' (Lansing State Journal 2009: 6A). The editorial went on to suggest that school districts should be allowed to raise more funds. Interestingly, it made no mention of addressing the structured inequities or the market-based aspects of Proposal A. Nor was there a suggestion of adopting a new funding model similar to that used in the state of Vermont, whereby the state collects the revenue based upon local property taxes and redistributes the funds nearly equally to all school districts in the state. Instead, the hope was that a special session of the state legislature would reform the act towards allowing wealthier communities to levy higher taxes on themselves thereby increasing their resources over other school districts.

As Michigan has the nation's worst economy, the per pupil allotment from the state has not kept up with rising retirement and health care costs and thus districts throughout the state have been cutting programmes. School boards throughout the state attempted to forestall more disastrous cuts by bringing bond proposals before voters to cover costs allowed under the law. Often, as in this case, they did this by articulating a vision of stronger schools as both a hope for children's future success and as a way to slow declining home values.

At the public forum I attended, many people voiced support for this logic. I sat there listening to the discussion just feeling sadder and more frustrated by the moment. These are people whom I have come to know as, for the most part, quite thoughtful and well-meaning. They really want to be helpful. Yet, the only strategy being articulated was accepting the 'new reality' and engaging in individualised coping strategies such as training students to invest in maintaining their relative white and class privileges.

Trying to keep in mind that my children need to go to those schools, and also wanting to build relationships for collaborating together over the coming years, I tried to be diplomatic. I raised my hand and said how I appreciated the snapshot of the political economic challenges of today and that those were indeed troubling dynamics. I then asked, though, if there perhaps was another way of both thinking about the current situation and of educating students to respond to recent social and economic restructurings. I suggested that what was being described as 'the new reality' was, in fact, the outcome of particular practices and policies that were not some sort of natural occurrence that existed beyond the reach of human agency. Therefore, perhaps a large group of humans could actually change the world but only if they worked collectively to remake that 'reality' and produce one with more equality and democracy. I suggested that educating students that the only 'rational' or 'logical' approach to deal with these circumstances was to embrace individualism and accept that they needed to compete in that 'reality' would, in fact, contribute to reproducing modes of governance of the self that reinforce structures of inequality. Alternatively, perhaps we could think about how to educate students on how to analyse the class dimensions of globalisation and organise collectively to transform those conditions. Public education might educate students for something beyond how to compete with billions of other potential workers in a constricting labour market. And that if we wanted to address the problems facing the schools and the students' future, we could not just look within the schools. Instead, I argued, what was causing the stress and insecurity locally was a result of a broad range of neoliberal social and economic restructurings across the globe and that much work needed to be done collectively outside of the schools to transform an increasingly unequal, authoritarian, and class exploitative society.

Of course, the initial response was silence. Quickly, the meeting was brought back on track to the notion that the best hope for the future of residents of the community was to support increased funding for more technology. A presentation that began with the idea that a small group of citizens can change the world ended with a sentiment that a local community is powerless to alter broad global, political economic forces: thus, the only reasonable strategy is to embrace the market and to maximise individuals' chances for success. Of course, given that this meeting was largely set up as a venue for building parental support for promoting investments in their children and the local community in an increasingly hostile global economy, this was about the only imaginable response at that moment.

However, over the course of the following years, the conversations continued in all sorts of community settings. What became increasingly clear was that, while not always using the same terms, there was fairly widespread agreement that the current funding model within the state was not working well. There was also a commonly articulated understanding about a class dimension to recent restructurings and that the future was looking increasingly insecure. What people were expressing was not a lack of understanding so much as a pragmatic hope that education might work. More importantly, what was most widespread was a sense that there was no other reasonable alternative. It appeared to be commonsensical to follow the ideals of privatisation and market driven educational initiatives while striving to produce neoliberal subjects who respond to the economic crisis in individualised manners. This is not uncommon. As Zizek (2008), drawing upon the work of Jacques Lacan, argues, it is misplaced to understand such responses as a consequence of people not knowing about structures of inequality. Rather, he suggests, people learn to not know what they understand they cannot change. When people have seen other efforts result in failure or punishment and given the lack of spaces and places for effectively addressing growing global inequities, it comes to make good sense for subjects to embrace local and individualised efforts.

However, those plans have not worked out well. The spring of 2009 saw school boards throughout the state voting to close schools to save money. Despite the passage of the technology bond, Okemos continued to lose students and engaged in a contentious school board-led process of balancing the budget. I, along with hundreds of other community members, spent much of the spring of 2009 in a series of public and school board meetings, which eventually resulted in the closing of two of the district's six elementary schools. Interestingly, the two schools slated to be closed were those that had the most ethnically diverse student bodies and the highest percentage of students qualifying for free or reduced lunches. Despite testimony from an assistant superintendent stating that the academic research showed that such transitions affected poorer students most negatively, the school board voted to punish poor students and privilege the well-off in the district while embracing 'schools of choice'.

As Saltman (2007) has suggested, 'schools of choice' is just one part of the neoliberalisation of public schools. Under the guise of more freedom of choice for parents and students and with the logic that more competition will push schools to educate better, many regions in Michigan embraced the 'school of choice' model. Of course, transportation to school is the student's responsibility, which limits this 'freedom' for those unable to afford the time or expense of such travel in a region with poor public transportation.

In Michigan, school districts announce each spring how many openings they will have for each grade for the following year and students can apply to attend any of the schools. Some districts developed specialised, more costly programmes that they marketed to students living in other areas in order to attract those students. Such programmes included public Montessori schools, language immersion programmes, and schools focussed on science and technology. The goal is to compete in the market for students. This follows the market-based educational strategy that Arne Duncan, President Obama's appointed head of the Department of Education, practiced with the Chicago schools (Saltman 2007) and articulated as his vision. One of Duncan's first suggestions in office was for performance-based pay for teachers. Again, the plan is to pursue market-driven competition among workers rather than to address the structural inequities within the educational system itself. Given the existing funding structures within the state, school administrators describe trying to persuade students from other school districts to enrol in local schools through the 'schools of choice' programme as simply a reasonable response. In Okemos, many people did voice concerns regarding the pursuit of 'schools of choice' students. However, the argument articulated was most often not against the neoliberal model but because the district received less money from the state for students living in other school districts.

The liberal notion of education as a solution to economic distress is expressed at both the local and state levels in Michigan. For example, Democratic Governor Jennifer Granholm's state of the state address in 2008 laid out her plans for pulling the state out of economic recession by transforming the automobile manufacturing state to 'the education state'. Laying out an agenda for changes in education, she emphasised that the new global, knowledge-based economy required a renewed focus on education in Science, Technology, Engineering, and Mathematics (STEM) for the state to remain competitive in attracting private capital and for individuals to market themselves to potential employers.

The 2008 plan articulated by Governor Granholm developed out of an earlier effort. In her ongoing quest to respond to the long term economic difficulties facing the state of Michigan, Governor Granholm formed the Lieutenant Governor's Commission on Higher Education and Economic Growth in June of 2004. Under the leadership of Lieutenant Governor John Cherry, this commission brought together elected officials, academics, and heads of state governmental departments to identify strategies for doubling the number of Michigan residents with college degrees within ten years. In announcing the commission's formation, Governor Granholm (2004: 1) stated its rationale as follows: 'If we want a high-performance economy, we must work to improve the strength, depth, and adaptability of our colleges and universities'. The commission developed a set of proposals for improving preparation, expanding participation, helping students complete degrees, and maximising economic benefits. Curricular changes included more stringent math and science graduation requirements for high schools and increased opportunities for dual enrolment and advanced placement classes to allow high school students to do college work. The most widely promoted aspect of the commission's plans, however, were those focussed on maximising the economic benefits of education.

The coupling of educational reform with hoped for economic development appears prominently throughout the commission's final report. An argument was put forth that, while Michigan once was able to thrive with a largely manufacturing economy that required little formal education for many workers, the global economy had shifted in such a way that in order to compete with global competitors, the state must have a highly educated populace. The report emphasised how only 26 per cent of Michigan residents had a bachelor's degree or higher in 2000 while arguing that such a lack of higher education explained why per capita income growth in Michigan had declined relative to the U.S. average over the previous three decades (Cherry Commission 2004: 6). Simply educating more people was not the goal. The commission argued that the state's colleges and universities need to be 'aligned' with perceived future employment opportunities. This was to be done primarily through developing closer working relationships between public colleges and universities and private industry and through the promotion of particular degree programmes. Investing in STEM programmes was represented as key to future economic well-being for residents of the state.

Interestingly, despite proclamations about the need for Michigan to switch from a concentration on automobile production towards embracing education, enhancing education, itself, has not been carried out in practice. A 2009 report from the Center for Michigan demonstrated that 98 per cent of public schools in the state offered fewer than 180 days with an average of 1,066 hours of instruction (below the state recommended 1,098 hours). Okemos Public Schools had 172 school days scheduled with 1,054 hours of instruction during the 2007 to 2008 school year (Center for Michigan 2009). And, yet, this shortcoming in the education offered locally was never mentioned by anyone other than me in any of the dozens of public meetings I attended.

This is just one more example of the inconsistencies between stated intentions and actual practices. There remains a clear contradiction between the educational desires of those faced with insecurity and the availability of ways of responding that might actually address the very factors crafting their problems. Instead, well-meaning social actors are tending to embrace the very sort of market-driven, individualised practices that have contributed to producing the systemic conditions that have resulted in the loss of stable, well paid jobs. I have seen this contradiction especially clearly among students in my university classes.

Neoliberal globalism or class interventions in the classroom

In one of my recent upper level undergraduate anthropology classes, we read Sherry Ortner's article 'Generation X: Anthropology in a Media Saturated World' (1998). While this is not exactly the focus of the article, Ortner does describe a situation of the children of upper-middle parents being frustrated at knowing they would not be able to achieve their parent's standards of living as their belief in generational upward mobility was declining. When I walked into class that afternoon a discussion was already in progress. Three students were discussing their attempts to find jobs and were relating their frustrations to the subjects of Ortner's work. Soon, almost the entire class had joined in with everyone agreeing that the only opportunities seemed to be in food services. I asked if anyone felt they would reach the standard of living of their parents. Everyone except for one student said, 'no'. Her response was 'yeah, when they die'.

This kind of conversation is an increasingly common occurrence in my classroom. Many students seemingly find it quite simple to understand the range of factors involved with the loss of middle-class lives. Perhaps this is because they have experienced this directly in their own lives and/or in the lives of their families and friends. As mostly members of white, middle-class families, they describe knowing that the middle class is being decimated. They can easily construct a fairly complex global and local analysis about it. What they cannot figure out is if there is anything that can be done.

Many students also display a complete disgust and distrust of any sort of political solution. They articulate an understanding of the political process as fundamentally flawed, corrupt, and serving the interests of the wealthy. And, again, for them, there is no realistic alternative. When, for example, we discuss the recent move towards authoritarianism and the decline of direct democracy, there is a palpable sense of disappointment, but even more predominant is their feeling of frustration and resignation.

When I ask if the conditions discussed make them angry, it often leads to an echoing of the ideas expressed in bell hooks' book, *Killing Rage* (1995). They agree they suppress the feelings or use outlets like exercise or drug/alcohol use as ways of not admitting to being angry. After reading hooks' work in class, I suggested that it may be that they, too, might learn to embrace rage and use it as an organising tool. I most often get a response indicating a sense that I just do not understand today's world. They'll often say, 'Yes, that's a great idea, but where are we going to find these other people who will work with us? Because otherwise we'll just be these angry people that no-one wants to be around'.

Even when confronted with empirical examples of more collective contemporary organising efforts taking place elsewhere, the possibility that such strategies will work locally is often dismissed. For example, I recently spent a week discussing the recovered factories movements in Argentina in my large introductory class. A very spirited discussion followed regarding the many shuttered factories in Michigan. I mentioned the possibility of a city or the state using eminent domain to take over closed auto factories and have the laid off workers run them as a public entity. Despite my best efforts to provide a hopeful outlook, the general consensus was that this was unworkable as the idea of a public, rather than private, capital-driven good was antiquated. Similarly, the vast majority of students felt that workers in the U.S.A. would never think it was possible to pursue factory recovery efforts.

As Bourdieu (1998) has argued, neoliberalism is not limited to the policies and practices that promote privatisation and deregulation. These practices also have the material impact of breaking apart communities and disrupting the possibility of collective mobilisations. In the process, individualism and selfishness are transformed into virtues. Most of my students agree with that, but also express the belief that knowing so doesn't change anything. This, then, is another dynamic I hear over and over again. There is a general sense of despair and frustration where they suggest that knowledge can actually seem disempowering because it just makes them upset about things they have no control over. What is particularly frustrating in this context is that many of these students are members of the very same social class of people who are being most deleteriously affected through the economic restructurings. Many students come from families of former manufacturing or agricultural workers and are often the first generation in their family pursuing a university degree. The university is also not particularly demanding with admissions requirements and, while we end up with many excellent students, very few spent much time in their earlier years building records to compete for admission to elite institutions.

Often, my initial reaction to my students' responses is one of frustration; 'What is wrong with these people, how can they be so self-involved and unengaged with challenging what is happening to their future?' But, then, with some effort, I begin to remember that perhaps what is important to consider is how these subject positions have come to make so much sense to them. When I do challenge students to consider what can be done beyond feeling powerless and frustrated, I most often hear a belief that there are only two rational, reasonable strategies worth pursuing to achieve 'success' today. Some argue for fleeing the state in search of better opportunities elsewhere while others argue for embracing individualised access to privilege.

Of course, migrating out of Michigan will not alter what is a much broader global restructuring to the detriment of working people. Recently, for example, I provided students with research documenting the growing inequality in New England states and the increase in the homeless population and in severe poverty across the nation as evidence that what is occurring in Michigan, while extreme, is part of a general trend occurring nationally. While agreeing with my point, students, perhaps rightly so, point out there still are more jobs elsewhere and, since they are not going to change the world, they might as well individually seek out the remaining jobs wherever they are located.

The second 'response' is even more challenging. Many students have embraced a dominant message that the only reasonable thing to do is compete individually in the marketplace. To do that successfully, they need to embrace a set of individualised strategies to maximise their attractiveness to potential employers. For example, we recently discussed

George Lipsitz's (1998) article 'The Possessive Investment in Whiteness' in another class. One student, who had earlier expressed many heartfelt responses against racial and ethnic inequities, asked me, 'I just do not understand this article. He seems to be saying that it's a problem for people to invest in whiteness. But, isn't that what you're supposed to do? Isn't that what everyone does? How else are you going to be successful?' A discussion then ensued where most students agreed that engaging in 'white cultural practices' is just rational, reasonable behaviour as it is the only logical way to survive economically.

What is interesting is how this belief intersects with a very popularly expressed belief in fairness and equal treatment. Almost all of my students clearly express anti-racist sentiments. But, many also express support for the 2006 popular vote to ban affirmative action in the state. Some explain that since race is not 'real', affirmative action just reaffirms unfairness. Other students are just frustrated at what they see as unfair advantages based on race while they, too, suffer economically.

A similar sentiment is apparent in discussions about migration and immigration. This is where student discussion becomes most disturbing. Students who are quite concerned about growing economic and social insecurity begin to articulate the sort of xenophobic anti-affirmative action, anti-immigration and anti-gay rights sentiments that are becoming increasingly popular throughout the nation. In fact, I would argue that the recent increase in hate crimes and the legislative efforts to attack 'unfair' benefits for gays and minorities in Michigan are part of the same trend towards vigilantism against immigrant workers sweeping much of the rest of the country. As Giovanni Arrighi (2005) has argued, economic devastation often brings about the 'self protection of society' efforts in both progressive and reactionary forms. It is not difficult to see a similar set of circumstances unfolding throughout both Michigan and much of the nation with the growth of active movements by middle-class people responding to the new hardships confronting them by working to punish immigrants and to support religious fundamentalism. The loss of security by members of the middle class may precede social actors' decision to collaborate with their exploiters in the hope that it will allow them as individuals some return to a more secure economic position (Hedges 2007; Buck 2008).

Again, it would be an error to read these responses as those of people who are simply being fooled into some false consciousness. For example, when we discuss migration, students easily understand the limitations in the xenophobic perspectives offered by Lou Dobbs or the New Minutemen (http://www.minutemanproject.com). What they do not see is any alternative to Dobbs' anti-immigrant message for protecting their middle-class way of life. Thoughtful students are thus in a quandary. They know the strategies they are embracing are not likely to address adequately the systemic difficulties they and others face, but yet they see little choice.

As Wolff (2007) has noted, this all leaves many members of the middle class in a quandary. Students (and often their parents) understand that there are increasingly fewer opportunities for economic security in waged labour in the U.S.A. and believe that the key to achieving some sort of stability is through pursuing higher education. But, they are also faced with the declining quality of education at public universities produced through the administration's embracing of neoliberal corporatist models, as well as the declining availability of middle-class jobs. Still, students and their families 'know' that they need to obtain a university degree. This is especially timely in places like Michigan where a high school diploma was, until very recently, adequate for obtaining a secure and relatively prosperous life working in manufacturing. But, as the state support for education has declined, costs to students have increased while the quality of education has decreased. Students are paying more money for larger class sizes, and for faculty who are less approachable due to the demand to speed up the production of their teaching, research and service. While just a few decades ago many public universities educated students as well, if not better, than their private counterparts, Wolff (2007) argues that this democratising feature of public education is also becoming a thing of the past. If students think about it, they will soon realise that they are paying more to participate in a system of separate and unequal education. But, what are else are they to do? What alternatives are available to them except to struggle along with an individualised strategy of credentialising themselves while hoping and praying that they will be among the lucky ones?

As the former middle class find themselves losing their ability to find stable, well-paying jobs, frustration and anxiety is created. In the absence of an organised left offering a possibility of collective mobilisations and economic transformations, it is easy for that anxiety to become directed towards resentment against the even lower working class and towards populist messages, such as those articulated by the opponents of affirmative action or by television personalities like Lou Dobbs. In the absence of 'realistic' or 'reasonable' alternatives, support for investing in one's whiteness and for nascent fascism become understood as rational responses to current capitalist practices which are causing economic and psychological insecurities and disorder.

Despite my analytical insights about the current situation, I often find myself feeling similar anxiety and insecurity along with the frustration about the lack of any other alternatives. Having two children, seeing the support for even their relatively good quality schools erode on a yearly basis, speaking with school-board members who readily acknowledge the existence of many pedagogically proven programmes they wish they could afford to incorporate (such as full-day kindergarten and offering instruction in languages other than English in elementary school), and seeing little hope for quality jobs and communities emerging in Michigan in the next decade, I often find myself discussing how to flee the state before it gets even worse, our state-funded jobs disappear, our home loses even more value, and our kids' education suffers so that they will not be able to compete well in the market twenty years from now. This, of course, creates all kinds of emotional and intellectual dissonance as what I want to believe analytically flies in the face of what we emotionally know to be the most rational way of responding to today's insecurities if we want to be 'responsible' parents: that is to embrace our white and class privilege. If we, as the relatively privileged, experience such emotions, it is easy to understand how other members of the middle class also respond to what is occurring in similar ways.

In the absence of any alternatives in the form of collective social movements, such individualised responses make increasing sense as the most reasonable way of responding to 'the new reality'. Very few middle-class residents of Michigan may be consciously engaging in organising global alternatives to the recent state interventions creating increased inequalities and authoritarianism in the state and across the globe or the type of deliberative, reflective effort to build an alternative, non-capitalist economy advocated by Gibson-Graham (2006). Yet I have found that most are very aware and concerned and are responding in ways that make sense to them. The challenge then, as always, remains how to create the possibility for alternative practices to become imaginable.

We can work to make new imaginings possible by critically engaging with community members with the hope that new practices might then become thinkable and emerge. But, when people express an agreement with the critical analysis, but still understand their selves powerless to act against the combined efforts of the state and corporate elites, such work may not be transformative. When social and economic forces are disrupting community, producing economic and emotional insecurity, and promoting individualism and selfishness as virtues, teaching how to analyse social processes critically offers little hope to those who despair and feel themselves disempowered economically and politically. It certainly does not, in itself, help produce the possibilities of collective mobilisations sufficient to alter the material realities under which increasing numbers of people are struggling.

With this in mind, during the spring 2010 semester, I attempted a different teaching technique for engaging the students in both my introductory cultural anthropology course and my upper-level ethnographic theory and methods class. About halfway through the semester, the students were asked to interview four people they knew who had been impacted by recent social and economic restructurings in Michigan. They were to ask what the interviewee thought was producing the problems confronting people in the state, what should be done regarding those problems, and what they themselves were doing. The notes from approximately 150 interviews were then posted on an electronic page for everyone to analyse and discuss. What quickly became obvious to students were the levels of despair, distrust of governmental solutions, blaming of unions and tax policies, and misinformation about levels of taxation. With some prodding from me, students also noticed how these were, almost universally, individualised responses, such as trying for more education or retraining, getting a second job, moving, or starting a home-based business. We then compared that with the recovered factories movement in Argentina and discussed the possibilities of how such efforts might become possible. Students in the introductory class began to consider how ethnography might be done in ways that went beyond simply documenting inequalities and began working collaboratively with community members to rethink resistance possibilities.

In the upper level class, we spent the last half of the semester working on four collective ethnographic research proposals focussed on the issues raised in those interviews. This was a class of 19 students, almost all of whom were anthropology majors. Several of the students had previously taken classes with me and, consequently, were familiar with much contemporary Marxist and anarchist social theory as well as calls for a more activist ethnography. As with all collective efforts, there were challenges. Living in the U.S.A. and attending public schools, they had learned well the habits of individualism and learning as passive receptors of other people's knowledge. I also had to give up past habits. In a class that always had received very positive student evaluations in the past with a format of students reading, discussing, and writing papers, critically analysing several thousand pages of contemporary ethnography and social theory, I had to let go of my accustomed method of leading seminars. Instead, we spent many class periods building skills at working collectively. Eventually, students produced proposals for collaborative ethnographic projects with community members to promote collective responses to local manifestations of broader economic and environmental challenges. Each of the proposals, from a project to help the local food cooperative develop community gardens in low-income areas, to work with a group of homeless activists and community based co-housing advocates to develop cooperative housing options locally, focussed on working collaboratively with community members and a team of researchers. There was no time in the semester to actually carry out the projects and some students graduated at the end of the semester. However, perhaps more importantly, rather than expressing despair or cynicism, almost all of those students embraced an appreciation for new understandings of the enhanced potentials from working collectively and doing anthropology in new, more collaborative ways. Several students continue to plan how to do the work with community members in the near future. Producing proposals in this one class did not in itself transform the local community but it did begin to transform how the students thought of both anthropology and the possibilities of collective actions.

If we hope to do work to actually challenge and transform today's world full of increasing exploitation and inequality, we will need to develop such concrete practices for actualising cooperation and for reviving direct democracy. Imagining is fine but we must also begin to create alternatives. To do that, we need to confront and transform both ideas and structures of power; not just ideas. To create a post-capitalist world, we need to begin creating that world and not just developing more sophisticated analyses of today's exploitation (Gibson-Graham 2006). As citizens and educators, we must begin rethinking our practices in the classroom and as we work with the broader community. As the 2008 report by Pew (Pew Research Center 2008) suggests, middle-class Americans are increasingly troubled by the impacts of recent economic and social restructurings. What is not yet clear, however, are the complex ways in which they understand and respond to those conditions. What I have tried to outline in this paper is a preliminary understanding of the ways in which some middle-class people in one location are articulating and responding to those conditions. They are responding in multiple ways which have one thing in common: they do very little to challenge the types of processes that have produced the increased insecurities within which they find themselves. What I want to suggest is that those of us who are concerned about inequality, poverty, exploitation, and democracy cannot be content with analysing those inequalities or dismissing middle-class subjects as misguided or ill-informed. New subjectivities are being produced through the changing realities of their lives. As Haq and Hyatt have argued (2008), the recent neoliberal policies, which have supposedly freed people from overbearing state interventions and 'liberated' people to provide for themselves and for their communities' own needs, have, in fact, created the groundwork for an even more authoritarian intrusive state whose interventions have actually helped make grassroots activism less possible.

Engaged, activist, ethnographic work with members of this increasingly economically and emotionally insecure middle class (which includes many university students) has the potential to broaden understanding of today's world and generate collective responses to contemporary conditions. There are no guarantees that the nascent class awareness discussed earlier in this chapter will develop into class-based social movements rather than the continued embracing of neoliberal interventions. Such work would not be easy, but as I argue in this chapter, the alternatives are far worse.

◆

Vincent Lyon-Callo is Professor of Anthropology at Western Michigan University. His research in Michigan and Massachusetts has focussed on homelessness, class inequalities, responses to neoliberal restructurings and the possibilities of activist ethnography.

Notes

This chapter originally appeared in *Learning and Teaching: The International Journal of Higher Education in the Social Sciences* Winter 2010, 3(3): 63–90.

References

Aronowitz, Stanley (2001) *The Knowledge Factory: Dismantling the Corporate University and Creating True Higher Learning*, Boston: Beacon Press.

Arrighi, Giovanni (2005) 'Hegemony unraveling', *New Left Review*, 32: 23–80.

Bernstein, Jared, McNichol, Elizabeth and Nichols, Andrew (2008) *Pulling Apart: A State by State Analysis of Income Trends*, Washington DC: The Center on Budget and Policy Priorities.

Bourdieu, Pierre (1998) *Acts of Resistance: Against the Tyranny of the Market*, New York: New Press.

Bousquet, Marc (2008) *Higher Education and the Low Waged Nation*, New York: NYU Press.

Bowles, Samuel and Gintis, Herbert (1977) *Schooling in Capitalism America: Educational Reform and the Contradictions of Economic Life*, New York: Basic Books.

Buck, Pem Davidson (2008) 'Keeping the collaborators on board as the ship sinks: towards a theory of fascism and the U.S. "Middle Class"', *Rethinking Marxism*, 21, no. 1: 68–90.

Center for Michigan (2009) 'School daze: Michigan's shrinking school year', < http://www.thecenterformichigan.net/tcfm/docs/School%20Daze%20Report.pdf?PHSESSID = 719244137482e17c911b229b2086ce8a > (accessed 17 May 2009).

Cherry Commission (2004) Final Report of the Lt. Governor's Commission on Higher Education and Economic Growth, http://www.cherrycommission.org/docs/finalReport/CherryReport.pdf (accessed 11 May 2009).

Gibson-Graham, J. K. (2006) *A PostCapitalist Politics*, Minneapolis: University of Minnesota Press.

Giroux, Henry (2007) *The University in Chains: Confronting the Military–Industrial–Academic Complex*, Boulder: Paradigm Publishers.

Haq, Jaqueline and Hyatt, Susan Brin (2008) 'Paradoxes of progressive government: urban policy under New Labour and the decline of grassroots activism', *Urban Anthropology*, 37, no. 2: 211–249.

Hedges, Chris (2007) *American Fascists: The Christian Right and the War on America*, New York: The Free Press.

Holderbaum, Josh (2009) 'Professor calls for rethinking education', *Western Herald*, 4 August.

hooks, bell (1995) *Killing Rage: Ending Racism*, New York: Henry Hold and Company.

Kozol, Jonathan (2005) *The Shame of the Nation: The Restoration of Apartheid Schooling in America*, New York: Crown Publishing.

Landauer, Bettie-Menchik (2006) 'How segregated are Michigan's schools? Changes in enrollment from 1992–93 to 2004–05', < http://www.epc.msu.edu/publications/REPORT/PR27%20Segregation%20D4%20FINAL%20Feb06%20wlogos.pdf > (accessed 20 May 2010)

Lansing State Journal (2009) 'Use a special session to fix Proposal A', *Lansing State Journal*, 8 April: A6.

Lipsitz, George (1998) *The Possessive Investment in Whiteness*, Philadelphia: Temple University Press.

Lyon-Callo, Vincent (2008) 'Cool cities or class analysis: exploring popular consent (?) to neoliberal domination and exploitation', *Rethinking Marxism*, 20, no. 1: 28–41.

Michigan Catholic Conference (2008) 'Poverty in Michigan: grief, anxiety, and suffering on the rise', *Michigan Catholic Conference Focus* 36(1): 1–5.

Orfield, Gary and Lee, Chungmei (2006) 'Racial transformation and the changing nature of segregation', < http://www.civilrightsproject.ucla.edu/research/deseg/deseg06.php#fullreport > (accessed 8 April 2009)

Ortner, Sherry (1998) 'Generation X: Anthropology in a media saturated world', *Cultural Anthropology*, 13, no. 3: 414–440.

Pew Research Center (2008) 'Inside the middle class: bad times hit the good life', < http://pewresearch.org/pubs/?Year = 2008 > (accessed 14 May 2008)

Ravitch, Diane (2010) *The Death and Life of the Great American School System: How Testing and Choice are Undermining Education*, New York: Basic Books.

Russom, Gillian (2010) 'Obama's neoliberal agenda for education', International Socialist Review, 71, < http://www.isreview.org/issues/71/feat-neoliberaledu cation.shtml > (accessed 29 May 2010)

Saltman, Kenneth (2007) *Capitalizing on Disaster: Taking and Breaking Public Schools*, New York: Paradigm Publishers.

United States Department of Education (2010) *The Condition of Education 2010*, < http://nces.ed.gov/pubsearch/pubsinfo.asp?pubid = 2010028 > (accessed 1 June 2010).

Wacquant, Loic (2009) *Punishing the Poor: The Neoliberal Government of Social Insecurity*, Durham, North Carolina: Duke University Press.

Willis, Paul (1977) *Learning to Labor: How Working Class Kids Get Working Class Jobs*, New York: Columbia University Press.

Wolff, Rick (2007) 'The decline of public higher education', MR Zine < http://mr-zine.monthlyreview.org/wolff170207.html > (accessed 12 May 2009).

Zizek, Slavoj (2008) *Violence*, New York: Picador.

CHAPTER 4

Reading neoliberalism at the university

BOONE W. SHEAR AND ANGELINA I. ZONTINE

◆◆◆

'Whose university? OUR UNIVERSITY!
Whose university? OUR UNIVERSITY!
Whose university? OUR UNIVERSITY!'
A thousand voices echoed through the corridors of the University of
Massachusetts Amherst administration building. Undergraduate and
graduate students, as well as some faculty and community activists,
sat shoulder to shoulder, lining both sides of the narrow hallways and
spilled out into the lobby. Student 'marshals' and organisers walked
through the maze of bodies assessing the action and giving updates
to protest participants. Protestors, soggy but resolute after the cold and
rainy half-mile march from the student union to Whitmore Hall, clapped
and stomped along with the chants. Others beat makeshift drums, played
bells and blew whistles. Students danced through the aisles, transforming their anger and anxiety into a celebration of empowerment. As one
student put it, 'it felt good to feel like we actually had some influence
over what happens in this place'.
    In early November of 2007, spurred by frustration over the lack of
movement on issues that students (and some faculty) had been cam-
paigning about for years, a hasty coalition of undergraduate and graduate students began to plan for a large, coordinated action on four
demands: a rollback of student fees, increased and accountable funding
for student diversity, student control over student space and a halt to
unwarranted police searches. Organisers asked students to forgo classes
for two days and instead attend a number of on-campus events including teach-ins, a press conference and the march. Even with limited time
and planning, the strike was able to generate significant support from
both students and faculty. In addition to the students who marched on
Whitmore, hundreds more attended workshops over the course of the
two-day strike and many instructors cancelled classes or chose not to
attend. The strike, and the brief occupation of Whitmore, ended with
administrators agreeing to a series of meetings to discuss the four de-

mands (a somewhat ambiguous and indeterminable outcome) and gave rise to an ongoing coalition of undergraduate and graduate students.

The general student strike at UMass is just one example of the growing concern and resistance from students, staff and faculty to problematic and changing conditions on campus.[1] Throughout the U.S.A., student unions are organising at an accelerated pace, lobbying efforts are increasing and marches, protests and demonstrations are commonplace. Labour and human rights issues have been met with hunger strikes at Purdue University, University of Vermont, Columbia, Georgetown, and Harvard University, among others. At the University of Virginia, 17 students were arrested in 2007 after a sit-in as part of a Living Wage campaign. In May 2008, 16 students protesting fee increases were arrested at a University California Board of Regents meeting (Gardner 2008). That December, students occupied the New School of Social Research in NYC, barricading themselves into the Graduate Faculty building and demanding more transparency and democracy in university operations. Recent budget cuts to higher education, which politicians sought to justify by referring to the global economic crisis, have further fuelled student opposition. In the first four months of 2009, there were protests and demonstrations at the University of North Carolina, at Middle Tennessee State, New York University, the University of Massachusetts, City University of New York and Penn State University as well as large organised actions in the state capitals of Arizona, Massachusetts and California.[2] Resistance in Europe has been even more active, as European Union member states scramble to restructure and standardise their educational systems in efforts to make Europe 'the most competitive and dynamic knowledge-based economy in the world'.[3] Reforms in Europe and the U.S.A. are presented under various banners, from calls for 'autonomy' in France and 'rationalisation' in Italy to catchphrases like 'world-class education' at the University of Arizona or 'high quality education' at UMass Amherst, but the policy changes bear marked similarity: an interlinked set of transformations put forward in the name of global competitiveness that some critics have dubbed 'university corporatisation'.

Neoliberal restructuring and higher education

By university corporatisation we mean a set of profound, interrelated changes at universities taking place over the past few decades in association with contemporary class restructuring. These changes include: an increase in contingent faculty, the proliferation of corporate-university ties, a focus on commercialisation of research and commodification of knowledge (with the associated devalorisation of research that is not easily commodifiable), privatisation of space and services, the proliferation of corporate and market logics in both policy and everyday discourse, decreasing democratic governance and a shifting of operational costs from the state to individual students and families. In sum, universities are extensively bound up with corporate interests and universities are largely imagined by decision and policymakers as for-profit corporations that are in the business of producing particular types knowledge, relationships and people capable of attracting and benefiting private capital.

The integration of private corporate monies and interests as well as the restructuring of universities towards a corporate design are symptomatic of contemporary class restructuring. Indeed, we understand the corporatised university to be materially and discursively caught up in processes of freeing capital from constraints, processes that work to reinvigorate the dominant class through privatization, deregulation, and the withdrawal of the state (alongside selective intervention) from certain social service provision tasks. This broader project has intensified exploitation and oppression in many places and particularly in the global south, extracting resources and surplus to the global north and disproportionately impacting people of color.

These processes and trends are widespread although not total, homogenous, or unopposed. As Slaughter and Leslie show, by the end of the twentieth century 'a quiet revolution' was already taking place in which 'market and marketlike behaviors' (1997: 11) were coming to dominate academic, labour and administrative practices in English-speaking industrialised countries. The contemporary discursive and material construction of a globalised knowledge economy positions higher education as a primary means and agent of economic growth both within and between nations, even though policies and practices differ in both form and effect in different locations (see Canaan and Shumar 2008 for examples). In this paper we concentrate on the particularities of a specific case, the University of Massachusetts in Amherst (UMass), the flagship campus of Massachusetts' state university system. While we draw on the growing body of scholarship analysing (and criticising) the various aspects of university corporatisation, we shy away from the inclination of some scholars to treat university culture as a previously free and static body of values and practices that is being (or has been) irreparably altered. Historians have argued persuasively that the very development of the American university system, as well as public education in general, has been engineered so as to serve the different needs of the capitalist class in different historical periods (see, for example, Barrow 1990; Bowles and Gintis 1976), and it may well be disingenuous to consider an idyllic period of greater federal funding as simply serving the common good.

Even if the shaping of higher education according to corporate interests is not unprecedented, we find current trends disturbing. It is not necessary to fall back on rosy visions of what the university once was to argue that current developments are not positive. As part of ongoing changes in global relations of production, they demand our critical attention and responses; we suggest that paying close attention to how people experience and imagine themselves in relation to these processes may also provide insights into possible interventions.

In this article we describe and assess corporatisation unfolding at UMass during the latter half of the 2000's. We examine one project mounted in response: an ad-hoc reading group formed by students and faculty in the Department of Anthropology. We draw on our own experiences with the group as well as interviews with other participants to help us analyse the constraints on engaged academic practice. We outline some of the contours of a contemporary academic habitus that we found discourages and suppresses efforts to intervene in the political economic processes of corporatisation and to see a way forward despite – or across – these constraints.

University corporatisation at UMass

While demonstrating awareness of the multiple impacts of university corporatisation, the most pressing concern of many student campaigns has been the cost of education. Issues of access and affordability are particularly urgent at UMass. From 2001 to 2004 Massachusetts reduced its investment in higher education more than any other state in the U.S.A., and Massachusetts now spends more on incarceration than on higher education (PHENOM 2006: 5). As education costs escalate, much of the financial burden has been shifted to students and families. Overall costs for in-state undergraduate students have jumped from $1,573 from 1977 to 1978 to $19,317 from 2006 to 2007, an increase that has outpaced inflation by three to one since 1978 (Wolff 2007). Graduate students have seen mandatory fees grow from $595 to $7,252 since 1987. Rising costs, along with a defunding of outreach programmes and need-based state grants, has made attending UMass a particularly difficult proposition for poor people and members of marginalised groups

(PHENOM 2006; Clawson and Lieblum 2008). Students who are able to enrol are accumulating more and more debt. Indeed, public university graduates in 2004 had on average more than twice as much debt than students graduating in 1993 (Project on Student Debt 2007), an aspect of corporatisation that has received less attention from scholars but which significantly affects students' lives (Williams 2006, 2008).

The university is also increasingly invested in commercialisation and technology transfer (that is, the transfer of ideas and processes developed at the university to private and corporate buyers). UMass currently ranks in the 'top 15 [of academic institutions] in the country in licensing revenue [from intellectual property]' (University of Massachusetts 2006). The passage of the Bayh-Dole Act in 1980 is sometimes identified as a turning point in the development of university knowledge commercialisation, as it allowed universities more readily to own the federally funded products they develop (Minsky 2000).[4] Universities could then more easily establish exclusive licensing agreements with corporations thereby providing a financial incentive to both universities and corporations to invest in this relationship. The implementation of this act has worked to harness the productive activities of university actors into market processes and commodity circuits and to shift public resources towards the private sector.

Universities today are marketed and managed as revenue generating engines of economic growth. For example, during the latter half of the 2000's, Massachusetts Governor Deval Patrick pushed a $1 billion life science bill intended to direct hundreds of millions of public monies to the private sector through tax incentives. The bill also aims to establish collaborative relationships between higher education and industry, reflecting the view espoused by both the state government and UMass administrators of the university as a prime economic driver in terms of innovation, job creation, and workforce development.

Market logics and associated material conditions have also thoroughly penetrated the university's internal operations. Labour conditions and bureaucratic infrastructure are significantly changing: the numbers of contingent faculty are on the rise and the democracy of decision-making processes is deeply compromised. At UMass, the percentage of tenure-track positions among full time faculty has steadily declined from 92 per cent in 1990 to 83 per cent in 2009 while the number of poorly paid non-tenure-track instructors has increased. As Clawson and Lieblum point out, the population of 'clerical and maintenance workers' (2008: 20) is decreasing even as the amount of work that they are expected to complete increases: as a result, at least part of this work then falls to faculty members. Meanwhile, UMass upper level administrators are becoming more like the CEOs of large, for-profit corporations. Between 2003 to 2004 and 2006 to 2007, the number of UMass personnel in top administrative roles increased by 21 per cent, and their salaries grew by 25 per cent on average and 51 per cent overall. At the same time tenure-track faculty saw a slowdown in hiring and comparably modest salary increases (6 per cent from 2003 to 2004 to 2006 to 2007) (Luce 2007). Along with these changes in pay, many faculty note that the university's bureaucratic structure has become more centralised and less democratic – in other words, more structured like a corporation – with associated transformations in university governance. In the words of one tenured professor in the Anthropology department, 'the people up top are not interested in any information flow coming up. Everything flows down'. The professor said that whereas in the 1990s the provost hosted a retreat for new faculty at her own house and was 'very hands on and encouraging', faculty relations with the current provost are quite different: 'Now, if I send an email [directly] to the Provost I'm going to get disciplined for it because I'm stepping outside the lines of communication'.

The character and function of space at UMass is also changing. On one hand the university is creating new buildings and features designed specifically to appeal to the cultural consumptive tastes of a desired population of students, such as elite residence halls with apartment-style single-occupant rooms constructed 'with the explicit aim of attracting affluent out-of-state students' (Clawson and Leiblum 2008: 16) and a new $50 million recreation centre (UMass 2007). This is as much a political and cultural project of producing 'distinction' and changing the racial and socio-economic composition of the student body as it is an economic project intended to bring in more funds; in a revealing quote attributed to a former top administrator, the University seeks to make the student body 'less Old Navy and more Abercrombie and Fitch'.[5]

On the other hand, public space on campus is diminishing and what remains is subject to increasing regulation. There are several ostensibly public and student-oriented complexes on the UMass campus, including an adjoining student union building and 'campus center'. On-campus bookstores are now run by the corporate behemoth Follet and the campus centre is managed as a revenue generating entity. For example, students who wish to utilise rooms for meetings must rent equipment through the campus centre or go without. Posted communications by students in the campus centre are relegated to enclosed glass cases and designated for officially recognised student groups only.

Over four hundred surveillance cameras monitor and record student behaviour across campus. Moreover, the university is looking to extend more campus space for corporate involvement through 'industrial partnerships in new science buildings' (Holub 2009: 8) Attentive to the inherently political nature of the production of space, we see these developments as reflecting and engaging the changing power relations associated with the political-economic transformations we have described. It is no coincidence that space has become a key issue of conflict between students and administrators in this setting. In demanding student-managed spaces within key university buildings like the campus centre, students are also demanding that they be able choose how to use certain spaces. Students want to be able to enact social relations that are not determined by the planners and policymakers who regulate the uses of university spaces and that are potentially alternative to the prevailing market logics being produced elsewhere on campus.

Entrepreneurialism, human capital and everyday practice

Market-oriented and entrepreneurial language and habits of thought produced in the corporate sphere have been adopted by administrators and are becoming increasingly central to the practices of graduate students and faculty members as well. We see these processes as entrepreneurial in that each actor and/or sub-section of the university is encouraged to strive for ever-increasing economic self-sufficiency through various (non-mutually exclusive) strategies, including fundraising (preferably from outside sources such as corporations, private institutions, and alumni); administrative re-organisation and partnerships (both within and outside the university); and tailoring or re-framing academic initiatives to reflect new logics and accommodate new conditions. A senior faculty member described receiving one such lesson in entrepreneurialism when she tried to launch a new graduate certificate: 'So I meet with the Dean who said "Great, I'll support this graduate certificate" but then they turn to me and say, "so, where are you going to get the resources?" As if I control any resources!' She was made to understand that her role should properly include both tailoring her proposal to correspond to the strategic goals already defined by top administrators and acting entrepreneurially to unite human resources and capital in her proposed 'enterprise'.

While individuals, organisations and departments are encouraged and expected to generate revenue, specific practices of accounting, auditing and quantification are becoming more prevalent at UMass (as at other universities: see Canaan 2008, Shore and Wright 1999 and Thorpe 2008 on the U.K.). These assessment tools are often obligatory and mirror the strategies and discourses that are by now widespread in other public or state-funded spheres. They follow a logic that presents the free market as the model for the operation of public services and holds that state expenditures in every area must be justified according to the principles of efficiency, transparency and accountability (Shore and Wright 1999; Thorpe 2008). For instance, the department of Anthropology has invested considerable labour-time and resources in conducting periodic 'Academic Quality Assessment and Development' self-studies, in accordance with the recommendations of the university's 'Office of Academic Planning and Assessment'. Although the goals and progress evaluated in these studies are ostensibly set by departments themselves, the evaluation methods measure how well these goals correspond to the principles of 'quality and cost-effectiveness' as set by senior administrators. 'Cost-effective' departments are those that produce faculty research and teaching that improve the competitive profile of the department in relation to standardised criteria and quantifiable outcomes, and, as a result, the ranking of the university. In the spirit of 'transparency', all subsections of the university are invited in glowing, participatory language to collaborate in finding ways to implement strategic goals: however, the underlying logic of auditing and the parameters of success themselves are not up for discussion.

A recent document outlining a ten-year strategic plan for the University of Massachusetts clearly states that the productivity of faculty, measured in secured research funding, is a top priority. Faculty hires in the future should be clustered in 'the better funded research areas'. Education is a concern, but 'instructional needs cannot be the sole factor in deciding where to allocate new positions'. Instead, 'we will want to consider what sort of return we are going to receive in terms of teaching, research, and service' (Holub 2009: 4). It is precisely this specific definition of 'return' on investment that we are concerned with. Aside from the question of whether or not evaluation itself may be reasonable, we take issue with the lack of democratic participation and the over-representation of corporate interests in the parameters themselves. Audit functions as 'a means for imposing governmentality and transforming culture' (Thorpe 2008). The institutionalisation of these priorities through the coercive diffusion of auditing and assessment tools creates the conditions within which faculty and students are forcefully encouraged to adopt such corporate logics and market-based visions of higher education at the level of subjectivity and habitual practice. This has the potential to marginalise or co-opt other possible conceptuali-sations of what higher education might consist of and produce, such as research that does not further (and may even call into question) the agendas of corporate actors, collaborative working relations, particular types of politically engaged initiatives that reach outside the university, or pedagogical methods that give rise to transformative experiences for students rather than quantifiable skill sets.

Rather than bemoaning how university culture is being lost or de-graded, we instead propose to look closely at what is currently being instilled, produced, and valorised. From this perspective we argue that the most worrying aspect of university corporatisation is not that it represents a shift away from time-honoured intellectual parameters for judging the worth of research, curricula or initiatives, but rather that it represent a shift towards beliefs, practices and subjects produced through market logics, corporate interests and neoliberal discourse.

Neoliberalism is not simply about liberating market mechanisms: rather, it is a way of imagining and enacting the world that requires intensive intervention on bodies, both individually and collectively. Foucault posits that an invariable analytic of neoliberalism is the pro-duction of subjects who are imagined and imagine themselves as en-trepreneurial, revenue generating 'ability-machines' (2008: 226–233). Individuals invest in themselves over their lifetimes. This process of investing in individuals through environmental stimulus, training and support can also be seen at the level of the population, in that policy-makers champion such programmes as a means to stimulate economic growth and successful innovation and ensure the health and wealth of society. In other words, the pursuit of neoliberalism includes an imagin-ing of individuals and populations as human capital. Formal education is perhaps the most straightforward way in which technologies can be deployed on the body to produce particular ways of knowing and being and to invest in human capital, but, following Foucault's concept of governmentality, we are interested also in routine practices, policies and regulations that shape actors' ways of thinking and performing their roles in the space of the university.

At UMass, students and faculty are discursively constructed as en-trepreneurial subjects through everyday routinised practices. Like other workers, as academics we find ourselves responding to the increasing drive to accumulate credentials, certificates and other markers of our diverse and flexible competencies in order to sell ourselves more ef-fectively in the academic marketplace. As Zygmunt Bauman argues, this drive constantly to reinvent oneself as a desirable commodity can be seen as a key aspect of contemporary subjectivity (2007). Given the increasing insecurity of the conditions of academic labour outlined above, it is no wonder so many early career academics flock to various credentialising and 'retooling' schemes in the hopes of increased employability. This trend is experienced by many graduate students and faculty members as a coercive process in which they are being hailed as new kinds of subjects with new roles and responsibilities – fundraising, development, reframing one's own competencies and professional initiatives for improved 'marketability' – that are not what they were trained for or sought when entering higher education. In the words of one faculty member, 'this talk and justification is now having to happen at the individual faculty level so you've got to figure out how your projects contribute to the university's mission, which is a different speak, it's a different language, it's an administrative language, not argued necessarily on [the] intellectual merit of the project'.

One of the more remarked upon and problematic imaginings associated with university corporatisation is that of students as consumers, in which education is cast as a market transaction. In this model, universities sell their products to students and students choose which products – degrees and accreditations – will most benefit them in their aim to produce future revenue. Indeed, anthropologist Art Keene, who has conducted ethnographic work with undergraduate student informants, concludes that students at UMass 'commonly [see] their education in … reductionist terms – not so much a process of learning and exploration and growth but simply a case in which they must pay to play' (2009). Another instructor at UMass opines that, 'with increasing fees and costs to do with higher education, it becomes more and more instrumental, like "I need a degree in order to just get a job"'. With the pressure of escalating loan debt weighing on graduate and undergraduate students alike, this way of thinking is commonsensical even to those who might on principle oppose its logic. As one graduate student instructor of critical pedagogy explains, even though she finds consumer processes in education abhorrent 'I'd never tell them [her undergraduate students], do not accumulate degrees, because they have to do that in the system'.

While students and faculty are enlisted as entrepreneurial subjects through everyday, academic practices, broader discourses and policies relating to understandings of human capital and higher education establish the discursive parameters in which social imaginings take place. In today's globalised knowledge economy, good universities are those that not only generate particular types of knowledge-products and economic relationships but also particular types of subjects who can successfully compete in the global marketplace. In the United States, this view is commonsensical and is largely presupposed by policymakers, politicians and student activists alike. A recent speech by President Obama promoting his education platform exemplifies this logic:

> In a twenty-first-century world where jobs can be shipped wherever there's an Internet connection, where a child born in Dallas is now competing with a child in New Delhi, where your best job qualification is not what you do, but what you know – education is no longer just a pathway to opportunity and success, it's a prerequisite for success ... It's time to demand results from government at every level. It's time to prepare every child, everywhere in America, to out-compete any worker, anywhere in the world. It's time to give all Americans a complete and competitive education from the cradle up through a career (Obama 2009).

In Massachusetts, it is taken for granted at all bureaucratic levels that the primary purpose of education is to invest in human capital. This is codified in Governor Deval Patrick's comprehensive education plan, the 'Readiness Project', which promises to 'guarantee that the Massachusetts educational system will graduate students who will be able to compete for any job in the new economy and that Massachusetts will assert itself as a world center of the twenty-first century innovation economy'. To accomplish this, the project calls for restructuring that would prepare students for the demands of employers in the global economy through proper curriculum alignment, global standards, and accountability measures. Efforts to instrumentalise education for the purpose of economic growth are made even more commonsensical given the impacts of the current economic crisis. From March 2008 until the end of 2009 Massachusetts lost over 136,000 jobs and the unemployment rate had reached 9.4 per cent (Gavin 2010).

Conditions at public universities today are in many ways being restructured by global relations of production and students and faculty are being pulled into discursive practices that in some ways help to naturalise and sustain those conditions. As our own account suggests, the sum total of these processes appears quite coherent and unyielding, its reach extensive and totalising. And yet we suggest that this very conceptualisation of the phenomenon can contribute to the relative paucity of engaged, oppositional responses. We now turn to an exploration of one attempted intervention in the Anthropology Department at the University of Massachusetts Amherst in order to analyse some of the constraints that complicate critical responses to university corporatisation. Drawing on recent theorising by Gibson-Graham (2006)[6] about the way that actors' conceptual 'dispositions' shape the range and character of their responses to political-economic constraints, we argue that, counter to intuition and common wisdom, we might find more effective avenues of intervention if we let go of our totalising conceptualisations and instead approach the problem with what Gibson-Graham term 'weak theory'. By this they mean, for instance, that instead of working to understand the processes of 'corporatisation' as parts of a structural and all-encompassing whole, we instead think of them as contingent outcomes played out in local spaces: this move towards 'weak theory' encourages us to consider spaces of possibility rather than knowing, ahead of time, how possible spaces of intervention are already co-opted and foreclosed.

Reading university corporatisation

In the fall of 2006, during a regularly scheduled departmental meeting, the anthropology department hosted a presentation by a representative from the administration about the benefits and opportunities of teaching on-line courses. Unsurprisingly, the presentation failed to address the troubling implications of the move towards online education and the part it has been made to play in the commodification of knowledge and restructuring of academic labour (Noble 2002). More worryingly, there was not much critical discussion of these issues around the department either. This small episode signalled a larger lack of theorisation of and opposition to the myriad changes at the university that we were caught up in and were often helping to naturalise and reproduce through our everyday practices as academics, students and citizens. We (the authors) began to incite discussion about what we were coming to know and refer to as 'university corporatisation' and we tried to gauge ideas for and interest in potential departmental responses to what was happening around us. In collaboration with a faculty member, we organised the Reading Together Project (RTP), a departmental reading and discussion group intended to address these changing conditions by spurring discussion and building community in the department and ultimately serving as a platform for intervention(s). Over the next two years, an ad-hoc group of graduate students, faculty and sometimes undergraduates met in a variety of locations to discuss readings, ask questions and present ideas about neoliberal restructuring and university corporatisation.

Each year we chose a primary text to provide us with a theoretical and political anchor: the first year, David Harvey's *A Brief History of*

Neoliberalism (2005) helped us theorise and historicise broad political-economic and cultural processes, and the following year, Henry Giroux's *University in Chains* (2007) located the university as a site of hegemonic struggle. We also read numerous articles and book chapters suggested by members of the RTP. With these readings as our foundation, members of the RTP addressed themselves to the questions: What is neoliberalism? How are universities being restructured, and what relation does this have to larger political-economic and cultural processes? What are the possibilities and limitations of academic practice apropos these changing conditions? What are the political-ethical responsibilities of academics in this context? And, finally, how can anthropologists, our department and our group respond? Although RTP membership fluctuated and we never officially defined our goals, our efforts converged around gaining an understanding of how we were caught up in and reproducing the conditions around us and, with this understanding, formulating responses and interventions.

Strategy and praxis

During the second year of the RTP, we organised a two-day symposium featuring three activist anthropologists from outside UMass to discuss different aspects of neoliberal restructuring and academic practice. Public presentations to a large, general audience on the first day preceded a more intimate discussion with members of the RTP; this event was designated as a 'strategy session' that would help the RTP to begin to concretise and enact interventions. At the very beginning of the strategy session, one of the visiting anthropologists asked the group to discuss some of the interventions that we had engaged in or were planning. A Ph.D. student who had been consistently involved in the RTP over the previous two years swiftly responded, 'We haven't done anything to respond, we haven't done anything at all!'.

Her assertion captured the frustration and disappointment some of us were feeling over the RTP's outcomes. Although many of us in the group consider ourselves to be politically engaged or activist scholars, RTP discussions about concrete collective initiatives never seemed to gain much traction. In contrast, we had made significant gains in understanding and theorising what was going on around us. RTP members are quick to talk about this side of the group. According to one participant, it 'helped me to put those [conditions at UMass) in larger context and made me think about what I could do, you know like what's my place in it'. The readings 'really helped [me to think about and theorise some of the changing conditions at the university]', affirmed another. In the words of another participant: '[The RTP] made me more aware of the structural changes that have taken place in the past 28 years or so. It allows me to understand my position in the university as a neoliberal subject in terms of the different types of interactions I have with co-workers, students, faculty [and] colleagues; so it contextualised what it is I do at the university'. Members pointed out that the group had been 'really productive' in terms of enhancing their research and teaching. As a result of the RTP, one faculty member developed her public anthropology seminar around the themes of neoliberalism and university corporatisation. Members of the group organised and participated in at least three conference sessions dealing with neoliberalism and academic practice. We had great success in working towards understanding what was going on around us. However, the authors and some other participants looked on these outcomes as insufficient and suspect, produced out of the very material conditions we were seeking to oppose and contributing to career building and auditable production rather than to the oppositional political action we had intended.

Dispositions and stances

There are a number of fairly evident reasons for the discomfort and challenge we felt in trying to move towards a more engaged political praxis that speaks to the constraining and productive forces in which our project was embedded. As (relatively) overworked students and faculty at an underfunded public research university it was difficult to find time to meet, let alone collectively organise. For example, one faculty member told us that, even though she was very certain that the RTP was 'politically really important', she had trouble even attending meetings, given the professional demands placed on her. Caught up with auditing and accounting tasks on one side and the anxious urge to invest in themselves as academic human capital on the other, it was hard for us to prioritise an apparently non-quantifiable project such as the RTP.

Taking a more phenomenological approach, we might even more usefully look to the habits of thought and action that we brought to the project, such as the way some participants imagined themselves and the RTP as part of a disengaged, academic project even while participating in conversations about possible collective action. This fascinating contradiction can be seen in RTP participants' answers to our question, 'why have we not been able to generate a collective political response [to university corporatisation]?'. One participant responded that she was 'joining a reading group, not a political party', suggesting that a group of academics would intrinsically carry multifarious political agendas and thus have a difficult time mounting a collective response. Another replied that 'the group was very academically focussed ... this was not a group that was like "we're going to be an activist group". This was a group that said, "we're engaging in academic exploration of these forces and how we are implicated in these forces"'.

These responses struck us precisely because many of us in the group, including one of the participants quoted above, had consistently stated the intention that the RTP be part of a political praxis that would transform our collective analysis into collective interventions. Moreover, while having trouble envisioning and enacting responses in the RTP, many of us in the group were also participating in union work and activist efforts on campus. We can perhaps read this discursive disconnect of the interviewees, as well as the group's overall drift towards conventional scholarly work, as reflective of an academic habitus in which academic beliefs and practices are carried out in accordance with an imagined 'sacred boundary ... between scholarship and commitment' (Bourdieu 2003: 24). Conventional and disengaged academic work – 'disinterested scholarship' – is supported by and is part and parcel with the interests of the 'educational bureaucracy', which are often thrust upon and/or 'internalized in the motivations of the scholar: promotion, tenure, higher salaries, prestige – all of which are best secured by innovating in prescribed directions' (Zinn 1990: 9). In sum, we can begin to understand the group's efforts in relation to our individual investments in sustaining and developing our careers: or more bluntly, in our various investments in white and/or class privilege.

From our perspective, it is clear that a deeply held academic habitus and the class positions of RTP members – including ourselves – played a significant role in shaping and constraining the outcomes of the project. Academia is no less compromised than other spaces and, within an increasingly corporatised university, academics are significantly constrained and encouraged to act more thoroughly as 'traditional intellectuals' and 'the functionaries of elite interests' (Shear 2008: 54, citing Gramsci 2003: 12). At the same time, as numerous anthropologists have demonstrated, our position in academia also gives us the opportunity to make interventions in all aspects of our work (Davis 2003, 2005), engage in innovative and radical pedagogy (Addes and Keene 2006; Hyatt 2009), construct alternative histories (Buck 2001), and enact collaborative and politically engaged research projects (Hale 2006; Hemment

2007; Lyon-Callo and Hyatt 2003). The RTP, however, seemingly failed to move in this direction. There was something intriguing about the way that some of us, perhaps the authors in particular, were talking about and theorising social and economic conditions and processes at the university that made it difficult even to imagine effective interventions. Conversations about 'what to do' were often haphazard and emotionally deflating. Indeed, we were frequently frustrated by suggestions from group members (including ourselves) that we perceived to be limited, parochial or reformist rather than transformative. At one meeting, for example, talk about how to respond turned to specific teaching strategies that might get students interested in anthropology. Initial queries about potential group or department responses sometimes devolved into personal complaints of exploitation and mistreatment by the university administration. At these times we would suggest that we needed to keep in mind how changes at UMass are part of a larger, global project of neoliberal capitalism that was resulting in devastating inequalities, cultural and political oppression, domination and structural violence. We needed to think big; we had to work towards dismantling this capitalist system and/or building something else in its place.

This suggestion was usually met with awkward laughter and/or uncomfortable silence. Indeed, this proposal – to 'dismantle capitalism' – is seemingly so far removed from our everyday practices that we felt somewhat uncomfortable or ridiculous even voicing it. In reflecting on this dynamic, one RTP participant said 'I think that [people in the group laughed] because part of them know it's true but they are not going to do shit about it'. Another agreed that 'probably most of us, especially after reading Harvey, agree with you but nobody has any idea how [to proceed in dismantling capitalism]'. One participant expressed this feeling of bewilderment in the face of such a prospect: 'I do not know what to do; I do not know what's effective. I do not have anything to go on or basis for action. And it just seems to me like short of a bloody revolution there is not really a whole lot you can do'. Another member explained, 'It's so deeply engrained, you know, its commonsensical to all of us, it's the wallpaper that surrounds us, because of the success of neoliberal projects'.

For many of us in the group, the 'spectre' of capitalism presented an unyielding, inevitable and near totalising system. The more we understood and emphasised our understandings of neoliberalism and university corporatisation, the harder it was to bring to mind realistic responses. At the final strategy session, this dynamic nearly brought us to an impasse. A faculty member who had participated in the visiting scholars' presentations voiced the critique that the racial processes of economic restructuring had not been sufficiently addressed by the work of RTP participants and argued that the label of neoliberalism itself needed to be discarded because it conceals the true aim and consequence of these shifts, that of enlarging white supremacy. This inspired an intense discussion about what overarching label and theoretical framework best captures the sum of recent political economic and cultural transformations. Unsurprisingly, this exercise in totalising thinking in place of the hoped-for strategy session left many of us feeling frustrated and impotent.

Capitalocentrism and weak theory

If we look to our habits of thought and perception as part of the problem, we might also look to changes in these habits as a first step towards praxis. It is not uncommon, argues J.K. Gibson-Graham, for the left to theorise capitalism as a totalising, global container, system or structure in which social relations, discourses and actions are subsumed (2006). Capitalism thus becomes 'extradiscursive': it is given the status of being real, irrespective of discourse, and therefore there is nothing outside of it; every social relation, act or subject is reflective of, subsumed within, compromised by, or supplemental to capitalism. These 'capitalocentric' modes of thought can be described as 'strong theories', ways of thinking that can explain everything and 'make all phenomena bear on a core thesis' (Gibson-Graham 2006: 212n6). The explanatory power and reach of such 'strong theories' seems at first glance quite an attractive proposition. Indeed, the authors vividly recall the sense of satisfaction emanating from many RTP meetings as we worked together to identify and intellectually master the myriad changes going on around us, casting our analytical net ever wider to draw in more and more processes and trends that could be explained as part of the neoliberal project of university corporatisation. In the face of the impotence and hopelessness inspired by many of the material changes we describe above, this was heady stuff. We had immersed ourselves in strong theory with the hopes of understanding our place and position in relation to the conditions around us.

It then followed that, considering our position (and most likely subjectivity) as already produced through and reproducing an oppressive and exploitative global political-economic and cultural system, the only effective response was to organise against and subvert capitalism. This is, to say the least, a daunting task. With this habit of thought, all the responses we imagined seemed incremental and tedious, supplemental, or already compromised. Indeed, the pitfall of 'strong theory' is that explaining all existing and potential social phenomena actually works to close off possibilities, in that 'while it [strong theory] affords the pleasures of recognition, of capture, of intellectually subduing that one last thing, it offers no relief or exit to a place beyond' (Gibson-Graham 2006: 4). The emotional and affective result is that we tend to view any intervention short of revolution as insufficient and therefore pointless, thus making it difficult to imagine any effective alternative to 'the system' unless and until that system is destroyed.

But what if we choose to think about neoliberal restructuring at the university in a different way? What if we were to 'act as beginners', and refuse to already know everything about our situation (Gibson-Graham 2006: 8)? As a way out of the discursive dominance of strong theories of capitalism (and capitalocentrism), we could approach 'the economy' with 'weak theory'. Weak theory is an approach that allows for contingency and possibility. 'By exploring the unknown, rather than extending and confirming the known … weak theory can be strong politics: it opens up social options that would be inaccessible to a theorist intent on eliminating surprise' (Gibson-Graham 2006: 205n15). In this imagining, social processes and arrangements are not structured or produced through 'capitalism' but are over-determined by a multiplicity of factors that coalesce around a particular place and time. Thus social phenomena, processes and places are 'empty' categories that can become, and in fact are, locations of political possibility. With this orientation to possibility, there is not one legitimate course, that of building a coordinated oppositional politics that might lead to revolution: we can also (or instead) work on cultivating and fostering non-capitalist relations and new subjective orientations right now, where we already are.

If we were to approach the transformations that were happening around us with weak theory, what would we have envisioned for our project? One possibility is that we might have taken up Gibson-Graham's project of building alternatives to neoliberal capitalism in the here and now. We might have imagined the task of undermining the discursive dominance of neoliberalism as fundamental to our project and developed pedagogies and curricula to help foster non-capitalist imaginings and practices. However, a prescription of weak theory opens up a range of political possibilities. Since weak theory doesn't 'know that social experiments are already co-opted and thus doomed to fail or reinforce or to reinforce dominance' (2006: 8) we can be hopeful and enthusiastic about possible action. Of course this does not mean that we could not or should not be vigilant and thoughtfully critical while undertaking new projects or that we should not be critically reflexive and strategic in our efforts. But it does let us entertain the possibility of emphasising and amplifying particular practices that under strong theories might be predetermined as supplemental or already co-opted and therefore not worthy of pursuit.

To take one example, we might rethink and revalue particular aspects of the RTP itself. When asked why they joined the RTP, all of our interviewees talked about community or collegiality as a primary draw and an important outcome of the project. Students admitted they were pulled to the group in part for the chance to 'hang out with friends' while doing interesting work. One participant said that 'just getting people together outside of a seminar or department meeting was really huge' while another pointed out that 'we're never able to have discussions like that and talk about ideas outside of the department'. In the words of one faculty member: 'For me, that was a treat to hear from colleagues, to hear from students, in different positions, you know, undergrads come in, so it was neat. I was very enthusiastic about it'. In particular more senior faculty emphasised the importance of social interaction outside more structured academic settings.

Within a capitalocentric framework, this type of community building might be presumed to be apolitical, supplemental to capitalist processes or helping to naturalise the conditions that create the need for this type of intellectual and social community in the first place. However, assessing this outcome with a 'weak' theoretical framework, we might imagine a number of possibilities in which the RTP is itself a valuable product. The meetings helped to interrupt the commodification of knowledge and the coercive changes in academic working conditions. As one of the RTP members said, one notable aspect of the RTP was 'just the fact that we are getting together and having embodied encounters with one another! It's working against this trend of these forces that are [acting] on us'.

Indeed, the group's social practices and academic work were done collectively and without regard for – and in defiance of – productivity markers, intellectual property and entrepreneurial investment. If we had put more emphasis on this part of the project perhaps we would have expanded and made habitual the group's practices. And if we had worked to sustain and build this community, our membership might have grown, new social relationships and social understandings might have emerged and our group might now be in a new, potentially stronger and more radicalised position with new possibilities to imagine and enact collective interventions.

While it is potentially exciting, we must admit to reservations about this proposition of 'weak theory'. Strong theories of neoliberal capitalism that emphasise linked processes have led us to view changes in the university as connected to other political economic processes in other sectors, to examine our complicity and location in these processes, and thus to recognise the grounds for action and solidarity with differently positioned populations and actors. With a 'weak' theoretical lens, might we lose track of these connections? Might we end up leaving our difficult, radical projects to fall back on the already familiar (and conveniently valorised) conventional academic practices? These are concerns: yet it is true that when the RTP repositioned group members and enrolled them in new practices and social interactions, new possibilities emerged.

For us, an approach involving weak theory does not necessarily need to supplant the insights provided by 'strong theories'. Rather, weak theory lets us imagine possibility rather than certainty and enables us to make political decisions and move forward rather than already knowing the limits and impacts of our actions. We do not want to suggest that building community around a departmental reading group is necessarily a revolutionary project. But we do believe that the RTP, like every social practice, relationship or condition, has the potential to lead to new, potentially transformative social imaginings and enactments. For academics who are interested in transforming global relations of production and related cultural forms of oppression, we suggest that it might make sense to spend more time thinking about ways in which we can emphasise and amplify projects that are truly doable at the present time, while still maintaining a critical eye. Anthropological practice lends itself well to this possibility and provides a vehicle for approaching real life, on-the-ground processes with weak theory. Indeed, one strength of ethnography (both as methodology and representational tool) is that, the more local and specific your lens, the more it is possible to see the local manifestations of, responses to, and slippages in larger processes in everyday actions and talk. 'Systems' that from afar seem totalising and seamless might break down, slip off the tracks and fail to reproduce themselves as anticipated. With this orientation to possibility and an ethnographic eye to local disjunctures and slippages, we might see more avenues of possible action and fewer dead ends.

Conclusions

In this spirit of possibility, we should like to close by outlining some of the areas in which we might realistically intervene with the hope of exploiting such disjunctures and interrupting the reproduction of the processes we have described above, opening the possibility of contributing to the production of new ways of imagining and enacting the world.

In the area of theorisation, we propose that academics might work on building up awareness around selected issues, both their own awareness (through informing themselves about the specific trends in their local settings) and a larger awareness, through communicative projects both in and outside of the classroom. As part of these efforts, we might work together to develop and cultivate ways of describing and characterising what is going on so as to help us to imagine possible interventions and to direct out attention and efforts more effectively. We might look to some of the oppositional discourses being produced throughout Europe in order to approach the discursive logics of university corporatisation as less commonsense and inevitable. We can also reconceptualise who *we* are: as many collective interventions into university corporatisation have shown (see, for example, White and Hauck 2000) we can usefully seek allies not just among colleagues but also among differently positioned actors in the university, including administrators, faculty, graduate and undergraduate students, adjunct instructors, and other workers both in and outside of the university. While changing labour conditions at the university may feel unprecedented and painful for many academics, they are hardly new for many other kinds of workers, and responses that seek only to protect professional privilege are obviously glaringly insufficient.

In the classroom, we can incorporate materials about these processes in their local, national and global aspects into our curricula. We can work with students to theorise economic and cultural shifts beginning from the everyday firsthand experiences of students: from parents at risk of losing their jobs to the pressures they may feel to use higher education to arm themselves for success in the contemporary workforce. We can encourage and reward learning projects for our students that both document or theorise and engage directly with the processes we seek to interrupt. Students can be encouraged and rewarded for research and engagement projects that, for instance, address local manifestations of larger policy developments or delve into the local histories of struggles over corporatisation processes. We can stress the relevance of our analyses and fulfil an ethical mandate to students by helping them to see their own location in these processes by focusing on concrete struggles and instances of conflict in our shared settings, from movements in opposition to corporate contracts, like those with Coca Cola, to the historical development and current conflicts around specific spaces on and around campus. And through radical pedagogical methods we can try to establish alternative social relations in the here and now.

In the institutional sphere, we can participate in and encourage – or establish, where lacking – efforts to mentor and support colleagues, and especially junior faculty members, to share strategies of constructive interruption or creative avoidance, for instance to evade, locally devalorise or propose alternatives to coercive auditing processes in teaching and research. Faculty members participating in tenure reviews can work together to argue for the validity of those outputs that may not be measured by prevailing instruments, and advance alternative parameters of evaluation. We can also think about what kinds of worker-controlled spaces or structures can or maybe already do exist, perhaps under other names, in the university environment, and give our support to and/or participate in these.

The university is inextricably and dynamically linked to cultural and economic processes that have created vast inequalities and insecurities in the world. At the same time, the location of the academy and the multidimensional nature of academic practice offer a powerful location from which to launch projects for intervention and social transformation. If we choose to re-imagine the university and our practices as locations of possibility rather than already compromised by and reproducing capitalist relations, openings for intervention emerge all around us. We can begin to see and help enact alternative ways of working and/or controlling labour conditions and profits without thinking of a wholesale systemic change as a necessary precondition.

To be clear, although we understand academia as a location of possibility for revolutionary politics, we are not advocating for any one particular path or particular course of action. And it is not our goal to offer or even suggest a programme or theory that can link the small scale interventions of engaged academics to larger social movement: although working as part of, alongside or in solidarity with social movements is a salient feature of effective intervention. We do, however, intend to suggest that politics begins in place. Different places have different histories, sets of conditions, social actors and different possibilities. If we look for the ways that even seemingly 'small' practices and projects can interrupt the discursive dominance of capitalism, rather than decrying their ineffectiveness or already 'knowing' their collusion: we might be able to better envision and cultivate counter-hegemonic dispositions and initiatives as part of a broader, ongoing 'war of position'.

Acknowledgments

Boone Shear and Angelina Zontine wish to thank the participants of the Reading Together Project for their ideas, energy and friendship. In particular, we want to thank Art Keene, one of the founders of the group who was instrumental in building and maintaining interest around the project. We also want to thank the following people for their support, insights and efforts around this paper: Dana-Ain Davis, Juan Florencia, Art Keene, Julie Graham, Julie Hemment, Sue Hyatt, Vin Lyon-Callo, Graciela Monteagudo, Jackie Urla, and the editors of the journal *Learning and Teaching: the International Journal of Higher Education in the Social Sciences*.

◆

Boone Shear is a Lecturer in the Anthropology Department at the University of Massachusetts, Amherst. He is on the editorial board of the journal Rethinking Marxism, a member of the Community Economies Collective, and the author of several articles that lie at the intersection of academic engagement, economic subjectivity, and development.

Angelina I. Zontine earned her PhD in 2012 from the University of Massachusetts Amherst with a dissertation focused on the forms of collective political engagement practiced at occupied, self-managed social centres in Bologna ('Remaking the Political in Fortress Europe: Political Practice and Cultural Citizenship in Italian Social Centers', available online at http://scholarworks.umass.edu/open_access_dissertations/526/). She now lives in Bologna, where she works as a freelance editor and translator.

Notes

This chapter originally appeared in *Learning and Teaching: The International Journal of Higher Education in the Social Sciences* Winter 2010, 3(3): 32–62.

1. See Clawson and Lieblum (2008) for a brief outline of recent such campaigns at UMass.

2. These events were covered in many media sources, see, for example, http://www.fightbacknews.org/2009/03/wave-of-protests-against-cuts-to-education.htm
3. As articulated on the official EU site, http://ec.europa.eu/employment_social/knowledge_society/index_en.htm
4. This account is specific to the U.S.A., but various genealogies can be proposed for the political-economic processes that comprise specific aspects of university corporatisation and in specific settings. See, for example, Thorpe (2008) for a compelling argument that the rise of audit systems and the marketisation of academic knowledge production in Britain can be traced to a postwar disassociation of capitalism from liberal humanism that redefined intellectual freedom and hence the place of academics vis-à-vis the state and civil society.
5. For readers not fully versed in the finer details of young people's fashion, Old Navy is a chain of clothing stores featuring low prices and 'mass' styles, while Abercrombie and Fitch is a brand that seeks to distinguish itself with significantly higher prices and claims of higher-quality materials.
6. The political geographers Katherine Gibson and Julie Graham writing under the joint pseudonym J.K. Gibson-Graham.

References

Addes, Danyel and Keene, A. (2006) 'Grassroots community development at UMass Amherst: the professional classroom', in Edward Zlotkowski, Nicholas V. Longo and James R. Williams (eds) *Students as Colleagues: Expanding The Circle of Service-Learning Leadership*, Boston: Campus Compact, 227–240.

Barrow, Clyde W. (1990) *Universities and the Corporate State: Corporate Liberalism and the Reconstruction of Higher Education, 1894–1928*, Madison: University of Wisconsin Press.

Bauman, Zygmunt (2007) *Consuming Life*, Cambridge: Polity Press.

Bourdieu, Pierre (2003) *Firing Back: Against the Tyranny of the Market 2*, New York: The New Press.

Bowles, Samuel and Gintis, Herbert (1976) *Schooling in Capitalist America: Educational Reform and the Contradictions of Economic Life*, New York: Basic Books.

Buck, Pem Davidson. (2001) *Worked to the Bone: Race, Class, Power and Privilege in Kentucky*, New York: Monthly Review Press.

Canaan, Joyce E. (2008) 'A funny thing happened on the way to the (European Social) Forum: or how new forms of accountability are transforming academics' identities and possible responses', in Joyce E. Canaan and Wesley Shumar (eds) *Structure and Agency in the Neoliberal University*, New York: Routledge, 256–277.

Canaan, Joyce E. and Shumar, Wesley (eds) (2008) *Structure and Agency in the Neoliberal University*, New York: Routledge.

Clawson, Dan and Leiblum, Mishy (2008) 'Class struggle in higher education', *Equity and Excellence in Education*, 41, no. 1: 12–30.

Davis, Dana-Ain (2003) 'What did you do today? Notes from a politically engaged anthropologist', *Urban Anthropology* 32, no. 2: 147–173.

Davis, Dana-Ain (2005) 'What did you do today? Notes from a public anthropologist', paper given at Public Anthropology Conference, American University, 15 October.

Foucault, Michel (2008) *The Birth of Biopolitics: Lectures at the College de France, 1978–1979*, (trans.) Graham Burchell, Basingstoke: Palgrave Macmillan.

Gardner, Eric (2008) '16 arrested at UCLA protesting fee increase', *FightBack! News*, 20 May, < http://www.fightbacknews.org/2008/05/uclaprotest.htm > (accessed 20 July 2010).

Gavin, Robert (2010) 'Mass. unemployment rate rises to 9.4 per cent', *Boston Globe online*, 21 January, < http://www.boston.com/business/ticker/2010/01/mass_unemployme_24.html > (accessed 20 July 2010).

Gibson-Graham, J. K. (2006) *A Postcapitalist Politics*, Minneapolis: University of Minnesota Press.

Giroux, Henry (2007) *University in Chains: Confronting the Military-Industrial-Academic Complex*, Boulder, CO: Paradigm Publishers.

Gramsci, Antonio (2003) 'The Intellectuals' in Q. Hoare and G. Norwell Smith (eds) *Selections From the Prison Notebooks*, New York: International Publishers, 3–23.

Hale, Charles (2006) 'Activist research vs. cultural critique: indigenous land rights and the contradictions of politically engaged Anthropology', *Cultural Anthropology*, 21, no. 1: 96–120.

Harvey, David (2005) *A Brief History of Neoliberalism*, New York: Oxford University Press.

Hemment, Julie (2007) *Empowering Women in Russia: Activism, AIDS, and NGOs*, Bloomington: Indiana University Press.

Holub, Robert C. (2009) *Framework for Excellence: The Flagship Report Spring 2009*, < http://www.umass.edu/chancellor/pdfs/frameworkreport2009.pdf > (accessed April 2009).

Hyatt, Susan B. (2009) 'Creating social change by teaching behind bars: the Inside-Out Prison Exchange Program', *Anthropology News*, 50, no. 1: 24–28.

Keene, Art (2009) 'Students as neoliberal subjects', paper presented at the Society for Applied Anthropology Conference, Santa Fe, New Mexico, March.

Luce, S. (2007) 'No money for 250 plan … but lots for administrators', *MSP Chronicles* February: 8, < http://umassmsp.org/sites/umassmsp.org/files/Feb07.pdf > (accessed 15 July 2010).

Lyon-Callo, Vincent and Hyatt, Susan B. (2003) 'The depoliticization of poverty: activist Anthropology and "ethnography from below"', *Urban Anthropology*, 32, no. 3: 175–204.

Minsky, Leonard (2000) 'Dead souls: the aftermath of Bayh Dol', in Geoffry D. White and Flannery C. Hauck (eds) *Campus, Inc.: Corporate Power in the Ivory Tower*, Amherst, NY: Prometheus Books, 95–105.

Noble, David (2002) 'Technology and the commodification of higher education', *Monthly Review*, March, 53, no 10.

Obama, B. (2009) Speech to the Hispanic Chamber of Commerce, transcript at < http://www.nytimes.com/2009/03/10/us/politics/10text-obama.html > (accessed 20 July 2010).

PHENOM (2006) Advancing Public Higher Education in Massachusetts: A Roadmap for Governor-Elect Patrick, Massachusetts: The Public Higher Education Commission, < http://geoumb.org/start/images/PDF/phenom-advancing.pdf > (accessed 11 July 2010).

Project on Student Debt (2007) 'Quick Facts about Student Debt', < http://projec tonstudentdebt.org/files/File/Debt_Facts_and_Sources.pdf > (accessed March 2009).

Shear, Boone (2008) 'Gramsci, intellectuals and academic practice today', *Rethinking Marxism*, 20, no. 1: 55–67.

Shore, C. and Wright, S. (1999) 'Audit culture and Anthropology: neo-liberalism in British higher education', *Journal of the Royal Anthropological Institute*, 5: 557–575.

Slaughter, Sheila and Leslie, Larry L (1997) *Academic Capitalism: Politics, Policies and the Entrepreneurial University*, Baltimore and London: The John Hopkins University Press.

Thorpe, C. (2008) 'Capitalism, audit, and the demise of the humanistic academy', *Workplace*, 15: 103–125.

UMass Office of News and Media Relations (2007) 'UMass Amherst holds groundbreaking ceremony for new, $50 million recreation center', Press Release, 2 November.

University of Massachusetts (2006) *UMass: A Strategic Investment: a Critical Asset for the Commonwealth's Economic Future*, < http://media.umassp.edu/ massedu/econdev/umass_economic_impact.pdf > (accessed March 2009).

White, Geoffry D. and Hauck, Flannery C. (eds) (2000) *Campus Inc.: Corporate Power in the Ivory Tower*, Amherst, NY: Prometheus Books.

Williams, Jeffrey (2006) 'Pedagogy of debt', *College Literature*, 33, no. 4: 155–169.

Williams, Jeffrey J. (2008) 'Student debt and the spirit of indenture', *Dissent*, Fall.

Wolff, Rick (2007) 'The Decline of Public Higher Education', *MRzine*, February, < http://mrzine.monthlyreview.org/wolff170207.html > (accessed 20 July 2010).

Zinn, Howard (1990) *The Politics of History*, 2nd ed., Urbana and Chicago: University of Illinois Press.

CHAPTER 5

So many strategies, so little time . . . making universities modern

JOHN CLARKE

◆◆◆

An academic sits in front of her computer. On the screen is a programme that invites her to allocate her working days of the last year
to a range of categories (34 in total). She puzzles over how to allocate
her time between these classificatory distinctions: was the time spent
with a colleague over a hastily purchased lunch 'Administration' and
if so, was it 'Administration related to Teaching' or 'Administration related to Research' (they talked about both)? Or was it 'Personal Development'? Or perhaps ... In the end she settles for making the numbers
add up, and not looking too different from last year (although just
different enough).

She then turns to projections of her time for the following year,
feeling strangely puzzled by the surreal quality of this task. These
constructed numbers will be used by her institution to make judg-
ments about workloads and the distribution of scarce resources, and
to produce official accounts of the university's expenditure on teaching, research and administration. She wonders if anyone knows how
the basic data is generated in the first place. ... The exercise is badged
as TRAC (Transparent Approach to Costing) and uses an electronic
system developed for HEIs (Higher Education Institutions) by JCPSG
(the Joint Costing and Pricing Steering Group) in collaboration with a
consulting company and in use by 165 HEIs since its introduction in
2000. (Details at http://www.jcpsg.ac.uk/guidance)

In this chapter I explore the multiple, overlaid and condensed processes of reform that have been 'modernising' higher education in the
U.K. for the last three decades.[1] I try to emphasise their heterogeneous
and sometimes contradictory character, rather than viewing them as
emanating from a singular and coherent political project. I suggest that
their condensed combination is, at best, incoherent and more properly
should be viewed as making higher education a site characterised by
what the French Marxist philosopher Louis Althusser described as 'contradiction and overdetermination' (1965: English edition 1969). The

processes, strategies and practices of reform have become condensed and compounded in institutional and organisational sites: producing pressures, tensions and antagonisms. They also produce what might be described as collective psychic states among those who inhabit these spaces. This is not a psychosocial essay, but I do want to borrow a few terms to illuminate the experiences of inhabiting the modernised university: for example, states such as fantasy, dissociation and melancholia. But that will come later: let us begin instead with the problem of defining the time and place of reform.

The thirty-year drive to modernise universities in the U.K. began as one element of the Thatcherite or New Right project of transforming public institutions. This project sought to subordinate them to market-centric and managerial modes of coordination (Clarke and Newman 1997). The New Right combined a variety of contradictory political tendencies: linking neoliberal approaches to deregulation, anti-unionism and state reform with profoundly conservative social, moral and cultural orientations. Despite the relatively narrow and elitist character of university recruitment and practice in the U.K., universities found themselves aligned with other public institutions – most notably the BBC – as part of the socialist/social democratic/progressive 'consensus' that needed to be dismantled to liberate enterprise and enterprising individuals while restoring 'traditional values'. A number of key reforms were elaborated: for example, the abolition of academic tenure, the dissolution of the binary divide between universities and polytechnics, enlarging the number of institutions who could call themselves universities and the creation of a quasi-market in students between 'competing providers'. The 1980s also saw the entry of versions of the New Public Management to both the higher education system and the organisation of individual universities as the pursuit of 'economy, efficiency and effectiveness' was driven by central control of funding regimes and lodged in expectations that universities would make 'efficiency savings' in their internal arrangements.

Higher education shared such innovations in common with most other public services in this period. Indeed other areas probably suffered more dramatic and sustained dislocation and reform through marketising and managerialising processes. But the Conservative-led reforms created some of the elementary features of a new landscape for higher education: features that subsequent Labour governments developed, enhanced and expanded (Wright 2004). New Labour changed the landscape in other ways: not least through the processes of constitutional, political and policy devolution within the U.K., establishing new arrangements for Scotland, Wales and Northern Ireland. These diverse arrangements have produced further diversity in policy and practice, making it more difficult to speak of a coherent higher education sector or a single higher education policy. The funding and regulation of higher education is now conducted through separate funding council for each of the four 'nation regions' and other policy distinctions have emerged (e.g., in 1998 the first New Labour government introduced the requirement for students to pay university fees, while the Scottish Parliament took Scottish universities out of this arrangement in 2002). In England and Wales, universities were empowered to set their own fee levels subject to a capped upper point (sometimes known as 'top-up fees') from 2004. I have no intention of trying to survey the complete field of differences across the four nation regions, but it is important to take account of how the processes of constitutional devolution have produced a much more differentiated landscape of policy and practice, making it difficult to talk about U.K. higher education in general.

Interwoven with these processes of recomposing the national political and policy field, higher education has also been reworked through its insertion onto the combined and contradictory processes of Europeanisation and globalisation (Dale and Robertson 2009). Dale and Robertson argue that such changes make it necessary to challenge three methodological and analytical conventions in social science approaches to education: methodological nationalism, methodological statism and methodological educationalism. Each of these, they suggest, tends to take particular historical constructions – nations, states and the institutionalised practices of education – as the framing devices for investigation and theorisation (see also Clarke 2004). In what follows, I focus mainly on the emerging governance of universities within the recomposition or re-assemblage of nation, state and higher education (Newman and Clarke 2009).

Making a mass of things?

There have been a number of consistent – or at least recurrent – elements of government strategy for higher education across this period. The creation of a market-like or market-mimicking mechanism that treats students as choice-makers or consumers and universities and other higher education institutions as service providers, has remained a core conception of how the sector should be organised. Such market mechanisms have been subject to refinement and elaboration, with shifting views about the proper role of government in establishing, regulating and managing such a market (see HEPI 2009: Rutherford 2005). Over the period, governments have combined profoundly centralist direction and intervention about policy, governance and key areas of practice with a laissez-faire approach to specific disputes (e.g., insisting that governments could not intervene in the closure of departments in specific universities, ranging from physics to Chinese, because governmentally defined 'national interests' could not override 'market dynamics').

A second persistent theme has been the expansion of higher education, moving it away from recruiting students from a relatively narrow spectrum of class origin towards a 'mass' system. Not surprisingly, progress has been neither smooth nor simple, particularly so after the introduction of a student fee and loan process in place of publicly funded grants and the removal of public funding for the teaching of 'non-STEM' subjects (Arts, Humanities and Social Sciences). Universities have consistently complained about the 'funding gap', as increased recruitment was accompanied by a declining unit of resource (the funding paid per student). Arguments have raged about whether the introduction of tuition fees has dissuaded students from poorer backgrounds from applying (with government claiming that means-tested financial support has offset such changes). Despite that, the last two Labour governments put extra funding into 'widening participation' schemes targeting a range of socially and educationally disadvantaged groups in line with New Labour commitments to create a more socially inclusive foundation for a 'knowledge society' and a globally 'competitive' national economy. Such commitments predated the global financial crisis of 2008 to 2009 and the subsequent arrival of a Conservative–Liberal Democrat coalition government committed to taking 'hard decisions' to reduce public spending.

The future of the national economy – and its competitive global framing – has been another recurrent thread in higher education policy. Several initiatives have been launched to teach 'enterprise' (as an ethic, orientation and set of practices) across the curriculum. Equally, government research funding has been directed to thematic national priorities and increasingly required forms of partnership, engagement or involvement with current or potential 'users' in a series of models ranging from dissemination to knowledge sharing to co-production. Most recently, universities have been invited/instructed to develop approaches to 'employer engagement' in governance, curriculum design and student recruitment.

Finally, there has been a persistent commitment to 'improving' the governance, administration and management of universities, most recently in approaches to developing the capacity for 'leadership' at senior levels (Deem and Parker 2008). I will be returning to this theme later in the paper because it is managerialism that provides the 'glue' that connects and orders multiple priorities, pressures and problems into an apparently coherent organisational project (Clarke and Newman 1997). By managerialism I mean to refer to a discourse that promotes the social and organisational role and power of management, containing a view that 'more and better management' is the way to resolve organisational, institutional and public problems. Managerialism was renewed and reinvigorated in the 1980s by the drive to liberate management from the institutional constraints that inhibited 'the right to manage' (Clarke and Newman, 1993; Pollitt, 1993). This 'liberation' sought to enhance the range and scope of managerial power in the pursuit of corporate excellence, success and – the 'bottom line' – profitability. Public sector organisations were increasingly incited to model themselves on the dynamic, innovative and competitive organisations of the private sector – and to make themselves 'business-like'. 'Business-like', in this moment, encapsulated the imaginary characteristics of the ideal capitalist organisation: dynamic, competitive, lean and mean in its internal processes, customer-facing, and shaped by a strategic vision of corporate survival and success. In the following section, I reflect on some of the ways in which universities and other higher education institutions are produced as manageable sites, particularly through the conception of a higher education 'system' in which universities can be imagined as small to medium sized business (SMEs), each with its own distinctive corporate strategy.

Striving for success: the reinvention of the University

Of course, universities and other institutions (polytechnics, colleges, university colleges, etcetera) were always separate organisational entities with their own charters, constitutions, identities, apparatuses of internal governance and so on. But what is distinctive here is the construction of a new 'system' (see Stan 2007, on the significance of 'system' as a governing category). A system in this sense is a field of entities (agents, agencies) defined in a specific set of relationships that can be viewed, managed, assessed and directed as if it formed a coherent and integrated network. Higher education is grasped as a national system, framed and ordered by central government policy, funding and forms of regulation. It is also, as I noted earlier, a multi-national system within the devolved U.K., and is – in some ways – an international system (in terms of collaboration, competition and the attraction of students and other valued resources). But its framing as a system is primarily national: and this national framing establishes the fundamental organising principle of the system as one of competition.

Currently, universities are framed by a variety of logics of competition: competition for students, for research funds, for 'success' in various performance evaluation systems (teaching quality, research quality, student evaluations, etcetera). While some of these logics of competition take market-like forms (attracting students, for example), these are better seen as market-mimicking devices (in which the value of students is partly established by government). As Janet Newman and I have recently argued (2009), in the remaking of public services a variety of such market-mimicking devices have been invented and put to work: whose main effect is to encourage actors (organisations, managers, staff, users) to think of themselves as economic agents engaged in market-like relations, practices and calculations. This is, we think, different to creating markets in any simple sense.

Although these devices are significant, they form only one of the competitive logics that provide the dynamics for the higher education system. Competition for research funds, for example, is organised through research councils in which 'peer evaluation' combines with central imperatives about topics, modes of working and the forms and uses of knowledge that are desired. It is further structured by the national processes of research evaluation (the Research Assessment Exercise), replaced for 2013 by the REF (Research Excellence Framework) in which the work of all departments that are identified as research active is compared and evaluated: with rankings attributed at the end of the process. Here again, central imperatives (mediated by the different 'arms-length' agencies) combine with forms of peer review to establish 'quality' distinctions.

Teaching has been subjected to a variety of evaluative instruments – inspections, audits – to produce benchmarks, quality marks and rankings. These are overlaid with surveys of student opinion (to gauge 'customer satisfaction') about the quality of both the university experience and of teaching in specific subjects (see the Quality Assurance Agency: http://www.qaa.ac.uk/). In these processes we see what might be called mixed modes of governance – inspection, audit, customer surveys, peer review – that contribute to what I have described elsewhere (Clarke 2005) as a 'performance-evaluation nexus' in public services. In the higher education system, it is possible to see the accumulation of different competitive framings that position universities as competing enterprises, for whom 'success' is necessarily a critical organisational objective. Eschewing the pursuit of success is not a possible option: success is the route to resources, whether it is defined in terms of research quality, or attracting students, especially international students (and their extra cash value). The competitive logics, especially those embodied in the devices and practices of performance evaluation and resource allocation, demand that each higher education institution understands itself as a competing enterprise.

This conception of a system is not unique to higher education (in the U.K. it has been applied in some form to most public services), but it is a powerful way of framing the internal worlds of universities, demanding their adaptation to compelling external imperatives. So, higher education is expected to conform to a number of strategic demands: promoting national competitiveness, creating a 'knowledge economy', producing 'useful knowledge', enlarging 'access' to higher education, or delivering 'enterprising selves'. At the same time, it is subject to the obsessions of performance management: the requirements of efficiency, economy and effectiveness, or Value for Money that have been attached to the use of public funds. Finally, universities are expected to demonstrate the conventional features of 'good governance': those forms of transparency, accountability and effective internal processes that are held to be the marks of 'well-managed' organisations (see Ball 2008: 41–54 on policy technologies).

These strategic demands are distributed through mediating institutions (the funding councils, research councils, and organisations that promote 'best practice' and benchmarking). The demands are also 'incentivised': funding, other resources and 'reputation' are more or less tightly coupled to compliance with such objectives. They are lodged in the agencies of evaluation and inspection that assess the (comparative) performance of each university. Together these strategic objectives and the apparatuses of distributing and policing them create the 'system' as the field of relations and imperatives within which individual universities can choose how to act. It is a field that distributes 'relative autonomy'. Each university must imagine itself as a corporate entity, geared to competitive success, and needing to develop its own unique 'strategy'.

Managing to succeed?

This systemic organisation of competition incites universities to think of themselves as competitive organisations, characterised by corporate objectives, strategic leadership and a 'business-like' approach to managing their internal and external environments. Achieving success (or even just survival) requires the managerialisation of each institution. The organisation must have effective strategic direction (sometimes known as 'leadership') in order to plot its course through the shifting possibilities and problems that constitute its environment. But it must also have rigorous internal management systems to ensure the effective and purposive coordination of its internal resources in pursuit of the corporate mission. So universities must learn to be – or at least present themselves as – well-managed organisations (although this does not mean that they are). There are two important aspects of this process of corporate managerialism: the intersection with older arrangements of internal governance and the emergence of incorporating logics of calculation and action.

In higher education as elsewhere, the arrival of managerialism is not the simple establishment of a new mode of organising or coordinating institutions. Rather the drive for more and better management enters a landscape already filled with logics and practices of organising: from the quasi-democracies of professional decision-making to the bureaucratic logics of legal administration. The expansion of managerial logics thus involves the displacement, subordination and/or co-option of existing logics (Clarke 2003; Kirkpatrick, Walker and Ackroyd 2004). The results are best understood as hybrids or contradictory and strained assemblages in which modes of organising become mixed together within the guiding framing of corporate managerialism (Newman and Clarke 2009). So professionalism is enrolled as a source of values, orientations and reference points of quality (most notably in the persistence of many forms of peer review). Administrative logics are sometimes transformed by the quest for innovation, risk-taking and enterprise: but also become the mode through which managerial direction and scrutiny are installed (what some have described as the re-bureaucratisation of organisational life, e.g., Travers 2007). In the process, many previous positions, practices and languages persist during this transformation but are systematically rearticulated with the logics of managerial governing. They acquire new value, significance and effectivity as they are subordinated to managerial imperatives (on articulation and assemblage as ways of thinking conjuncturally, see Newman and Clarke, 2009).

As a result, these processes of hybridisation or assemblage make the world of the modernised and managerialised university a peculiarly condensed and compound organisational space. Many 'professional' conceptions, orientations, tasks and practices persist alongside, albeit usually subordinated to, the new logics. So, academics continue to teach although they may be described as promoting or facilitating learning. In such processes, they may well be engaged in interacting with students who may nevertheless be identified as customers. They might be engaged in research and publishing – though the processes through which they do such activities are more managerialised and more competitive. They might also find themselves expected to engage in knowledge transfer or even knowledge co-production with users, beneficiaries, or collaborators. Quality is one of the nodal words through which professional and managerial logics intersect and are articulated. So, in the apparatuses of performance evaluation of teaching and research, peer review becomes combined with centralised standards and managerial mechanisms. Quality has also tended to become institutionalised in profoundly bureaucratised practices and devices: forms, archives, documents and so on (Travers 2007).

Such traces of the past tend to obscure the depth of the transformation that managerial modernisation has wrought. The processes of displacement, subordination and cooption through which managerial logics have been installed have produced a systematic reworking of the internal world of the university. Compliance with the corporate mission and submission to new forms of work discipline have combined to produce an intensification of labour processes ('increased productivity'), a casualisation of the academic labour force (an increase in part-time, precarious and contingent contracts) and a subjection to new internal and external processes of direction and scrutiny over time use and labour processes (Gill 2009). This combination produces a simultaneous intensification and degradation of academic work: even through the depth and intensity may differ between institutions.

At the same time, practices and processes of collaborative academic decision-making (the quasi-democracies of the college) have tended to be displaced by, or subordinated to, the logics of corporate management that determine the business of the university and establish the business plan for its successful accomplishment. These logics also become institutionalised in the apparatus of forms (for course proposals and course assessment, for permission to bid for external funds, for promotion cases) in which the specific academic or academic practice is to be framed by, or tested against, the strategic objectives of the university. It is here, in the tiny devices and minute organisational practices that we can see the full multiplicity or heterogeneity of the reforming impulses that combine to make up the modern university. Table 1 below lists some of these impulses, composed by the author from initiatives at his own institution and elsewhere.

Table 1 Our Objectives Today

Increasing Access/Widening Participation
Improving the quality of teaching and learning
Increasing external research funding
Increasing 'world class' publications
Increasing international collaboration
Increasing student numbers
Increasing international student numbers
Innovating subjects to be taught
Expanding 'employer engagement'
Delivering more vocational/professional education (foundation degrees, post-
  qualifying courses, etc)
Innovating in teaching methods (especially forms of e-learning)
Improving organisational systems
Increasing accountability/auditability
Improving efficiency
Strengthening line management
Improving strategic capability
Developing leadership capacity
Addressing diversity
Transforming organisational culture
Enhancing staff development

In this list, we can see the blurring of professional and managerial logics. But each of these objectives is located within the strategic framing of the university and each is embedded in a variety of devices and techniques for making them manageable. This modernisation through managerialism produces a strange paradox in relation to the boundaries of the institution as a corporate entity: they have become simultaneously more and less permeable.

On the one hand, staff (and students) of the University are increasingly invited to see themselves as 'contributing to the mission'. Internal communications stress 'cascading' the objectives, visions and strategies of the 'leadership' down to staff via line management systems. Their identifications and attachments are expected to be corporate and systems of management (workload planning, performance evaluation, rewards and promotions) are increasingly framed by corporate considerations. This implicitly – and sometimes explicitly – diminishes the complex network of personal and professional affiliations to the 'academic community' beyond the university.

However such affiliations persist, albeit subject to the new dominant logics. Professional, disciplinary, collaborative and collegial connections have not been abolished: rather they are instrumentalised, rendered calculable as means of achieving the corporate objectives. At a recent research management meeting, a controversy broke out when the person responsible for research funds announced that the University now doubted the value of funding academics to give papers at national and international conferences. In the internal world of the well-managed university, costs of travel and units of academic time are made calculable and manageable. As a consequence, a specific activity – giving a conference paper – incurs costs without giving rise to calculable outcomes. In this meeting, I heard the institutional view that 'there is no evidence that giving conference papers delivers benefits': an idiosyncratic, if thoroughly normalised, conception of evidence-based policy-making. Since no-one had ever bothered to gather evidence on the issue, the absence of evidence was readily converted into 'there is no evidence'. This conception of value is framed by the corporate calculus: only benefits which can be realised in the corporate logic could count or could be counted.

At the same time, however, the boundaries of the university are more permeable, to processes that we might describe as domestication, nationalisation and internationalisation. Both Gill (2009) and Gregg (2009) have shown how the boundary between academics' work and home has been made more permeable by the ways in which intensified labour and more extensive ideas of working time have combined with new technologies that facilitate the flexible arrangement of time and place. This pattern of working builds on existing academic dispositions (to work as vocation, or to the home as a 'space' to think, read and write, for example) and articulates them to the intensive and extensive demands of 'being successful': or, at least 'keeping up'.[2]

The international permeability of the university in the form of international alliances, collaborations, markets and policies registers the importance of sites and subjects of potential value: they become the means through which institutions might create 'room for manoeuvre' against the centralising/nationalising tendencies of higher education policy, funding and regulation. For example, Dale argues that

> A further direct and practical consequence of globalisation and Europeanisation within higher education sectors has been for universities to become more international in their reach and student body, and for regional organizations like the EU to encourage increased mobility amongst students to further European social and economic integration (2009: 16).

So, British universities develop partnerships, engage in recruitment drives, and create 'overseas' offices, missions and even locations (e.g., the University of Warwick in Venice: http://www2.warwick.ac.uk/international/world/venice).

University boundaries are also more permeable in nationalising terms. The combination of funding, policy direction and the elaborated systems of performance evaluation, guidance/best practice dissemination both penetrate deep into institutions and render them transparent in particular ways (Stan 2007). In Michael Power's phrase (1997; see also Strathern 2000), universities have been made 'auditable': open to, and self-aligned with, the calculations of performance, value and conduct that are the current objects of governmental desire. But it is important to understand how 'audit' has been extended beyond its financial origins to a capacity to survey and evaluate any desired aspect of organisational performance (Clarke et al. 2000).

This form of 'relative autonomy' (what in other settings has been called 'centralised localism', Lindsay et al. 2008) is a characteristic form of modernisation in the U.K. It combines the creation of a space for 'leadership' or 'strategic management' in corporate form, while framing the exercise of that judgement by centralised direction of funding and policy, and ensuring compliance through the apparatuses of performance evaluation. But it does need the ambiguous, contradictory and paradoxical space of 'leadership', in which the autonomy counterbalances the controlling logics and apparatuses. As with so many other features of public and social policy in the last three decades, the illusion of choice needs to be more than mere illusion. People – especially, but not only, 'leaders' – must be incited to exercise their judgement and believe that the choices they make will be consequential (see Newman and Clarke 2009; O'Reilly and Reed 2008).

Dissolving the academic community?

Let me begin from another ethnographic vignette. In a room, a group of academic staff sit (somewhat sullenly) being introduced to the latest thinking on pedagogic techniques, which their university hopes will transform their rather out-of-date commitments to 'teaching their subject'. Invited to contemplate a more 'student-centred' approach to learning strategies they become a little restive, suggesting that they are, in fact, supposed to be teachers, not learning facilitators. The sense of disquiet deepens when one of the advisers (a learning technologist) suggests it would be better to think of 'chunking' the rather large pieces of knowledge that they have been used to into smaller pieces or 'gobbets' that could be more readily digested by students. The meeting descends into anger when it is suggested that the course (or module) as a focus of teaching and learning ought to be supplanted by pointing students at a variety of 'learning objects' and letting them put them together and make sense of them as they can. The voiced objections (and there were many unvoiced ones) ranged from 'bloody Wikipedia is what we'll get' to the more polite-sounding: 'Are learning objects what we used to call reading lists? Only we couldn't get them to read any of them. ....'

This vignette exemplifies the impact of the multiple modernisations of the university, spoken in the name of the student-centredness, dressed in professional terminology (learning objectives, strategies and technologies) and centred on pedagogic progress. It exemplifies the sense of betrayal felt by many academics as their work (and its vast philosophical and pedagogic underpinnings) is undermined and rendered governable and technical. It represents the de-professionalisation of the academy and the academic. And yet, I will suggest, this is a rather one-sided reading of these trends in which we can imagine ourselves – perhaps too comfortably – as the victims of a new dominant project.

Indeed, one way of summing up these multiple and contradictory reform strategies and the agents, practices and techniques in which they have become embedded is to treat them as 'dissolving the academic community'. The degradation of academic work, the attempted displacement of professional identities and logics by corporate ones, the insistence on competition over collegiality, the centrality of metaphors of markets and enterprise, all point to a displacement of collegial and communal conceptions of academic life and of universities as the locations where they are (or were) enacted.

One recurrent – and recurrently contested – marker of this dissolution is the conceptualisation of students as consumers or customers. Such demanding and choice-exercising agents are a key figure in the reform of public services more generally (see Clarke et al. 2007; Needham 2007). In higher education reforms, this conception of the student has played a central role in thinking about competition between 'providers' (different higher education institutions) and between 'subjects', as the student-consumer chooses what and where to study. But the figure also reorganises the internal world of the corporatised university. It requires new forms of knowledge or expertise (marketing, customer relations management, etcetera) and new techniques and tools (the menu of modular choice: the customer satisfaction survey, the student charter and so on).

Here we can see the most developed aspect of the transformation of the university to the image of a corporatised enterprise. The distinction between consumers and producers is a fundamental ordering principle articulated by Public Choice theory as a way of thinking about – and reforming – public services (e.g., Dunleavy 1991; Finlayson 2003 for different views). But it is echoed in the managerialisation of the internal world of the university/provider organisation. The elevation of the Vice-Chancellor/Principal to Chief Executive Officer: the conception of the senior management team as providing strategic vision and leadership; the elaboration of hierarchicalised forms of line management through which resources, communications, directions and objectives can be 'cascaded'; and, in turn, the image of the staff of the university as human resources that are to be 'valued', 'developed', 'appraised', 'enabled' and 'empowered'. Of course, the introduction of these conceptions and their materialisation in offices, positions, documents, training schemes and meetings has been a deeply uncomfortable – and often contested – process. Academics, like other professionals, have been a mixture of enthusiastic adopters (who wouldn't want to work in a 'well-managed' university? Who wouldn't want to be a leader?); outright resisters (demanding academic freedom or respect for academic values); grudging compliers (is grumbling a new art form?), engaging in passive consent or what Jeremy Gilbert (2009) nicely called the relation of 'disaffected consent'. For most people in universities it may be that Mrs Thatcher's idea of 'TINA' rules: the sense that There Is No Alternative. But it would be difficult to envisage these spaces as populated with enthusiasts or newly minted enterprising subjects taking their places in the newly corporatised or neoliberalised world.

On the contrary, I want to speculatively suggest that these processes of reform have produced a variety of collective adaptations that are troubling in themselves. These are what I can only describe, rather clumsily, as cultural-psychological conditions that are both an effect of, and a response to, the contradictory assemblages and positions within them associated with the modernisation of the university. The following comments are speculative, but seem to me to mark at least some of the ways in which we inhabit this brave new world. The modernised university is a powerful site of *fantasy*, emanating from many different sources: from national and international governmental projections to the plaintive desire of many for the experience of working in a 'well-managed organisation' (in which the desires of the managed rarely seem to coincide with those of managers). But fantasy is also visible in the aspirational strategic objectives and visions that permeate the corporate university culture: becoming the 'world-class university', achieving top 5 ranking in something or other and so on. Such fantasies have their other side, their echo or mirror, in the *dissociative* states that organise the working lives of many academic staff. Sometimes these are forms of privatised retreatism (the desire to be 'left alone' with one's work). Sometimes they are the immobilising sceptical or cynical states induced by the disjuncture between grandiose claims of visions and mission statements and the minutiae of bureaucratised, scrutinised and budgetary conscious organisational life. Here is the surreal dislocation with which I began: the puzzled performance of a subject of performance management. I suspect that dissociation as a collective psycho-cultural response is intimately linked to forms and practices of managerialism and especially to 'leadership' varieties that seek to inspire, enthuse and energise a workforce that appears reluctant.

Surveys of university staff in recent years have reported high levels of perceived stress and distress in their working lives. The University and College Union (UCU) recently published such a report:

> A damning report on U.K. universities reveals today the levels of stress in higher education are considerably worse than recommendations from the Health and Safety Executive (HSE).
>
> The 'Tackling stress in higher education' report from UCU lists individual institutions' stress scores and paints a worrying picture of a higher education sector that is failing to meet standards of psychosocial working conditions set out by the HSE.
>
> In the report individual institutions are ranked by an overall average for scores on each of the seven HSE stressors: demands, control, managerial support, peer support, relationships, role and change. On all of the stressors, apart from control, higher education institutions on average reported lower well-being than the levels recorded in the HSE report 'Psychosocial Working Conditions in Britain in 2008' (UCU 2008).

The responses to such occupational stress are various: anger, despair, withdrawal and the development of a variety of devices for micro- or self-management in a stressful environment. But the UCU study – and others like it within and across higher education institutions – point to a working environment in which the processes of 'disorganised governance' (Clarke 2006) have had profound impacts on the experiences, relationships and forms of conduct that were supposed to characterise being part of an academic community. In particular, it has driven the processes through which the stresses of this environment and the search for solutions to them, have been fundamentally individualised and privatised, evoking what Ros Gill calls 'a panoply of privatised responses for managing the unmanageable' (2009: 259). Nevertheless, there is something about this imagery of the academic community that troubles me.

Is now the time for nostalgia?

At the heart of these troubles are some questions about the relationship between professionalism, managerialism and politics. I have a suspicion that academics – like other public professions – may be experiencing a sort of collective professional melancholia (my use of this term is inspired by Paul Gilroy's writing about 'post-colonial melancholia', 2005). Gilroy suggests that former metropolitan societies of empire are wrapped in a collective psychology of loss that they cannot resolve: because the loss involves the dissolution of formations of power, authority and superiority whose character cannot be admitted even as their loss is powerfully felt. In this context, the 'academic community' – and the ethical orientations, relationships and practices that the term is intended to invoke – needs to be understood as playing a critical role in the professional melancholia of the post-welfarist era. Universities, like other public institutions, have been subjected to the new logics of calculation and coordination, and the idea – the imaginary – of the academic community has come to function as a powerful signifier of what has been lost (see the differently suggestive reflections on nostalgia as a political relation presented by Boym 2001; and Navaro-Yashin 2009).

As academics we should be attentive to the complex, contradictory and potent history of the word 'community' as a political and cultural signifier. We have many guides to such a view: from Raymond William's writings about the organicist conceptions of the imagined community in *The Country and the City* (1985) to more recent studies of what Gerald Creed nicely terms the 'seductions of community' (2007; see also Mooney and Neal 2009). The image of the 'academic community' is part of this repertoire, drawing on the appeal of community as the integrative, organic, harmonious other to the brutal worlds of economy, politics and mere association. It also shares the characteristic concealments of the discourse of community: rendering power, hierarchy, inequality and injustice invisible or at least treating them as secondary and exogenous misfortunes.

In this sense, conceptions of the academic community form a central part of a professional romance: the story that assures us of our shared history, orientation, and values and invites us to remember the shared glories of a collegial past. This, following Gilroy, may mark the precise location of professional melancholia: a loss to which we cannot be reconciled, not least because our imaginings of what is lost conceal its political conditions. I am less than comfortable with this imagined academic community, not least because the generational cultural and academic politics in which I was formed took shape in critical engagements with that imagined community and what it concealed. Remembering those politics indicates a further set of problems about the complex and contradictory assemblage of the modernised and managerialised university.

So, for some of my generation, we (and I recognise this 'we' is also an imagined collectivity) were against the apolitical character of the academy, not least the pretence that knowledge could be divorced from politics, either in its formation or its uses. We encountered a political project – the New Right – that explicitly insisted on subjecting the production and use of knowledge to political and economic purposes. We challenged the elitism of the university: not least the skewed recruitment of staff and students and the cultures of paternalism, patronage and patriarchal authority in which that elitism was embodied. We encountered political projects – especially New Labour – that were committed to challenging elitism and promoting social inclusion, and which sought to 'value diversity'. We challenged the artificial separation of the political and the personal, private and public. We encountered a governmental project committed to the personalisation of all public services, including the experience of higher education (Clegg and David 2006). We attacked the ideological biases of the organisation and production of knowledge (the conservatively conventional weight of traditions, canons and disciplinary inheritance). We have encountered political projects that have demanded multidisciplinary, problem-centred innovation in academic work (Strathern 2004). We challenged the parochial, national and imperial character of much scholarship and have encountered political projects that seek to internationalise 'engagement' and 'empowerment' through the intensified production and distribution of knowledge. Finally, we challenged the structured subordination of students to the authority of the professors. We have encountered political projects that have 'empowered' the student as consumer and disparaged the academic staff as mere knowledge providers and learning facilitators.

The modernised university is thus the site of political paradoxes in which critical demands and orientations have been absorbed and re-articulated, alongside older versions of academic professionalism. The resulting policies are both strangely familiar and deeply disconcerting in their embodiment in governmental and managerial objectives and devices. The languages, dispositions and even energies of critical movements have been enrolled into dominant political and governmental assemblages: rendered technical in the forms, instruments and data collection systems of managerialised modernisation. Let me draw out three final points about this conception of this paradoxical, contradictory and tension-ridden process. The first is that it points to the importance of thinking of political and governmental projects as heteroglossic in a Bakhtinian sense, rather than singular and coherent. Hegemony, to use an older term, was never the imposition of a block of dominant ideas on the subordinated. On the contrary, Gramsci pointed to work of building hegemony as a process of articulating 'fragments'; or 'traces' of existing common senses into new alignments: stitching them into apparently coherent and purposive directions. Here, in the modernised university, we discover many traces – of older academic professionalism, of critical challenges to older academic professionalism, of progressive discourses of equality, internationalism and engagement – being translated into a project of modernisation.

Second, this project of modernisation has been dynamic and adaptable, rather than a singular and static programme. It has been flexible over time and between specific sites (different higher education institutions have been 'accommodated' within it and even encouraged to develop their 'unique' style and selling points). But it matters that this project has a double character. On the one hand, it is *political,* lodged in and articulating a view of the world and how universities must conform to present needs and assist with the construction of a particular sort of future (in which national 'knowledge societies' are to be inserted in regional and global formations). But it is also *governmental* in a Foucauldian sense: embedded in 'technical' apparatuses, discourses, tools and devices. Its dominant mode is that of corporate managerialism, framed by 'competitive' calculations of global, national, sectoral and organisational performance. This mode installs the political project in the minute ordering of the interior world of the university as enterprise (but in all its paradoxical and contradictory forms).

Finally, this is not the time for nostalgia. The story of a modernising and managerialising dissolution of the 'academic community' is not, I think, a narrative that will help us make a different future, even if it provides moments of comfort and a familiar and affective language. I should confess that this has been the focus of many arguments with friends and colleagues about ideals, engagements and commitments.

And, indeed, it has some appeal for me: the ethics of collegiality, collaboration, the ideal of collective self-government and the political and intellectual thrills of intellectual work. And yet, for me professional melancholia (especially where it is locked into a romance of the lost community) is – like melancholia more generally – an immobilising condition. A more coherent accounting of what was lost, including a memory of why the university was the object of critical political engagements and mobilisations is a vital counterweight to nostalgia. I suspect it always was, but as the financial crisis of the globalised system deepens and redistributes inequality, impoverishment and insecurity, then thinking about different futures becomes more pressing. And as the financial crisis is converted into a fiscal crisis – centred on the problems of public spending and public debt – so the pressures on public services and the higher education system can only increase. Universities will be expected to absorb different aspects of the crisis, such as reduced public financing alongside further expansions of student numbers to increase employability or just keeping people off the street. The 'system tools' exist for such developments: competition and performance-evaluation will be perfectly adapted to ensuring an internal world of compliance with next year's strategic objectives. Escaping nostalgia may enable us to move beyond TINA: and imagine alternative ways of making communities.

◆

John Clarke is Emeritus Professor of Social Policy in the Faculty of Social Sciences at the Open University in the U.K. where he previously worked for over thirty years. He is also a recurrent Visiting Professor in the Department of Sociology and Social Anthropology at Central European University. His work has explored the political and discursive struggles involved in remaking the relationships between people, welfare and states, with a specific interest in the place of managerialism, consumerism and Austerity in these changes. His most recent publications include: Making Policy Move: Toward a politics of translation and assemblage (with Dave Bainton, Noémi Lendvai and Paul Stubbs; Policy Press 2015) and Disputing Citizenship (with Kathy Coll, Evelina Dagnino and Catherine Neveu; Policy Press, 2014).

Notes

This chapter originally appeared in *Learning and Teaching: The International Journal of Higher Education in the Social Sciences* Winter 2010, 3(3): 91–116.

1. The paper is a sort of participant ethnography, reflecting on the experience of working in, and talking about, the higher education sector in the U.K. during the period of reform that I discuss. Its evidence is, as result, local, particular, fragmentary and, almost certainly, unreliable. However, in reflecting on my experiences of being reformed, modernised, managed and led, I think it is possible to see some systemic tendencies and the conversations with friends, colleagues, collaborators – and even managers (who are sometimes the same people) – tend to reinforce this view of the direction and contradictoriness of reform. I am particularly grateful to Janet Newman for collaborations on modernisation and managerialisation; to my many colleagues who still insist on talking (both privately and publicly), and to last-minute exchanges with Ros Gill and Melissa Gregg which both reinforced my obsessions and drew me into new puzzles. The final paper has benefited from comments from many friends and colleagues, including the anonymous reviewers for *LATISS*.

2. There are equally important issues here about time and temporality. The university was never exactly the site of the normalised 'working day', even though it centred on professional conceptions of career and life's work. But the capacity for academic time to be simultaneously extended and intensified, and remade into different units and rhythms is striking. Gill (2009) talks about 'fast academia' and the shortening of both response and work times. I would also want to emphasise the dynamic of 'projectisation' and its implications for how time is calculated as work is organised in units that are briefer, and more disjunctured from other projects around. On projectisation in transnational policy, see Stubbs 2006.

References

Althusser, L. (1969) *For Marx*, (trans.) Ben Brewster, London: Allen Lane. First published in French (1965) as *Pour Marx*.

Ball, S. (2008) *The Education Debate*, Bristol: The Policy Press.

Boym, S. (2001) *The Future of Nostalgia*, New York: Basic Books.

Clarke, J. (2003) 'Doing the right thing? Managerialism and social welfare', in J. Reynolds, J. Henderson, J. Seden, J. Charlesworth and A. Bullman (eds) *The Managing Care Reader*, London: Routledge/The Open University, 195–203.

Clarke, J. (2004) *Changing Welfare, Changing States: New Directions in Social Policy*, London: Sage.

Clarke, J. (2005) 'Performing for the public? Desire, doubt and the governance of public services', in P. du Gay (ed.) *The Values of Bureaucracy*, Oxford: Oxford University Press, 211–232.

Clarke, J. (2006) 'Disorganizzare Il Publicco?', *La Rivista delle Politiche Sociali*, no. 2 (April–June): 107–126.

Clarke, J. and Newman, J. (1993) 'The right to manage: a second managerial revolution?' *Cultural Studies*, 7:3, 427–441.

Clarke, J. and Newman, J. (1997) *The Managerial State: Power, Politics and Ideology in the Remaking of Social Welfare*, London: Sage.

Clarke, J., Gewirtz, S., Hughes, G. and Humphrey, J. (2000) 'Guarding the public interest? Auditing public service', in J. Clarke, S. Gewirtz and E. McLaughlin (eds) *New Managerialism, New Welfare?* London: Sage/The Open University, 250–266.

Clarke, J., Newman, J., Smith, N., Vidler, E. and Westmarland, L. (2007) *Creating Citizen-Consumers: Changing Publics and Changing Public Services*, London: Sage.

Clegg, S. and David,. M. (2006) 'Passion, pedagogies and the project of the personal in higher education', *Twenty-First Century Society*, 1, no. 2: 149–166.

Creed, G. (ed.) (2007) *The Seductions of Community: Emancipations, Oppressions, Quandaries*, Santa Fe: School of American Research Press; Oxford: James Currey.

Dale, R. and Roberston, S. (2009) *Globalisation and Europeanization in Education,* Oxford: Symposium Books.

Deem, R. and Parker, J. (2008) 'Leading change in semi-autonomous public universities in England: following government agendas or subverting them?', paper presented at the European Group for Organisational Studies (EGOS) conference, Amsterdam, 10–12 July.

Dunleavy, P. (1991) *Democracy, Bureaucracy and Public choice: Economic Explanations in Political Science,* London: Longman.

Finlayson, A. (2003) 'Public Choice Theory: enemy of democracy', *Soundings,* 24: 25–40.

Gilbert, J. (2009) Presentation at *Culture (and Cultural Studies) After the Crunch,* an event organised by the Pavis Centre for Social and Cultural Theory, the Open University and the Centre for Cultural Studies Research, University of East London, London, 4 February.

Gill, R. (2009) 'Secrets, silence and toxic shame in the neoliberal university', in R. Ryan-Flood and R. Gill (eds) *Secrecy and Silence in the Research Process: Feminist Reflections,* London: Routledge, 253–264.

Gilroy, P. (2005) *Postcolonial Melancholia,* New York: Columbia University Press.

Gregg, M. (2009) 'Working with affect in the corporate university', in M. Liljeström and S. Paasonen (eds) *Working with Affect in Feminist Readings: Disturbing Differences,* London: Routledge, 182–192.

Higher Education Policy Institute (HEPI) (2009) *The Role of the Market in Higher Education.* Oxford: HEPI, < http://www.hepi.ac.uk/pubs.asp?DOC = Reports > (accessed 29 March 2009).

Kirkpatrick, I., Ackroyd, S. and Walker, R. (2004) *The New Managerialism and Public Service Professionals: Developments in Health, Social Services and Housing,* Basingstoke: Palgrave Macmillan.

Lindsay, C., McQuaid, R. W. and Dutton, M. (2008) 'Inter-agency cooperation and new approaches to employability', *Social Policy & Administration,* 42, no. 7: 715–732.

Mooney, G. and Neal, S. (eds) (2009) *Community: Welfare, Crime and Society,* Maidenhead: Open University Press in conjunction with The Open University.

Navaro-Yashin, Y. (2009) 'Affective spaces, melancholic objects: ruination and the production of anthropological knowledge', *Journal of the Royal Anthropological Institute,* 15: 1–18.

Needham, C. (2007) *The Reform of Public Services under New Labour: Narratives of Consumerism*, Basingstoke: Palgrave.

Newman, J. and Clarke, J. (2009) *Publics, Politics and Power: remaking the public in public services*, London: Sage.

O'Reilly, D and Reed, M. (2008) '"Leaderism" and U.K. public service reform', paper presented at European Group for Organisational Studies (EGOS) conference, Amsterdam, 10–12 July.

Pollitt, C. (1993) *Managerialism and the Public Services*. Oxford: Blackwell (2nd edition).

Power, M. (1997) *The Audit Society*, Oxford: Oxford University Press.

Rutherford, J. (2005) 'The market comes to higher education', *LATISS – Learning and Teaching in the Social Sciences*, 2, no. 1: 5–19.

Stan, S. (2007) 'Transparency: seeing, counting and experiencing the System', *Anthropologica*, 49, no. 2: 257–273.

Strathern, M. (2004) 'Social property: an interdisciplinary experiment', *PoLAR (Political and Legal Anthropology Review)*, 27: 33–50.

Strathern, M. (ed.) (2000) *Audit Cultures: Anthropological Studies in Accountability, Ethics and the Academy*, London: Routledge.

Stubbs, P. (2006) 'Aspects of community development in contemporary Croatia: globalisation, neo-liberalisation and ngo-isation', in L. Dominelli (ed.) *Revitalising Communities in a globalizing world*, Farnham: Ashgate.

Travers, M. (2007) *The New Bureaucracy: Quality assurance and its critics*, Bristol: Policy Press.

University and College Union (2008) 'Stress levels in higher education way above recommended levels', Press release, 11 December, < http://www.ucu.org.uk/index.cfm?articleid = 3647 > (accessed 29 March 2009).

Williams, R. (1985) *The Country and the City*, London: The Hogarth Press.

Wright, S. (2004) 'Markets, corporations, consumers? New landscapes of higher education', *LATISS – Learning and Teaching in the Social Sciences*, 1, no.1: 71–94.

CHAPTER 6

Constructing fear in academia: neoliberal practices at a public college

DÁNA-AIN DAVIS

◆◆◆

Introduction

Over the last decade anthropologists have engaged in robust inquiries into the meaning, impact and intrusions of neoliberal ideology and policy (see Goode and Maskovsky 2001; Hyatt 2001; Lyon-Callo 2004). Hyatt (2001) and Lyon-Callo (2004) explore how the tentacles of self-governance emanate from neoliberal ideology to shape the citizen subject; that is, how people end up policing their own behaviours in accordance with neoliberal ideology. Cumulatively, my own scholarship may be viewed as ethnography of particular instantiations of neoliberalism. I have argued that neoliberalism functions as a form of structural violence, particularly against women on welfare (Davis 2004). I have also suggested that advocates for the poor can create fissures in neoliberalism's architecture of governance by manipulating policies to address their clients' needs (Davis 2007a). I have also documented how neoliberal policies manipulate racism by championing a putative colour blind discourse thereby rejecting affirmative action policies that directly address racial disparities and are therefore categorised by opponents as 'racist' (Davis 2007b). The manipulation of racism, where victims of racism or supporters of anti-racist policies are labelled racist, serves to distract attention from the ways in which racism remains a very real lived experience in American society.

Increasingly, scholarly attention has focused on neoliberalism's penetration into public higher education. Academic institutions have embraced neoliberal positions in terms of privatisation and consumption as, for example, when services are subcontracted out to private entities. Students then become a captive audience for corporate interests, such as when mega-chain Barnes and Noble Booksellers are the primary on-campus option for the purchase of textbooks.

Since 1996 universities have been transformed into powerful con-sumer-oriented networks, where 'commercial sponsorship of school services in return for the guaranteed use of commercially sponsored materials is widespread, as is the privatizing of support services in schools and colleges, and the creation of internal markets within col-leges' (Lynch 2006: 5). Lynch astutely notes that 'corporatization pro-duces a commercially oriented environment where the university is pressured to shift from being an academic institution to one that is operational' (Lynch 2006: 6). In other words, universities become less important as places of education and more important as sites where market penetration can be achieved and profits can be accumulated. One way in which this is actualised is through the implementation of an 'audit' culture which, as Shore and Wright (1999) posit, serves to index productivity. Auditing practices and other indicators of produc-tion feed into the business model of what are presumably non-market activities such as securing an education.

Indeed, the neoliberal restructuring of higher education bleeds into the classroom in multiple, insidious ways. For example, Hartman (2009) argues that neoliberalism embraces curricular homogenisation by de-politicising certain identity-based programmes such as Latino Studies. Thus we find that particularities of difference are rejected in favour of broadly acceptable courses that generate intellectual uniformity. Other neoliberal strategies have resulted in many institutions raising tuition fees, and/or entering into research partnerships with industries, and hiring an increasing number of short-term adjunct faculty members as sources of flexible labour (Fish 2009). These and other actions have been deployed to address the decreased public funding of higher edu-cation (Doughtery 2004).

Despite critique and criticism of various aspects of neoliberal restruc-turing of the academy, higher education has become increasingly sub-ordinated to the requirements of capital by ensuring that opportunities exist for businesses to make profits from educational institutions (Hill 2007).

While many discussions focus on the macro-issues related to neo-liberalism, this article examines micro-expressions of governance that work to extend, naturalize or obfuscate neoliberal transformations spe-cifically in universities in the U.S.A.. In this article, in addition to refer-ring to the new emphases on marketing, corporatising and privatising American universities, I ask the question, in what other ways have neoliberal practices and policies been etched into public university systems? And, more importantly what pedagogical models can be used to elucidate the meaning and mutability of neoliberal ideology? The latter question moves this discussion beyond exposing the intersection where the academy and neoliberalism meet. Instead, it seeks to explore the way that neoliberal restructuring is borne out in the academy and, specifically, how it has influenced my teaching.

Mohanty offers an important perspective in this regard:

> Understanding the political economy of higher education at the beginning of the 21st century is about seeing and making visible the shifts and mystifications of power at a time when capitalism reigns supreme.... While we have access to a wealth of feminist and anti-racist, multicultural scholarship on curricular and pedagogical issues in U.S. higher education, there is very little scholarship that connects pedagogical and curricular questions to those of governance, administration and educational policy (2003: 171).

What follows is a reflection on three personal events that are methodologically and theoretically linked to my own autoethnography. Reed-Danahay notes that 'autoethnography refers to either ethnography of one's own group or to autobiographical writing that has ethnographic interest' (1997: 2). One of the more compelling aspects of the autoethnographic enterprise is that it interrupts self-erasure. Thus, an autoethnographic approach can provide valuable insights into the tensions between the neoliberal environment and being an academic in such a setting. While it is true that autoethnography is 'often deemed as non-scholarly or self-interested' (Brown 2008: 14) and is criticised for its sentimentality and embrace of the excesses of postmodernism, I posit that, as Ulysse (2007) points out, autoethnography also serves as an important site from which to vocalise conditions of vulnerability: in this case the vulnerability is created by administrators and institutions that embrace neoliberal practices. As academics critiquing neoliberalism in the academy, we can situate ourselves and draw from self-accounts in ways that do not undermine the authenticity and intellectualism of our analyses. Here, the narratives inform the argument, while simultaneously exploring the interpretive dynamics of subjectivity in relation to the context of neoliberal ideology. To that end, the first autoethnographic event reveals how fear coalesces around micro-aggressions, which I define as mundane indignities that are derogatory and communicate a subtext of hostility. These micro-aggressions operate as a form of neoliberal governance in which subtle intimidations encourage self-censorship. In the second event, I examine another element of neoliberalism, which rests on promoting 'homogeneity' and obfuscating difference. In this case the example is how the Global Black Studies programme at what I will call the College was simultaneously both embraced as a marketing tool and weakened as a viable, genuinely transformative project. Finally, I explore and problematise the seemingly innocent effects of a private-public university partnership. Comparatively speaking, the events are restrained examples of neoliberal ideology at work, but cumulatively they underscore the accrued toxic impact of administrators' seemingly harmless practices at the public institution where I used to work.

The 'governing' academy

The College is part of a State University system, founded in 1948. Currently it is an institution where students are offered education in both traditional liberal arts disciplines as well as in performance and studio arts. The composition of the student body is often touted as being 'diverse' according to a number of criteria, including the many students who are the first generation in their family to attend post-secondary education. The campus was built in 1971 under a master plan developed by a famous architect and sits on over 100 acres located in a very wealthy county outside of New York City. Upon entering the campus, which is in close proximity to several corporate offices of some of the U.S.A.'s global companies, it is not immediately apparent that one is on a college campus as the buildings look eerily like a prison. The campus is relentlessly sombre, so much so that even the College's President was prompted to admit that it looked 'depressing'. However, funds have been secured to enhance the College's visual appeal and the architect who has been hired plans to apply the planning concepts of New Urbanism to reconstruct the college's image, in the hope that it might ultimately lead to increased funding for the college.[1]

When I was hired I found that many of the faculty had been there practically since the College opened. The College had the air of an institution that held close the values of the Civil Rights, the Women's and the Lesbian and Gay Movements of the 1960s and 1970s. Many faculty members, especially in the Social Sciences, seemed to be predominantly liberal, leaning towards progressive positions on most issues. Vestiges of this political proclivity were evident in the administrative organisation of the departments. For example, we did not have paid

Department Chairs, but rather unpaid heads of Boards of Study. Also the College had a 2/3 teaching load that grew out of an expectation that faculty would work intensely with individual students as they completed their senior theses. Each faculty member was expected to work with approximately eight to ten students and the time spent with students was equivalent to teaching a sixth class.

Another area that seemed a placeholder of equality was the admissions criteria, with which I became familiar as a member of the Admissions Committee. It was my understanding that historically the College had been flexible in admitting students using a range of criteria, some objective and others subjective. But by the end of the 1990s, around the time of my arrival, the College, like many institutions, had begun the process of using selectivity models, based on a combination of grade point averages and standardised test scores, to determine who would be admitted. This process, which is rampant among colleges and universities, relies on test scores and statistical data, which are ostensibly objective, to support claims that admission is based on merit. However, processes represented as meritocratic often end up benefiting those who have access to the kinds of resources that will allow them to do well on tests. Therefore, the so-called meritocracy actually becomes a mechanism for exclusion. While the new audit norms that Shore and Wright describe are used to develop performance indicators that pit departments against one another (1999: 569), I want to point to how selectivity and performance indicators are also operationalised in the neoliberal environment of the academy in order to create a pecking order among applicants. The selectivity charts materialise as 'quantifiable score-cards' to determine admission decisions, which tend to favour those who have greater degrees of social, cultural and economic capital, that is, students from wealthier families and those who can purchase the power of programmes geared to help students become proficient test-takers. The use of these kinds of supposedly 'neutral' qualifications for admissions also serves the agenda of many institutions of higher learning, which is to boost the university's standing in national league tables, in the hopes that this will result in a more selective pool of applicants, another way in which working-class and other marginalised constituencies are potentially excluded.

Nonetheless, when I accepted the job, the College seemed to me a good environment for a newly minted PhD, whose scholarship resided at the intersection of academia, practical application of research and social justice activism.

Down these mean streets: an analysis of events through the lens of neoliberalism

The construction of fear: beware of the scholar

Glad to have found an academic home, I settled into the College's rhythm. Both students and colleagues were interesting and early on my interactions were stimulating and positive. I was one of three Black faculty members in the Social Sciences: two of us were in tenure-track positions and the third was nearing retirement. Inquiring about the tenure process, I had been assured by more seasoned faculty members that there was nothing to worry about, especially if I went through the third year review process with ease. The first two years flew by and soon the time came to prepare my reappointment file. Bolstered by sage advice from a senior faculty member, I felt confident in my professional scholarly achievements, college service and teaching accomplishments.

I carefully prepared my review file, documenting my service to the College, including having been the faculty advisor for several student groups and sitting on search committees. In completing my reappointment file, I underscored my teaching philosophy, which, like my scholarship, rested heavily on social justice issues and activism. In my statement I wrote that the point was to 'teach to transgress' (hooks 1994) and to help students recognise that there are goals and strategies to eradicate discrimination. Ultimately they can and should learn how to interrogate inequity. I used the classroom to encourage students to see how dominant ideologies are put into practice: not just 'out there', somewhere else, but also at the very institution where they were receiving an education.

Once the materials were submitted, I waited for letters of support from my colleagues. Upon receipt of those items, the file would be forwarded to the Provost who would then write a letter – hopefully recommending my renewal. After the Provost's letter was written, I could review the file in its entirety before it was sent to the President's office. This would allow me to address any irregularities. After two months, I was finally called to the Provost's office. I read all the letters, which were favourable, saving the Provost's for last. I smiled until I reached the second to last paragraph, which said:

> Such a record of academic and social activism is impressive, both for its scope and tone of persuasive well-researched advocacy; a matter to which she gives some attention in her excellently detailed statement. Professors who advocate for distinctive political viewpoints need, of

course, to be sure they do not close out students who may have alternative points of view. I am sure that with her impressive degree of
pedagogical self-awareness, Professor Davis is aware of these matters,
and will work hard to expect and encourage a fair exploration of multiple perspectives in her classes (6 June 2003).

Unable to refrain from rereading the lines, I became somewhat pan-
ic-stricken trying to figure out the subtext of his words. Only upon reflection did it sink in: I was being marked in the same characteristically
demeaning way that many political figures disparagingly refer to 'activist' judges whose decisions challenge conservative constitutional interpretation (albeit in my case with no comparable measure of success!).
By marking my political agenda as 'distinctive', about which I was not
shy, the Provost signalled suspicion regarding my ability to teach fairly
and impartially. To my knowledge, the Provost had no evidence that I
did not allow, 'alternative points of view', but his comment naturally
raised the concern that I did not allow for fair exploration of multiple
perspectives in the present or that I might engage in such classroom
censorship in the future. These subtle comments could raise a red flag
for the College President and/or the State University system when I
went up for tenure.

As David Price (2004) shows, activist anthropologists have historically come under surveillance and oppression in relation to the broader
social context. In the contemporary political and ideological climate
which tells us that politics should take a backseat to the realities and
logics of the market, the term 'activism' is viewed disparagingly and
as representative of a radical or progressive political agenda, which is
now considered suspect at the very least as it is constructed as in opposition to scholarship which passes as 'objective' simply because it does
not challenge the *status quo*. I did not expect this liberal college to be
concerned about activist scholars. But the Provost's letter was an early
sign of discourses that disparage activism. Rarely is the term 'activist'
associated with the actions of conservatives. The pejorative use of the
term 'activism' has emerged from the belief that there is no need for
social movements aimed at working for social justice; rather, neoliberal
ideology favours what Duggan (2004) calls non-redistributive forms of
equality. Part of what has spurred activists to organise internationally
has been the way that neoliberal ideology has positioned activism and
liberal, progressive or radical politics as unnecessary and a source of
harm. A recent *New York Times* op-ed by Stanley Fish (2009), for example, argues that faculty should refrain from taking political stands

and his tone suggests that the political stances that academics should renounce are those that gesture towards liberal, progressive or radical politics.

I was not alone in my concerns and paranoia about being viewed negatively as an activist. It seemed to me and some other colleagues that there was an unanticipated change in the political climate of the College. A former colleague who has been at the College for over 20 years shared with me that in 2007, just about the time I left the College, an official statement from the administration of the State University system was sent to all faculty members at the beginning of the academic year, reminding them that they were not to use the classroom as a political platform. This message came, some believe, to thwart 'bias' in anticipation of the upcoming presidential race. But some faculty viewed the statement with alarm, as an indirect warning to them personally.

This same former colleague also told me that she had attended a meeting during which she objected to some point made by the very same Provost who had written my letter. She later received a memo – slipped under her door – telling her she had been rude to challenge his point of view. In both her case and mine we found anxiety was produced by the micro-aggressions, which is some ways acted as disciplinary tools to ensure that we adopted the posture of supposed political neutrality and to minimise our potentially oppositional voices. Activism, opposition and progressive/left/liberal politics were ironically being disparaged by a college known for its proud history of precisely such activism. Inducing anxiety and constructing fear that there might be some negative consequence in being an activist, engaging in public opposition and participating in other-than-centrist or unbiased politics served to discourage such responses. Here it is useful to consider the angst generated by David Horowitz whose book, *The Professors: The 101 Most Dangerous Academics in America* (2006) argues that liberal bias in universities is equal to indoctrination and complains that conservatives are excluded from faculty appointments. Several colleagues from other institutions who were not tenured found themselves treading the academic waters and sharing their political perspectives very carefully for fear that they would not receive tenure. The problem is that Horowitz's point of view is not only concerned with the exclusion of particular political perspectives; his analysis is also in lockstep with tenets of neoliberalism, specifically in the ways that fear of professional retribution is used to suppress a particular set of political perspectives through inculcating self-governance among academics (Soss, Fording and Schram 2009: 5).

The Provost's reference to my activist politics and my colleague's unwillingness to toe the line were read as 'dangerous'. We both found his comments to be intimidating and viewed them as acts of micro-aggression. This form of micro-aggression is similar to the ways in which some welfare recipients in the U.S.A. experience departments of social services that intimidate and engender fear to ensure compliance with policies informed by neoliberal tenets. For example, my study of welfare recipients showed how the Department of Social Services induced fear among them by regularly sending letters to clients telling them they would lose their benefits if they did not comply with regulations (Davis 2004). In keeping with neoliberalism, the state's previous responsibility to provide resources for those in need has been cut back. This was achieved in part by making welfare recipients fearful of approaching the state for assistance and using tactics to deter people from applying for state benefits.

As a result of the Provost's comment, I became acutely aware of how any activist inclinations on my part might be interpreted. Second-guessing the appropriateness of my activist and political positions, in 2004 I was surprised to find myself questioning, for example, whether I should publicly support students who had organised in solidarity with food service workers' unionisation efforts. A series of events related to a demonstration connected to that issue ultimately involved some students being arrested and/or placed on academic probation. A few of the students involved wanted emotional and intellectual support for the decision they had made to stand in solidarity with the food service workers. In order to provide the students with a historical and theoretical context for understanding the risk and rewards of their choice to organise with and on behalf of food service workers, I offered to teach a course about activism titled *Pan-Africanism, Civil Rights and Radical Black Politics.* The course explored the roots of the Pan-African activism in the U.S.A. from the early 20th century to the late 20th century.

The critical pedagogical strategy that emerged out of that decision was to invite eight students who had participated in the union organising effort to take part in a dialogic class grounded in the work of Paolo Freire (2000). We examined non-violent organising and activism by examining three of the Black intellectual traditions that helped to shape them in the U.S.A.: Pan-Africanism, Civil Rights and Radical Black Politics. Four weeks were dedicated to each of these three topics. My role was to provide a lecture that contextualised each topic during the first session. For the remaining three sessions, groups of students were responsible for identifying readings and leading class discussions.

This approach was built on the model, in that students were not passive recipients of lectures; instead, we all shared the responsibility for teaching and learning.

This decision to teach students the history of their own activist practices perpetuated an activist tradition, which in this particular neoliberal climate, could not be taken lightly. I found myself caught in the tentacles of self-governance: I was thinking about what might be necessary in order to successfully compete for tenure and was wondering whether or not to teach the class out of fear. I was not that cautious in my concern about being viewed negatively, but I submitted to the neoliberal project of being referential and self-conscious in ways that reproduce the legitimacy of discipline. In other words, although I ultimately chose to teach the class, the very fact that I thought about the consequences *in relation* to the Provost's comments, exemplified the kind of self-governance that is part of neoliberal ideology.

The new abolitionist movement

During my tenure at the College I had also become an active promoter and contributor to the Black Studies Program, which had floundered a bit in the previous three years or so, prior to my joining the faculty. In the United States, Black Studies programmes emerged from the protest movements of the 1960s and highlighted group identity (Hartman 2009), but their historiography reaches back much further than that moment.

Shortly after my arrival at the College, a more senior member of the faculty, who was an Africanist, stoked my interest in working with three other faculty to redefine and expand the Black Studies programme, which students could choose as a secondary area of study but not as their primary focus at the time. After developing a more robust and cogent curriculum that moved across disciplines and included public programming, those of us who were on the ad-hoc committee were urged to apply for major grants. It seemed that the key to sustaining Global Black Studies (GBS), as we renamed the Black Studies Program, was to receive funding for it. The benefit of liberal education that includes Black Studies was being rationalised in terms of the amount of funding that could be secured to support such programmes. This was in contrast to other disciplines such as Literature and History, which were viewed as fundamental to the educational project and did not require external funding to justify their role in a liberal arts curriculum. At that time, with some unfounded degree of certainty that we would receive a couple of hundred thousand dollars in funding, we were also urged to apply to the state to revise Global Black Studies from its status as a minor (a secondary area of study for students) to a major (that is, a subject which they could choose as their primary area of study). But funding did not materialise and interest in submitting the application for it to be certified as a major quickly disappeared. A curious hesitancy loomed as some higher-ups in the administration tried to dissuade the application for GBS to be a major. In fact as I left a faculty meeting one fall day, a senior administrator whispered to me that I should 'hold off on filing for GBS to be a major'. Some light was shed on this turn of events when a colleague circulated, to the surprise of many, a 2002 newspaper article on the state of Black Studies programmes, featuring comments by Candace de Russy, a trustee of the State University system (Evans 2002). De Russy was also a member of the Trustees Advisory Council of the Council of Trustees and Alumni (ACTA) founded in 1995 by Lynne Cheney (the wife of former Vice President, Dick Cheney) among others.[2] ACTA attacked higher education, denigrating U.S.A. colleges and universities as biased institutions where liberal professors 'indoctrinated' students (Smith 2007: 1). In the article about Black Studies, de Russy criticises the State University's African American Studies programmes on several grounds, including such claims that they lack rigour and are feel-good programmes; that they have an anti-American bias; and that they do little to advance knowledge (Kurtz 2002). The reason for the managers' shift in attitude towards developing the programme had become clear.

By this time, I was teaching the *Introduction to Global Black Studies* class with approximately 45 students enrolled. In subsequent years I taught the same course with an enrolment of approximately 60 students and still another with approximately 35 students. That I am able to easily recall the number of students enrolled in the course reflects the fact that I was repeatedly asked to provide data on student enrolment and the number of students who declared GBS as a minor. Data mining of this sort illustrates that 'Black Studies are ensconced in institutions and increasingly act as a slave to neoliberalism. Black Studies faculty are compelled to rationalize their existence along neoliberal lines that include grants, [showing] how can the program serve public relations functions and [proving there are] enough students signing up' (Hartman 2009: 12–13). Shortly after being told to hold off on changing the status of Global Black Studies, I was then encouraged to expand the programme and give it a web-based presence. The 'market' rationale was working in one direction, but the political manipulation was going in the opposite direction. The College was simultaneously interested in using Global Black Studies to raise its public profile and possibly to attract students– a market-based interest – while simultaneously being unwilling to commit funds to support it, unless there was support in the form of external funding. Several years later, after it was determined that Boards of Study heads would be paid, I was the only Board of Study Coordinator who was not paid to do the job of organising the Global Black Studies programme. Ironically, I was then called upon to help develop a year-long college-wide initiative, *Africa and the African Diaspora: Traditions, Revolutions and Innovations.* This latter circumstance points to how programmes like Black Studies can be marginalised if their existence is based solely on the marketing function they may provide rather than on the value of the intellectual contribution they make. The focus on marketing functions serves the interest of public relations, an element of corporatisation (Hartman 2009: 13) that is imbued with neoliberal ideology.

As commitments to general education programmes rose, institutional support for Global Black Studies waned, revealing a conundrum. According to a former dean at the College, the institutional inertia around GBS played off of an earlier and nation-wide crisis; that is, the widely promoted belief that higher education had been 'victimised' by liberal political interests thereby compromising the quality of education that students were being offered.

Audit processes, such as measuring student learning outcomes and emphasising the importance of general education courses, converged around ensuring that students had something akin to a common educational experience centred on subjects like Western Civilization. Mandating that courses such as Western Civilization be taught actually forced areas of concentration (such as Black Studies) to be integrated into more general education courses. This move mandated that new faculty would have to be hired to teach those general education requirements. Global Black Studies courses were in a precarious position, as it seemed they could easily be denuded of the intellectual integrity that had made them so vibrant by incorporating them into courses that claimed to be more 'general', but that, in fact, reified 'the West'. I recall one meeting at which my interest in teaching a course on *Black Feminist Theory* was maligned. A colleague said to me, 'Why can't that course be *incorporated* [my italics] into the broader feminist theory class?' The more general feminist theory class placed Mary Wollstonecraft at the centre of theory and would have positioned black feminist theory as a sub-section of Feminist Theory rather than the progenitor of feminist theory in the United States in its own right. In other words, the shift would have orchestrated teaching feminist theory from a Eurocentric position rather than viewing a Black feminist intellectual tradition in the U.S.A. as the foundation of an equally important body of Black feminist theory. This tendency to flatten out differences and disrupt topical specialisations reveals the paradoxical way in which one Black Studies course, for example, was reassigned to an integrated intellectual inquiry that diminished its importance in the canon.

Several problems are made manifest under such circumstances, that is, when the homogenising tendencies described above leak into higher education. First, it is incredibly awkward to coordinate and teach in a programme with no dedicated funding commitments from the institution as it is easier to eliminate or sideline the programme than it is to revitalize and support it. Neglect of this sort exemplifies another form of micro-aggression. For, to ask a non-tenured faculty person, as I was at that time, to work towards programme expansion places that person in the precarious position of being evaluated on the success or lack of success of that programme, when its fortunes are tenuous due to a dearth of financial support and when there are ideological concerns about its very existence. Second, professionalism is undermined, as Shore and Wright (1999) argue, because of the discrete ways in which academics' work is inspected through the use of auditing technologies. Consequently, varying degrees of fear emerge due to the threat that teaching particular courses is neither valued nor legitimised. In other words, the number-counting game forces some of us to reconsider teaching particular areas of speciality or interest: in my case, Global Black Studies.

The unpredictable combination of interest in the marketability of Black Studies and concern about political criticism of such programmes came at the same time that General Education courses were being solidified. For example all new faculty hires had to teach these courses. One such course, *Western Civilization,* formerly known as *Culture and Society in the West,* was required for all freshmen at the College. According to Hedrick (2006), courses of this type are linked to notions of classicism and foster the idea that the 'West is the best'. General Education courses are pitched in contradistinction to Women's Studies, Black Studies, Asian American Studies, Lesbian and Gay Studies and Labour Studies. They attempt to represent the purportedly fragmented and specialised knowledge that comes with the 'particularity' of such intellectual traditions as partial, in contrast to the putative 'universality' of Western traditions. The whole point of general education is to integrate the interdisciplinarity of some courses and make connections in ways that – one might argue – subsume the 'other', representing yet another example of how neoliberalism is operationalised but this time in curricular contexts. Duggan (2004) eloquently postulates that neoliberalism glosses over difference in the interest of having particular political identities fade into the distance and in order to reassert or maintain the power and privilege of people who are ostensibly 'unmarked' (but who actually are marked by virtue of their location in positions of power).

My response, pedagogically, was to develop a comparative approach to address the awkward intersection of Global Black Studies and neoliberalism. I decided to directly raise the subject in classes, especially in the *Introduction to Global Black Studies* and in the *Black Popular Culture* courses, both of which only I taught. Students were introduced to neoliberal ideology by reading the article in which Dr de Russy laid out her opposition to programmes like Black Studies (see Evans 2002). They then developed a contextualised analysis by exploring the disappearance of other 'identity-based' programmes nationally (such as Latino Studies) and compared that to the re-emergence of mandated general education courses, such as Western Civilization.

I posed critical thinking questions to students such as: What does it mean to be at a liberal arts college that undermines the intellectual validity of programmes that were achieved during the Civil Rights movement? To facilitate students' ability to consider the impact of tentative institutional interest in Black Studies programmes in relation to broader neoliberal ideology, they read Stuart Hall's article *What is this 'Black' in Black Popular Culture?* (1993) alongside the article about de Russy denouncing Black Studies through a process I call 'article mapping'. Article mapping generates a visual interpretation of the main concepts of an article. It requires creating a sequence of questions that students answer prior to class that are then transposed onto the chalkboard. Specifically, in the course *Introduction to Global Black Studies*, Stuart Hall's article is used to theoretically situate some political and ideological elements that are foundational to neoliberalism. First, students are asked to conduct research and identify concrete examples of how marginalised citizens have asserted their interests in public forums. They are given time periods, such as the 1950s, 1960s and 1980s.

Students identify such movements as the Civil Rights, women's movements and reproductive rights movements. They are then asked to examine how those movements were translated into the academy in the United States, which resulted in such programmes as Women's Studies, Gay and Lesbian Studies and Black Studies. In class, we take several examples of each movement and map out various relationships between the movement and some of the concepts that Hall discusses. For example to understand marginal actors accruing power on the world stage, we explore the political and media voice of political movements. We also map out some of the ways those groups or marginal actors have decentred or challenged norms. To understand the expansive role of movement building and its political articulation in the academy, we map out the history of when some movements were legitimised in such a way that they were included in the academy as either programmes or disciplines.

To illustrate the relationship between politics and curricula, we examine how the academy has changed by reviewing previous course offerings at particular moments at various universities and colleges and what the political climate was during each time period. As one example one might examine the politics in the development of the curricular structure of Harvard University, which in the mid 19th century had a fairly secular curriculum. By the time we discuss the late 20th century, students are able to see various relationships between politics, ideology and the academy. Ultimately we reached a point where we were able to explore the relationship between Black Studies and general education (the broad requirements most colleges have designed to achieve the student learning outcomes in particular knowledge and skill areas).

Students began to see that Black Studies decentred previous curricula ideologies that privileged studies of Western Civilization. Then pursuing Hall's train of thought, even when such decentring occurs, 'it is matched, from the very heartland of cultural politics, by a backlash: the aggressive resistance to difference; ... the return to the grand narratives of history, language and literature' (Hall 1993: 107). In other words, the very fact that marginal voices, ideas or studies have accrued power mean they are susceptible to being dislodged when there is a demand to return to a Western-centric canon. I asked students to identify examples of the 'return to grand narratives' using their own educational experiences and the knowledge that emerged from their social networks. In response many students stated that the return to the grand narrative of history was evident in the fact that they had to take Western Civilisation courses in their freshman year. In terms of language, one student pointed out that 'we are required to take a language, but we are never offered languages such as Swahili: only the romance languages'. And in terms of literature, another student made the observation that *Harry Potter* books reinforce the Western canon by using 'lots of Latin'. If I may translate, the student was suggesting that *Harry Potter* books were praised for resuscitating interest in Latin because of the assumption that Latin was one aspect of the West's greatness.[3] Thus, the contours of neoliberal ideology become more visible in their translation in the academy as students are asked to map out or create grids that investigate particular relationships.

According to Marable (2000), Black Studies has an intellectual tradition that began its ascendancy with W.E.B. Dubois in the 1900s, as a way to develop a sense of identity and as a discipline with legitimate methodological strategies. By the 1960s, Black Studies was used as a tool for organising against inequality based on shared experiences of racism. The critical edge and saliency of Black Studies programmes waned, according to Marable (2000), as they became increasingly dependent on grant funding and marketing principles. From this reading, students are then able to explore the relationship between neoliberal restructuring and the decreased importance of, or conversely, the disabling of Black studies and other curricular programs built through social movements.

For We Are Sold, I and My People: public-private partnerships

A standard-bearer of neoliberalism is the valorisation of the public-private partnership. These partnerships help to extend corporate culture ever more deeply into the basic institutions of civil and political society with concomitant changes in access to public spheres, including public education (Giroux 2004). This transgression arrived at the department in which I worked, the Social Science division, in the form of furniture. More specifically it came in the guise of what I call the 'neoliberal chairs'.

In the summer of 2006 I attempted to enter the Social Sciences building as I always did from the side entrance, but it was locked. I walked around to enter from the front and found that the first floor was under construction. Then, just before the start of school that fall, again I walked into the Social Sciences building only to see two new maroon leather chairs in the lobby. The chairs represented an alliance between the College and a private wealthy university that was going to utilise space in our building for teaching night courses. After the arrival of the chairs came other gradual encroachments fomented by the public-private partnership. Faculty who had been in their offices for years, some over twenty, were told they would be relocated to new offices the next year to accommodate the private university that was renovating the space. On the surface this did not seem so bad: a fresh coat of paint, new state of the art classrooms and lovely carpeting could theoretically allow one to overlook the fact that the private university's recognisable insignia was conspicuously evident throughout the first floor.

As I walked to my office on the other side of the building, I felt disoriented and underwent a tremendous letdown because the renovation stopped right where the College's Social Science faculty offices began. We, the public professors, still had the same old paint, the same scratched-up wooden doors. The sharp contrast replicated Phillip Bourgois' vivid description of the malaise one feels simply crossing from one side of street to other, transporting you from the posh enclave of the upper east side of Manhattan to the dour, public housing scape of East Harlem where the wealth stops abruptly (1995). The 'renovation' primarily benefited the overclass, aptly described by Ruben (2001) who argues that gentrification disproportionately benefits the elite.[4] This description underscores how inequality is solidified and is, in fact, evidence of the broad way that Duggan articulates the neoliberalist reinforcement of inequity. Why was it that the College faculty were forced to stay in offices that were clearly inferior? What we did get? What we got were two large 'smart' classrooms that included the technology for teaching large numbers of students. Each room was designed to accommodate approximately 60 students, which certainly contrasted with the small class size that had hitherto been a hallmark of the College's education. Thus, this was another expression of the audit culture that Shore and Wright (1999) discuss because larger classes increase our Full Time Equivalents (FTEs).[5] Oh, and we also had lots of really nice chairs, which some faculty viewed so positively that they overlooked the broader expressions of inequality.

The private university's programme at the College was an outpost of its business school, which according to a June 2006 press release, would make an MBA (Master's in Business Administration) programme available to professionals living or working the same affluent suburb where the College was located. The benefits of this programme for 'regular' students at the College were only tangential. According to the President of the College, the private university's presence would allow students to gain awareness of the graduate programme offered by the private university. No consortium arrangements were available, however, which would allow the College's students the flexibility to attend the private university's programme (which costs approximately $16,000 for a fulltime undergraduate) at the State tuition rate, which at the time was approximately $4,400 per year. The students were not even really being invited to earn those credentials because the private-public partnership was only facilitating *awareness,* not participation. The message that students received was that they could partake in the *aspirations* of neoliberalism: they could hope to be admitted to the private university and might even envision themselves being business majors but there was no provision for actual *access* to the programme.

Although I am not prone to making biblical references, as I left the building that day, I could not shake from my mind the title of M. Patricia Fernández Kelly's 1983 book, *For We Have Been Sold, I and My People.* This title is a reference to Queen Esther who is married to a king who destroys people's lives on a whim.[6] In the context of its use here, I limit its utility to the literal: That we were sold by our 'king' (the President) who, according one faculty member, cut a deal with the private university and had them 'move in' over the summer. The feeling of being encroached upon by the 'private' did not go unnoticed by College students who sometimes commented on how students from the private university 'got the goods' (nice paint job, new offices, comfy chairs), while the College's students did not. Ironically, on the surface the College seemed 'lucky' to have an affiliation with such a well-regarded institution. At the same time it also seemed to consolidate peril in the form of diminishing the value of the public aspects of the institution.

Other examples of how the College embraced various corporate practices included a plan to develop an upscale retirement community on campus that would generate income for the College. Recently, Starbucks opened a store on campus that some argued diluted the College's liberal roots. Hyatt (2010, and this volume) examines such neoliberal strategies to commercialise campuses. Strident opposition, mostly by students, resulted in the store opening only after demands that Starbucks sell several blends of fair trade coffee were met. Reports in the school newspaper claimed that this made Starbucks at the College the only store in the country to do so.

While the impacts of neoliberal restructuring at the university continue to multiply – in terms of branding, commercialisation, consumption and corporatisation – neoliberal logics are insidiously reflected in spatial articulations, as was the case with the above 'takeover' of a small area of the College by the prestigious private university. In considering what forms of critical pedagogy can be deployed to teach about and counteract the spatial intrusion of neoliberal processes, one can look to Lynch (2006). Lynch argues that there is the hope and expectation of a widespread public trust and belief that the university employs scholars whose task is to undertake research and teach for the public good. In other words the underlying assumption is that academics will work for the good of humanity. This is why, as Lynch says, public funds are dedicated to college and university research. This assumption was being deeply challenged by the College's adoption of the practices described above.

According to Roy and Barsamian (2004), the accumulation of power can lead to the manipulation of knowledge. In order to at least understand how power operates in relation to neoliberal transformations, it is pedagogically important to facilitate students' ability to critique how people *live out* neoliberal policies. I chose to do this by structuring a course, *Urban Anthropology*, to investigate the spatial manifestations of neoliberalism, including poverty and gentrification. This was accomplished by having students engage in semester long research-based projects in a city I will call Cheston, New York, a small city near the College. On the surface, Cheston appears to be an affluent community with a compact commercial district that reveals both a manufacturing past and signs of current luxury commodities expressed, for example, in the conversion of a former candy factory into high-priced condominiums. The taken-for-granted affluence associated with Cheston belied the fact that neoliberal policy had played a role in the spatial configuration of the city. Students taking the *Urban Anthropology* course read anthropological treatments of poverty and gentrification and were then assigned to research how poverty, exclusion, inequality and dislocation were produced in the city of Cheston. Students received methodological training during class sessions that included community mapping, acquisition of census data, historical data, newspaper analysis, economic projections for the region and oral history interviews.

What resulted were rich presentations on how neoliberal policy and ideology were translated in particular spaces. Students documented such manifestations as community surveillance of the burgeoning immigrant population and the shift from a manufacturing to a service economy that kept certain residents in perpetually low-wage jobs. Students also became interested in an under-reported debate concerning the construction of a new mall in the city that was built on waterfront property. Their research illuminated the rise of poverty in Cheston and their interviews showed the spatial dissonance of poor and working class residents as compared to wealthier residents. Importantly some students focused on how neoliberal policy, specifically welfare reform, impacted on the lives of people receiving public assistance.

I have attempted to show, in discussing the development of private/public partnerships at the College and the way that commercialisation became incorporated into the public institution, that these processes represent subtle scales of neoliberal restructuring. Higher education drives the political, social, economic and cultural infrastructure of society. One way for academics to progressively engage with realising the goal of cultural critique through teaching is to move from 'a pedagogy of understanding to pedagogy of intervention' (Giroux 2004: 118). Giroux goes on to say that 'Our responsibility as public intellectuals cannot be separated from the consequences of the knowledge we produce, the social relations we legitimate and the ideologies and identities we offer up to students' (2004: 119). An important starting point for such pedagogy of intervention is to take into account how neoliberalism is translated spatially. As I have argued above, and as Hyatt also argues (this volume), one intervention is by teaching courses in communities, as they undergo change. This involves having students study privatisation and the proliferation of entities that increase consumerism in the interest of offering people pseudo-choices, so as to illuminate the economic inequities and subtleties that come in neoliberalism's wake.

Conclusion

Independently, the events described in this article may seem benign. But they accrue greater potency as the nuanced meanings of neoliberal practice in academe are consolidated into an analysis of its subtle articulations as experienced by an academic. I use these events to illustrate several consequences at an institution of higher education. One is the construction of fear by administrators who view 'political' faculty (assumed to be only those faculty with liberal or progressive leanings) as a threat. They also view faculty who challenge institutional decisions as dangerous. Questioning faculty members' politics, activism and our interest in voicing dissenting opinions, raises concerns because challenging the intellectual and activist integrity of faculty by resorting to using labels can impel us to retreat from being interested in academic governance issues. Just as important, our commitment to student engagement and teaching can also be compromised.

Beyond being compromised, the broader meaning of the first event when the Provost questioned my ability to allow different viewpoints in the class and then labelled me as an activist promulgated some degree of fear and anxiety. The academy's strategic production of fear in a neoliberal context operates at several levels. At the first level there is a crisis of illegitimacy (Holland et al. 2007) in that faculty can be dismissed and marginalised if they are seen as being activists. Being so labelled then positions us as potentially being an intellectual threat to students. A major consequence is that younger academics' participation as political and public intellectuals can be curtailed. The other level at which fear is operationalised can be read in the case of my colleague who received a handwritten memo slipped under her office door, chastising her for publicly disagreeing with the Provost. This form of micro-aggression was perceived as intimidating and is in keeping with the fact that neoliberalism employs tactics that silence critics (Maddison, Denniss and Hamilton 2004). Essentially, stoking fear was used to try and mute faculty and divert impulses to engage in healthy public dissent with the administration. While it is true that historically, muting dissent has been part of academic life, this is a moment when academics seem less willing to resist due to fear. It is a moment when public higher education is profoundly draped in the market-based principles of neoliberalism.

Teasing out the tensions between the Global Black Studies Program and the General Education Requirements in the second example underscores how audit practices at institutions of higher education appear to innocuously echo neoliberal strategies. The elision of the particular (for example the low number of students taking Black Studies courses or students with low test scores) with the dominant (for example large numbers of students taking Western Civilization courses or students with higher test scores) may be linked to the production of homogeneity. In other words, one aspect of neoliberalism is the production of homogeneity: of desire and of wants. By elevating consumerism of particular 'brands', what we think we want is manipulated through processes of undermining differentiation. It is, in essence the creation of general ideas, general wants, general knowledge. This process of creating more generalisable spheres means that colleges and universities can justify the elimination of programmes that are categorised as 'identity-based' or can initiate projects or plans based on numerical value. In either case there are outcomes that reify an intellectual and institutional homogeneity. Furthermore, in the case of the Global Black Studies programme, it was clear that the programme was volleyed about in a complex web of contradictions that are representative of neoliberalism's elusiveness and its power. Variously Global Black Studies was expected to receive new funding streams to justify its continuation and was simultaneously the subject of quiet political messages suggesting that the programme should be eliminated. Finally, when Global Black Studies served the purpose of potentially helping the College accumulate capital, it was drawn into the sphere of public relations and became part of the marketing campaign. When this article was initially written, there was still a Global Black Studies Program at the College. But through neglect, either benign or active, as of September 2010, the Global Black Studies Programme and the Minor had both been discontinued.

Finally, in the case of the 'neoliberal chairs', light is shed on the flexibility of neoliberalist practice and ideology in the realm of the private/ public partnership. Private/public partnerships are, as Holland et al. (2007) argue, the principle mechanism through which elites carry out the strategies to attain power. They exemplify a classic expression of how the privileged exert influence. The 'neoliberal chairs' have several possible interpretations, two of which I focus on here. The first and most obvious one is that they symbolise a strategy to replace decreased state resources. Alternatively, if funding was not the driving force behind the alliance, then the College gained status by its alliance with the private university, making it marketable in a different way. Both motivations reveal the private sector's 'occupation' of the public, whereby market interests can so easily dominate public entities.

What is important about this example is that in a neoliberal context, while many would want to suggest that public partnerships with private entities are the ironclad handmaiden of corporate culture, the partnership reveals a non-corporate mechanism through which elites express their power. In other words the private/public alliance may not always be a true corporate alliance. Since the academy is forced to market itself to overcome its financial short-falls, the entities with which they seek partnerships can vary. This case of a private/public arrangement exposes that there may be 'types' of privatisation that can increase the 'value' of a public institution. The other important point captured in this event is how there are varying degrees of invisibility when affairs are conducted for, but not by, the public. For example several faculty members confirmed that we were not consulted about the partnership between the College and the private university. It is important to examine the processes by which partnerships of this sort take place so as not to generate a monolithic interpretation of neoliberal practice, but rather to see how those practices are fluid and malleable. Although not unexpected, many aspects of neoliberal decision-making take place behind the scenes while presenting such *fait accompli* as the outcome of a process of participatory deliberations.

Each of these practices ghettoises broader visions of progressive politics in the interest of neoliberal values that manipulate identity-based concerns and inequalities in ways that undermine social justice and strengthen the privileged (Duggan 2004). Yet it is incumbent upon concerned faculty to develop pedagogical practices that interrupt neoliberal tendencies. A pedagogical cue may be taken from Giroux who argues that:

> In spite of the professional pretense of neutrality, academics need to do more than simply teach students how to be adept at forms of argumentation.... The pedagogy of argumentation in and of itself guarantees nothing, but is an essential step toward opening up the space of resistance against authority, teaching students to think critically about the world around them, and recognizing interpretation and dialogue as conditions for social intervention and transformation in the service of an unrealized democratic order (2004: 122).

Students should be encouraged to explore broader understanding (and questioning) of the effects of ideology and policy on theirs and others' lives. In part, this can be achieved by facilitating students' participation in political involvement. Intervening in any ideology or set of practices that undermine equity is important in the academy. What I am arguing here is that as scholars, we continue to resist the encroachment of neoliberalism. We can continue to assess structural inequality and promote critical analysis and action, and we can do this not only from the position of faculty governance, but also pedagogically in our classrooms. Staking out interesting ways to show the meaning of ideology and how it operates allows students to see how research and intellectual endeavours converge. Critical pedagogy can intervene in the neoliberal assaults on the academy and bring into bas-relief the relationship between 'out there' and the spaces students inhabit. According to Hill (2007), critical educators can agitate both in the classroom and within other sites of 'cultural reproduction' (2007: 131). By doing so the opportunity to construct new epistemologies is actualised and students are better prepared to simultaneously learn about, research and destabilise neoliberalist gestures in their many articulations.

These events, both the experience and the re-examination of them in this article, created a tremendous degree of personal discomfort and a dilemma. Experiencing the anxiety associated with fear of retribution – real or perceived – meant that I was for the most part, unable to fully enjoy my nascent entrée in the academy. I became overly concerned with how I would be judged and if that judgment was negative, then what would the outcome be? I negotiated these fears in relative silence not wanting to appear irrational. I also faced the dilemma of 'going public' with the same sort of trepidation one might have telling family secrets. It was not that the College was an inherently bad institution, but rather that it was caught up in the matrix of a particular political moment. Much of the work that I do, from a research perspective, centres on how people *live* policy: what their lives are like when policy is implemented. Overshadowing both my discomfort and the dilemmas therein, has been the necessity to interrogate how I lived some of the practices that are part of neoliberalism. Neoliberalism and its impact then, is not something that is borne out in the lives of others. It is also borne out in the everyday work experiences of academics, who are observing and analysing broad socio-political processes and who may or may not choose to integrate how those processes affect us and affect our pedagogical strategies. I chose to do so with all the tension it created because I am not academically or intellectually neutral. Neoliberalism matters to me, to my academic environment and to my pedagogy and therefore, it is incumbent upon me to make its effects visible in all of my work, both within the classroom and outside.

◆

Dána-Ain Davis is an Associate Professor of Urban Studies at Queens College and on the faculty of the PhD Program in Anthropology at the CUNY Graduate Center. Her research interests include policy, activist anthropology, race, class and gender. In addition to teaching she works with organisations that engage in community organising. She is the author of *Battered Black Women and Welfare Reform: Between a Rock and a Hard Place* (SUNY Press, 2006) and co-edited a volume with Christa Craven entitled *Feminist Activist Ethnography: New Priorities for Feminist Methods and Activism* (Lexington Press, 2013), and, most recently, with Christa Craven, Feminist Ethnography: Methodologies, Challenges and Possibilities (Roman and Littlefield 2016).

Notes

This chapter originally appeared in *Learning and Teaching: The International Journal of Higher Education in the Social Sciences* Spring 2011, 4(1): 42–69.

1. New Urbanism planning typically involves a mix of shops, offices and residences joined by narrow pedestrian-friendly roadways. Most often it is applied to residential areas (Brenner 2005).
2. In 1994, Ms Cheney, who was the former head of the National Endowment for the Humanities, wrote an op-ed in the *Wall Street Journal* 'The End of History'. That article critiqued the National History Standards and the Department of Education as a monument to political correctness (Nash 2004).
3. A *New York Times* article by Hu (2008) points out that Latin has benefited from a resurgent interest attributed to *Harry Potter.*
4. The overclass is conceptually explained in a *Newsweek* article (see Adler 1995). However, anthropologically, Matthew Ruben (2001) uses the term to discuss who benefits from gentrification.
5. FTEs are metrics used to measure how much a professor contributes to their institution. Most institutions expect a faculty person to contribute 20 FTEs,

which can be based on such activities as teaching classes and supervising research. FTEs can be increased by teaching larger classes, supervising more research projects, and similar activities.

6. The remainder of the quote is: 'for we have been sold, I and my people, to be destroyed, to be killed, and to be annihilated. Now if we had only been sold as slaves, men and women, I would have remained silent, for the trouble would not be commensurate with the annoyance to the king' (New American Standard Bible 1995). Fernández Kelly examines the hidden world of maquiladora factories on the U.S.A.-Mexican border.

References

Adler, Jerry (1995) 'The rise of the overclass: how the new elite scrambled up the merit ladder – and wants to stay there any way it can', *Newsweek,* 31 July, < http://www.newsweek.com/1995/07/30/the-rise-of-the-overclass.html > (accessed 18 January 2011).

Bourgois, Philippe (1995) *In Search of Respect: Selling Crack in El Barrio,* New York: Cambridge University Press.

Brenner, Elsa (2005) 'A softer look for a dark campus', *New York Times,* 24 July.

Brown, Ruth Nicole (2008) *Black Girlhood Celebration: toward a Hip-Hop Feminist Pedagogy,* New York: Peter Lang Publishing.

Davis, Dana (2004) 'Manufacturing mammies: the burdens of service work and welfare reform among battered black women', *Anthropologica,* 46, no. 2: 273–288.

Davis, Dana (2007a) 'Fissures in the architecture of governance: community-based advocate's responses to neo-liberalist welfare policy', *Sage Race Relations Abstracts,* 32, no. 2: 5–25.

Davis, Dana (2007b) 'Narrating the mute: racializing and racism in a neoliberal moment', *Souls: A Critical Journal of Black Politics, Culture and Society,* 9, no. 4: 346–360.

Doughtery, Kevin (2004) 'Financing higher education in the United States: structure, trends, and issues', paper presented at the Institute for Economics of Education, Peking University, 25 May, < http://www.tc.columbia.edu/centers/coce/pdf_files/c9.pdf > (accessed 31 March 2009).

Duggan, Lisa (2004) *The Twilight of Equality? Neoliberalism, Cultural Politics, and the Attack on Democracy,* New York: Beacon Press.

Evans, Martin C. (2002) 'Reviewing Black Studies: legitimacy of discipline taken to task', *Newsday,* 4 February, < http://www.goacta.org/press/Articles/2002Articles/02-02-04ND.pdf > (accessed 1 April 2009).

Fernández Kelly, M. Patricia (1983) *For We Are Sold, I and My People: Women and Industry in Mexico's Frontier,* Albany: State University of New York Press.

Fish, Stanley (2009) 'Neoliberalism and higher education', *New York Times,* 9 March.

Freire, Paulo (2000) *Pedagogy of the Oppressed (30ᵗʰ Anniversary Edition),* New York: The Continuum International Publishing Group Inc.

Giroux, Henry A. (2004) *The Terror of Neoliberalism*, Boulder, CO: Paradigm Publishers.

Goode, Judith and Maskovsky, Jeff (eds) (2001) *The New Poverty Studies: The Ethnography of Power, Politics and Impoverished People in the United States*, New York: New York University Press.

Hall, Stuart (1993) 'What is this "Black" in Black Popular Culture?', *Social Justice*, 20, nos. 1–2: 104–111.

Hartman, Andrew (2009) 'Black and Chicano power in the academy: the intellectual origins of identity politics', paper presented at U.S. Intellectual History Conference, 12 November, < http://ilstu.academia.edu/AndrewHartman/Papers/161687/Black-and-Chicano-Power-in-the-Academy-The-Intellectual-Origins-of-Identity-Politics- > (accessed 12 July 2010).

Hedrick Jr, Charles W. (2006) 'Ancient History and Western Civilization', *Occasional Papers of the American Philological Association's Committee on Ancient History Occasional Papers* 3, 1–18 American Philological Association, < http://www.thesagesshoppe.com/academia/CoAH/CoAH-OP/archive/20060301.pdf > (accessed 15 June 2010).

Hill, Dave (2007) 'Neoliberalism and the perversion of education', in E. Wayne Ross and Rich Gibson (eds) *Neoliberalism and Education Reform*, Cresskill, NJ: Hampton Press.

Holland, Dorothy, Nonini, Donald, Lutz, Catherine, Bartlett, Lesley, Frederick-McGlathery, Marla, Guldbrandsen, Thaddeus and Murillo, Enrique (2007) *Local Democracy under Siege: Activism, Public Interests and Private Politics*, New York: New York University Press.

hooks, bell (1994) *Teaching to Transgress. Education as the Practice of Freedom*, London: Routledge.

Horowitz, David (2006) *The Professors: The 101 Most Dangerous Academics in America*, Washington, D.C.: Regnery Press.

Hyatt, Susan B. (2001) 'From citizen to volunteer: neoliberal governance and the erasure of poverty', in Judith Goode and Jeff Maskovsky (eds) *The New Poverty Studies: The Ethnography of Power, Politics and Impoverished People in the United States*, New York: New York University Press.

Hyatt, Susan B. (2010) 'Universities and neoliberal models of urban development: using ethnographic fieldwork to understand the "Death and Rebirth of North Central Philadelphia"', *Learning and Teaching: The International Journal of Higher Education in the Social Sciences*, 3, no. 3: 6–31.

Hu, Winnie (2008) 'A dead language that is very much alive', *New York Times*, 8 October.

Kurtz, Stanley (2002) 'Candace under fire: SUNY seeks to dismiss a trustee for daring to criticize a Black Studies Program, *National Review*, 25, February, < http://www.nationalreview.com/contributors/kurtz022502.shtml > (accessed 30 March 2009).

Lynch, Kathleen (2006) 'Neo-Liberalism and marketisation: the implications for higher education', *European Educational Research Journal*, 5, no. 1: 1–17.

Lyon-Callo, Vin (2004) *Inequality, Poverty, and Neoliberal Governance: Activist Ethnography in the Homeless Sheltering Industry*, Toronto: Broadview Press.

Maddison, Sarah, Denniss, Richard and Hamilton, Clive (2004) *Silencing Dissent: Non-government organizations and Australian democracy,* The Australian Institute Discussion Paper Number 65, June.

Marable, Manning (2000) 'Black Studies and the racial mountain', *Souls,* 2, no. 3: 17–36.

Mohanty, Chandra (2003) *Feminism without Borders: Decolonizing Theory, Practicing Solidarity,* Durham, NC: Duke University Press.

Nash, Gary B. (2004) 'Lynne Cheney's Attack on the History standards, 10 years later', *History News Network,* 8 November, < http://hnn.us/articles/8418.html > (accessed 10 July 2010).

New American Bible (1995) La Habra, CA: The Lockman Foundation.

Reed-Danahay, Deborah E. (ed.) (1997) *Auto/ethnography: Rewriting the Self and the Social,* Oxford and New York: Berg.

Roy, Arundhati and Barsamian, David (2004) *The Checkbook and The Cruise Missile: Conversations with Arundhati Roy,* Cambridge, MA: South End Press.

Ruben, Matthew (2001) 'Suburbanization and urban poverty under neoliberalism', in J. Goode and J. Maskovsky (eds) *New Poverty Studies: Power, Politics and Impoverished People in the U.S.,* New York: New York University Press, 435–467.

Shore, Cris and Wright, Susan (1999) 'Audit culture and Anthropology: neoliberalism in British higher education', *The Journal of the Royal Anthropological Institute,* 5, no. 4: 537–575.

Smith, Craig (2007) 'Crib Sheet: The American Council of Trustees and Alumni. How their "Intellectual Diversity" agenda is advocating censorship', *Campus Progress,* 27 March, < http://www.campusprogress.org/tools/1489/crib-sheet-the-american-council-of-trustees-and-alumni > (accessed 12 July 2010).

Soss, Joe, Fording, Richard C. and Schram, Sanford F. (2009) 'Governing the poor: the rise of the neoliberal paternalist state', paper prepared for presentation at the Annual Meeting of the American Political Science Association, Toronto, Canada.

Ulysee, Gina Athena (2007) *Downtown Ladies: Informal Commercial Importers: A Haitian Anthropologist and Self-Making in Jamaica,* Chicago: University of Chicago Press.

CHAPTER 7

Autonomy and control: Danish university reform in the context of modern governance

SUSAN WRIGHT AND JAKOB WILLIAMS ØRBERG

---◆◆◆

Introduction

In November 2005, *Forskerforum,* a trades union magazine for academics and researchers in Denmark, published a front page account of what it called a secret meeting between the Minister for Education and the leaders of the Danish University of Education. The shock value in this story was that the Minister was not only trespassing onto the territory of his colleague, the Minister for Science, who was responsible for universities, but he was also trying to exert political influence over the research agenda of the university. Not long afterwards, the university substantially revised its draft Development Contract to reflect the Minister of Education's interests in research on public schools (*folkeskoler*), especially that which would increase their international PISA scores (the Organisation for Economic Co-operation and Development's Programme for International Student Assessment). The Ministry of Science then agreed the revised Development Contract as the basis of assessing the university's performance over the next three years.

This incident raised questions about the autonomy and independence of Danish universities, and the academic freedom of their staff, especially following a law to reform the universities in 2003 (Folketinget 2003).[1] Denmark adhered to the Bologna Process and the creation of a European Higher Education Area, in which universities would be characterised by greater autonomy from the state (European University Association 2003: 12). But what did this mean? The Danish government maintained that its university reform was setting universities free and strengthening their independence. How could the government at the same time endorse the political intervention of a Minister into a university's research agenda in this way? In this chapter we argue that the answer lies in seeing university reform in the much wider context of political projects to develop new forms of governance and a 'modernised' public sector in Europe. We explore what the Danish government's discourse about university freedom and self-ownership meant in terms of precise administrative and funding mechanisms. The chapter draws primarily on documentary research to uncover the rationalities of government that lay behind the Danish university reforms. We find a clear model for government steering of universities. But no rationality is ever completely coherent or closed: we also find other elements which confuse the model and point to possible ways that university leaders and academics may find room for manoeuvre.[2]

University autonomy

Autonomy is the term used in most international literature to refer to an ideal or an aspiration that the university protect its independence from the interests of the state and of the private sector in order to preserve the freedom of its academics. In Anglo-Saxon contexts, state influence over universities has been considered the greatest threat. Institutional independence from the state has traditionally been assured by establishing universities as public corporations, each with their own statutes and boards of governors, entirely outside state structures (even if, since 1919, U.K. universities have been increasingly dependent on state funding for teaching and research). In much of continental Europe, universities were protected from the influence of the private sector by being located within state structures, so that universities were part of the state bureaucracy and academics were employed on civil service contracts. Even though government set the universities' budgets, universities were self-governing before the 2003 Danish university law in that academics, administrative staff and students elected all of the decision-making bodies and leaders. Under the law the universities controlled their own research, granting of research degrees and appointment of academic staff. In principle, governments were meant to refrain from political influence over universities' research agendas.[3] When the Bologna documents called for more university autonomy, they meant a break with this location of universities in a protected space within the state. In Denmark, the law has been changed to make universities independent, self-managing organisations, placed outside the state hierarchy and empowered to write their own statutes within parameters set by the law. They are not however completely autonomous of the state. Their assets still ultimately belong to the state and the methods by which the state controls universities are set out in the new national law. As Scott (1997) says, autonomy is never absolute:

academics are always located in institutions with unequal relations of power to the state and to students, both of which involve negotiations between dependency, obligation and autonomy.

The derivation of 'autonomy' from Greek (*auto* meaning self, its own; *nomos* meaning law) contains a dual reference to the self-government and freedom of action of both institutions and individuals (OED).[4] This is echoed in the widespread assumption, held late into the 20th century, that university autonomy and academic freedom go hand in hand. If the governing bodies and leaders of the university saw it as their duty, and in their interests to maintain a position of independence from the state and from other interests, like political parties and capitalist organisations, then, it was assumed, the university's leaders would also protect the ability of individual staff to use their own judgement and to resist both internal and external pressures to choose particular research topics or manicure their research results. In the 1990s, however, there were reports that the interests of university leaders and of academics were no longer congruent. For example, Julie Marcus described how her university leaders in Australia used auditing procedures to pick on, harass and rid themselves of a professor whose research asked politically uncomfortable questions, and whose role, to create a new department out of fused units, ruffled feathers (quoted in Shore and Wright 2004). Tapper and Salter (1995: 60) argued that changes in government funding conditions for U.K. universities in the 1990s also meant that the link between the autonomy of universities and the ability of academics to control their own working conditions had been broken. The tension between defending academic freedom and university autonomy was further complicated by the 2003 university law in Denmark which gave universities' governing boards the legal duty to maintain the independence of the university at the same time as they were obliged to open the university to influence from the 'surrounding society', a category which included the government.

A further feature of academic autonomy is that the ingredients are not universally the same. For U.K. universities, for example, Farrant (1987: 48) lists the following components of academic autonomy:

- to appoint their own staff without external interference
- to decide which students to admit
- to identify what and how to teach
- to control their own standards
- to establish their own academic priorities
- to determine internally their own future development.

Here the focus is on teaching; research freedom is not named and is subsumed under 'academic priorities' and 'future development'. In contrast, in Denmark universities do not select their own students and the topic and content of new degree programmes have to be accredited and then approved by the Ministry. In 2005 all universities immediately complied with the Ministry's requirement to rewrite all their degree programmes according to a list of 'competences' that students should acquire. What in the U.K. would be considered deep intrusions into academic freedom are accepted unquestioningly by academics in Denmark, who associate their freedom entirely with the ability of researchers to select their own research topics and research methods.

Even if the meaning of, and referent for, autonomy varies by context, and even if the assumed congruence of interests between the institution and its academic workers is splitting apart, autonomy still features strongly in international discourses about universities as a term expressing an aspiration. It conveys an ideal of the university as an institution that protects its independence in order to ensure that external influences are not brought to bear on the professional judgement of academics about what and how to teach and research. Yet this meaning is not politically neutral: it may once have been a widely generalised idea about universities in Western societies, but it has most strongly conveyed the aspiration of the academics themselves. If the academic aspiration of autonomy is used for analysing university reform, it blinds researchers to other emerging uses of the term.

Other ideas of university independence were in play. These relate to the arguments, put forward by many European governments, that the world is set on an inevitable and immutable course towards a global knowledge economy. To succeed in this economy, the argument runs, countries will need universities first to turn their research ideas into enterprises and, second, through their teaching, to attract and produce the kind of highly skilled labour force that will create or attract internationally mobile knowledge industries. Universities are criticised for being ponderous organisations incapable of responding flexibly to changing social and industrial demands and to opportunities for teaching and research: universities need to reform their teaching and student management, their research priorities and organisation and their governance and strategic management.

There are two strands to this argument, and both speak of strengthening university autonomy (Wright 2004). The first strand paints a picture of future free trade in higher education and a need to make universities efficient and effective in competition with private corporations that purport to be in the forefront of the knowledge economy. These advocates of free trade look to the General Agreement on Trade in Services to provide the discipline needed to curb state interference in universities. To participate in free trade, say its supporters, universities have to become economically and politically autonomous of the state and able to prioritise their activities so as to optimise profits, not cluttered by social and public agendas. Autonomy in this sense means freedom for the institution to operate according to the profit motive.

The second strand, seen especially in the Bologna process, wants to maintain higher education as 'a public good and a public responsibility' (Bologna Process 2003: 1) whilst preparing universities for competition in the international knowledge economy. The Bologna process emphasises the need for European universities to coordinate, standardise and quality-assure their activities, so as to make Europe a leading provider of higher education and 'the most competitive and dynamic knowledge-based economy in the world' (Bologna Process 2003: 2). To achieve this, they also call for increased university autonomy. In many European contexts this means greater independence from state intervention, but what kind of relationship to the state does this imply? The third report to evaluate progress on the Bologna agenda found that increased independence from the state was generally accompanied by output-based funding, extended external quality assurance and greater influence for other stakeholders in society. Higher education representatives argued that replacing state intervention with state monitoring of outputs or the intrusion of other stakeholders with short-term interests would not increase universities' autonomy or increase their innovative potential (European University Association 2003: 13). What is going on here? How could a call for greater university autonomy be compatible with increased influence from external interests and government to steer academic activities?

For academics, autonomy may still be an aspiration for individual and collective self-government; for free traders it means freedom to operate according to a profit motive; and for modernising governments it somehow combines university independence with state control. The use of the word in any context becomes very complex as these three meanings weave around each other: discourses about releasing universities from state bureaucratic structures might chime with academic images of university freedom, whilst governments' new ways of steering universities depend entirely on them being independent institutions. In such circumstances, there can be a strong danger of misrecognition (Ohnuki-Tierney 2004; Wright 2005) whereby people (academics,

students) may hear their own meaning in others' discourse and un-
wittingly help translate that meaning into political and professional
practices to which they might otherwise be opposed.

It would be a misrecognition on our part to treat 'autonomous' universities as self-generating worlds. Our aims here are to ask what relationships and conditions are attached to the Danish government's
discourse about university independence, to discover the internal logic
of the modernising government discourse and to understand how the
apparently contradictory features of independence and control are reconciled. It is beyond the scope of this chapter (although it was a concern of our project) to follow the complex ways the government's new
conjunction of independence and control intersects with the very different histories and formations of particular universities and the ways
university leaders, academics and students respond. Here we confine
ourselves to exploring the internal logic and practical implications of
this Danish 'modernising state' discourse about autonomy.

Danish university reform

The 2003 University Law gave Danish universities a new status. No
longer part of the state hierarchy or included in government accounts,
universities became self-owning institutions ('selvejende institutioner')
(Folketinget 2003). 'Selveje' has positive connotations from a major
18th-century reform through which Danish peasants gained ownership
of their own land. It was these peasants that the priest-philosopher,
Grundtvig, mobilised in the 19th century to establish a flourishing
national movement for farmers' education and enlightenment. Graduates from the Grundtvigian schools formed cooperatives to process
their products and transformed the economy of the countryside. The
self-owning peasant is a proud icon of this Danish bottom-up organisation and democracy. It was in making universities into self-owning
institutions that the government claimed it was giving universities independence and freedom. But what does self-ownership mean in this
context? What kind of university subjectivity does it presuppose? What
kind of freedom?

The 2003 University Law does not define self-ownership. The Liberal-
Conservative government's explanatory memorandum (*bemærkninger*)
which sets out the background to the draft law, states that the concept
is well established and has been in use for 'about 100 years' (Folketinget 2002: 15). Documents about self-owning institutions produced in
the Danish public sector in the last three decades clearly reveal that the

concept was indeed not new in 2003 (Ministry of Finance 1996, Ministry of Finance 1998, Ministry of Education 1997), but they also suggest that much work has gone into defining and shaping the concept's use in the public sector throughout the 1990s and especially since 1995 (Ørberg 2006a).

In the months preceding the publication of the draft law, self-ownership was briefly discussed in *Forskerforum*, a trade union magazine for academics and researchers. But the concept and its implications were hardly discussed during the parliamentary debates on the university law. Most attention at that time was paid to associated provisions in the draft law:

- Governing boards, with a majority of members and a chairman from outside the university, replaced the elected senates. The governing boards were to set the university's priorities, agree a development contract with the government, hire the rector and ensure that the rector's budget reflected their priorities.
- An appointed hierarchy replaced the elected leaders (rector, dean and department leader) and allocated resources and managed staff so as to meet the board's priorities and fulfil the performance indicators in the development contract.
- Contributions to society's 'growth, development and welfare' (Folketinget 2003: paragraph 2, point 3) were to increase through relevant research, a faster throughput of students, and courses geared to employability.

The parliamentary debates focused on whether the new systems of governance and management posed a threat to freedom of research. Spokespeople for the governing coalition parties flatly denied that the law changed existing provisions on research freedom (Ørberg 2006b). What they did not discuss was whether and how, without altering the wording, the meaning and practice of academic freedom would change as it combined with the self-owning status of universities and the governance and management structures in a new assemblage created by the law.

Self-ownership and modernisation of the public sector

Self ownership took on new meanings when it became associated with the idea of converting the public sector into free agencies. This idea originated in the Ministry of Finance, and was in turn inspired by the work of the OECD's Public Management (PUMA) programme. The concept of free or self-owning agencies was not devised for universities specifically; it was already being applied to other parts of the education and health sectors in a thorough modernisation of the Danish state.

Following the oil and financial crises of the mid-1970s, there was a panic in many Western countries that public expenditure was out of control. As David Harvey has pointed out, many Social Democratic governments in the 1970s failed to produce viable solutions for this growing crisis and neo-liberal policies filled that gap (Harvey 2004: 4). In 1979, the Social Democratic[5] Finance Minister described Denmark as 'heading for the abyss' (Østergaard 1998: 12–13). Public spending was predicted to rise to 55 per cent of the GNP in 1985 and existing management and steering mechanisms were not considered adequate to control this trend (Østergaard 1998: 11). By turning its attention to devising new methods for managing the whole of the public sector, the Ministry of Finance sought to resolve this growing expenditure crisis, whilst reasserting its own dwindling influence at the same time.

The Danish response to the crisis came to be called 'Frame and aim steering'. Through the 1980s and 1990s this concept was passed like a baton from the Social Democratic to the Conservative/Liberal coalition (1983–1993) and again to the Social Democratic/Social-Liberal/Centre Democrat government (1993–2001) whose Finance Minister wanted to prove that the Social Democrats were a solid guarantee for good public finances. The fact that there was continuity among the senior officials who were in post in the Ministry of Finance throughout this period also contributed to the continuous development of initiatives to reform the financial and operational management of the welfare state (Østergaard 1998: 14).

To the Ministry of Finance, the main problem with the public sector was its bureaucratic command system and hierarchical decision-making structure. These systems were deemed no longer capable of managing the expanding welfare state. The Ministry of Finance's (1996) memorandum, 'Methods for management in the public sector', served as a 'retroactive manifesto' (Koolhaas 1978) for the policies it had devised over the past thirty years to drive the continuous modernisation and restructuring of the Danish public sector. The memorandum delineated three phrases, depicted and slightly adapted in Figure 1.

If Figure 1A represents the post-war welfare state as a monolithic system of hierarchical decision-making and bureaucratic service provision, the second diagram (Figure 1B), 'the 1960s and 1970s', shows ministers and politicians being detached from the actual process of managing

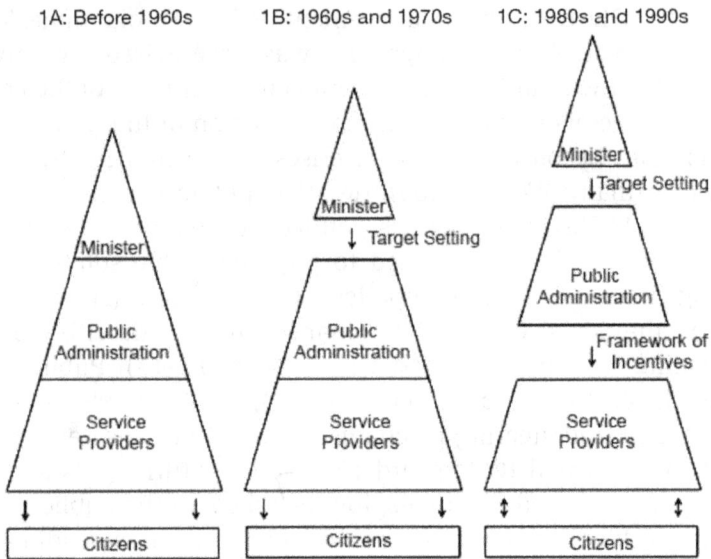

Figure 1 Methods for management in the public sector.

Adapted from 'Management systems in the public sector,' (Ministry of Finance 1996)

public services. They were to concentrate instead on setting the policy aims for the public services and the budgets through which those aims were to be achieved. That is, a space was created between the political leadership and public administrators. Politicians were no longer to row the bureaucratic system but to steer it (Osborne and Gaebler 1992). In the 1980s and 1990s (Figure 1C), ministries developed new administrative frameworks which would more efficiently and effectively achieve the politicians' policy aims. Central to this system was the purchaser-provider split, creating a space on the figure between public administrators and the providers of services. A ministry turns the politicians' policy aims and goals into contracts for services from independent providers. Parts of the state are turned into independent or self-owning institutions which in principle can compete for these contracts along with private-sector companies or non-government organisations. The quality and efficiency of these agencies' services are controlled through performance indicators and sanctions in the contracts and by payment by results. Quality and efficiency are also meant to improve in response to market competition and consumer choice. Citizens, represented by a two-way arrow in Figure 1C, are no longer to be passive recipients of services, but to exert their own pressure on service providers.

The overall aims of the reforms were to secure a closer correlation between the goals of the politicians and the behaviour of the providers, and a faster response by service deliverers when politicians changed their policy aims. To achieve this responsiveness to political goals, a bureaucratic command system has been transformed into one made up of self-owning, self-managing and self-disciplined independent contractors who are steered through market competition, contractual sanctions and rewards and output-based payment. This system is called decentralised, but it is designed to be more responsive and accountable to the top. It outsources to independent contractors, not only service delivery, but also responsibility for achieving the government's policy aims.

Through the 1990s the Ministry of Finance continued working out how to exercise control over these 'free agencies' without undermining their independence to a degree where they could no longer be held accountable for their actions (Ministry of Finance 1998: 44). At the same time, the Ministry wanted to stir up any pools of under-used assets to make sure they were deployed in a quick and effective response to current policy aims (Ministry of Finance 1998: 32–33). This meant realising any of the free agencies' under-used assets and returning them to the state, and accessing the substantial funds held in foundations that had been set up long ago for purposes which were now out of date. Once institutions no longer had untapped resources of their own, by implication, they would become dependent on a cash flow directed by the Ministry and allocated for specific outputs. By this means the Ministry would be able to link institutions' activities tightly to government policy.

Central to this strategy was the idea that 'free agencies' would have a contractual relationship with a ministry and become subject to the ministry's steering and scrutiny mechanisms. The Ministry of Education sought to be a front runner in making these changes. It called the resulting agencies by the existing Danish term, self-owning institutions (*selvejende institutioner*). Self-ownership was a term already in use in the education sector as many education institutions had originally been founded independently in the Grundtvigian tradition or by local entrepreneurs in response to local needs. These originally self-owning educational institutions had only later entered into relationships with the state in order to receive funds and authorisation. By the late 1980s, the Ministry of Education was seeking to standardise its relationships with this vast array of institutions right across the education sector. It reworked the concept of self-ownership in the light of the Ministry of Finance's model. Institutions were made independent of the central administration, while new steering mechanisms were to ensure that state funds were spent in accordance with the conditions under which they were provided (Ministry of Finance 1998: 94).

Throughout the 1990s the Ministry of Education continued to clarify the concept of self-owning institutions on which this new relationship would rest, and by 1997 the concept had taken on a consistent form (Ministry of Education 1997: 6–7). A self-owning institution is a legally independent organisation which can act like a legal person and which has responsibility for all its assets including buildings. It has to have clear purposes written into its statutes (*vedtægter*)[6] and an independent governing board with a majority of members from outside the organisation. It will not receive a state grant to support its existence, but will be paid for specified outputs and performance, and will be audited (*tilsyn*).

The legal obligation of the Ministry to carry out audits (*tilsyn*) was another important way in which its control was not diminished by this strategy. In general, *tilsyn* means not just auditing for financial probity, but scrutinising the institution to ensure it is fulfilling the conditions for its funding (Ministry of Education 1997: 24), including maximising the use of assets. *Tilsyn* carries features of the 'expanded' notion of audit in the U.K.: scrutiny of the organisation's finances, evaluation of the quantity and quality of the services provided, and assessment of the ability of the organisation's management systems to use state resources to provide good services effectively (Shore and Wright 2000).

In sum, agencies are detached from the state and turned into self-owning institutions in order to have a contractual relationship with the state. This contract reflects the politicians' policy goals and contains mechanisms for steering the organisation. These include the obligations written into the contract itself, payment based on outputs and performance, control of the organisation's liquidity and audit. In one sense, the institution is independent because the state is only concerned that the institution provides its contracted services efficiently and of a suitable quality; it is up to the institution how it achieves this. In another sense, the state's new steering mechanisms are deeply intrusive. Through *tilsyn*, the self-owning institution is not only made accountable to the Ministry, but the Ministry also fulfils its own accountability to ministers and parliament.

Self-owning universities

Universities were one of the last institutions in the education sector to be made self-owning. The idea had been put forward by the liberal Education Minister, Bertel Haarder, in 1991, but it was only in the late 1990s that it gained substantial support. From 1998 to 2000 the Ministry re-organised the Professional Education Colleges (MVUs) as self-owning, with their own assets, including the buildings in which they operated. This reform included the establishment of a new Danish University of Education, which was set up as the only self-owning university in 2000.

The same year, the Social Democratic Finance Minister, Lykketoft, reformed the administration of universities' real estate. State-owned property occupied by universities was transferred to an agency at arm's length from the state, from which universities were to rent their buildings on market-like conditions. The Ministry then funded the universities to pay this rent, but the funding was based on the university's output of students at a standardised rate. The system did not provide any compensation for universities located in areas of high property prices. Phased in over ten years, the system gave universities in the most expensive towns, notably Copenhagen University, an incentive to maximise the number of students and cut down their use of expensive space.

This reform of the way universities were funded for their premises brought to a head a financial crisis at the Technical University of Denmark (DTU). DTU had large research facilities but few students. Therefore, the funding they received from the Ministry to pay for their buildings (based on DTU's output of students) would be seriously inadequate in relation to the cost of the rent. In addition, DTU's facilities were outdated, and existing proposals from the ministry about how to finance their modernisation would further squeeze DTU's economy. Negotiations between the university and the Ministry concluded with the university asking the Ministry to re-establish it as the next self-owning university. As a self-owning institution, DTU bought its buildings from the Ministry by borrowing money against them. In addition, DTU expected to raise a mortgage on its buildings to pay for their modernisation and mark the birth of a new, bold DTU. DTU established a governing board, with a majority of external members, which had responsibility to manage these assets. The governing board then hired the rector (rather than the academic and support staff and students electing the rector, as previously). The arrangements immediately hit financial problems. The state's valuation of DTU's buildings and economic prospects was more positive than that of private investors and the state had to raise the annual subsidy to DTU to keep the institution from sliding back into financial turmoil. This experience sent shock waves through the sector, and other universities were reluctant to take these risks of self-ownership.

The Minister, who wanted to reform all universities, responded to the DTU experience by proposing that universities become 'self-owning without buildings'. They could continue to own whatever assets were already indisputably theirs but the ownership of the state buildings they occupied would not be transferred to them. Some universities had been bequeathed buildings or had other foundations attached to them, for example a foundation set up in relation to Århus University owned a large share of the agrochemical firm, Cheminova. Copenhagen University claimed that many of its buildings had been donated in the sixteenth to eighteenth centuries. But, after the British bombarded and ruined the city centre in 1807, the university, was rebuilt according to a state plan, and apparently nobody had been concerned about documenting who owned what. A dispute between Copenhagen University and the state lasted until 2006, when they reached a settlement that included state investment of 400 million kroner to modernise and reorganise the university's campuses (Ministry of Science, Technology and Innovation 2006). Universities which did not own the property they occupied became extremely dependent on a cash flow provided through state funding and thereby became susceptible to the conditions and steering mechanisms attached to it. Self-ownership without buildings had moved the concept a very long way from its origin in the peasants who came to own their own land and gain their independence through control of their own assets.

In 2002, the Rector of Copenhagen University had been sharply critical of 'self-owning without buildings'. She predicted that the state would continue to be the real owner of universities. All the existing regulations would continue, but on top of that funding would shift from being an appropriation on the state budget to becoming a grant paid to an institution outside of the state. This meant greater monitoring and auditing (*tilsyn*) of the universities' activities, not only by the state but also, as for private companies, by private auditing firms. Other rectors said the concept of self-ownership was ill-defined, and just saw it as a reward from the Minister for their willingness to reform and become more efficient and capable of strategic prioritising and development. Managers and staff in universities did not remark upon the way the draft law introduced a model of self-ownership and associated mechanisms for state steering that had already been introduced in the rest of the 'modernised' public sector (Ørberg 2006a). Several respondents to consultations and political speeches continued to claim that the concept of the self-owning institution was not clearly defined, but they did not explore this further. Instead, the clauses in the draft law about turning universities into self-owning institutions went through without serious debate in parliament or the press.

The 2003 law established universities as self-owning institutions with governing boards in a contractual relation to the state (via periodic Development Contracts). A hierarchy of hired leaders (rector, dean and department leader) are responsible upwards, to the governing board and thence the Ministry, to achieve the performance indicators set out in the development contract. The fact that very few universities have substantial assets of their own means that, as 'self-owning without buildings', they are very dependent on the state funding, which in turn means meeting agreed output levels, performance indicators and development targets.

The share-cropping university

For many years, there had been a shifting balance between two principles for funding universities. One was to provide a grant for universities to decide for themselves how to cover their basic costs (*basisbevilling*), which was a way of government and parliament valuing a national institution and keeping it going. The second method was for payments to be based on the delivery of outputs that the government desired from the sector. Since 1994 university teaching has been funded by the ministry entirely through output payments. A standard sum is allocated each time a student passes an exam for a module in a degree programme – and thereby clicks up one more payment on the so-called 'teaching taximeter'. Bonuses are also given for completing a degree programme within a set time, so as to encourage throughput. These taximeter payments are standard across universities, but vary enormously across disciplines. For example, in 2013 a university received 96,500 Danish kroner for a student passing a year's worth of exams in a 'wet' (laboratory) subject such as physics, and received 45,600 Danish kroner for a student passing a year's worth of exams in a 'dry' subject, such as Greek.

Research is partly supported by the basic grant (*basisbevilling*), with each institution deciding what percentage of a researcher's time is funded in this way for 'free research'. Other elements of state funding for research are channelled through the national research councils including programmes that are to reflect political priorities and national needs. Researchers supplement their 'free research time' by competing for funds from the national research councils, the EU and private and public foundations, as well as, increasingly, from competitive allocations of the basic grant within their own institutions. This competitive funding is intended to reward academic quality and social or economic relevance. The 2003 University law (Folketinget 2002) made clear that funding would be increasingly linked to the performance of institutions. In particular, the government envisioned an increase in university funding if they would become more trustworthy organisations, capable of delivering the instrumental research and employable graduates needed to spearhead Denmark's competitiveness in the global knowledge economy – the catchword for the 2003 reform was 'From thought to invoice'. In 2010 an algorithm was devised for the competitive allocation between the universities of part of this additional funding. It was based on a combination of output measures: points for research publications, income from external sources, numbers of student exam passes and numbers of PhD completions (Wright 2014).

The ministry's performance payments for teaching are allocated at the start of the year, based on the output of student exam passes that the university expects to achieve by the end of the year. The government makes these payments on a monthly basis and then settles accounts with the university on the basis of actual output at the end of the year. In contrast to Denmark's self-owning peasant, this system of payment is highly reminiscent of third world share-cropping farmers who take a loan from merchants at the beginning of the agricultural year, which they hope to be able to pay off at harvest time. Such 'farmers without assets', highly dependent on cash flow, know what it is to live with the continual risk of not being able to pay off debts raised on promises about risk-laden future harvests. They do not live in a system of overt domination: they are 'independent' and 'free' to choose how to deploy their labour, how big or small a production contract to engage in, and how big a mortgage to take out on the future. But their ability to free themselves from the status of dependent client is ultimately restricted if they lack other assets they can use to raise alternative sources of income.

The government's discourse about accountability further expressed the way risk is pushed down the system to the share-cropping university. Of course, in return for receiving state funding, universities have to be accountable, but this has taken on a new and very specific meaning. In an echo of Blair describing the modernisation of 'UK plc' (the equivalent would be Denmark A/S), the Danish government talks of self-owning institutions having to present an annual company (*virksomhed*) account to the ministry, which is referred to as the corporate level (*koncernniveau*). These metaphors refer to an important way that the private sector deals with risk: a parent corporation (*koncern*) sets up a subsidiary company to rid itself of the liability of engaging in, for example, a financially risky initiative. Each subsidiary company is an independent, self-managing (*selvstyrende*) organisation, set up in this way so that if it fails, it can be shed, and it does not take the parent corporation down with it. Individual universities are similarly economically self-managing, independent and free in the sense that they are responsible for managing their own finances, but the state has a strong interest in steering them tightly enough to avoid bankruptcy, as that would endanger the overall capacity to deliver on policy aims.

In practice, the treatment of a university as a company is no longer a metaphor, but an accounting reality. From 2005 all universities had to transfer from cash-based accounting to accrual accounting, and in 2006 universities presented their first annual 'company' reports based on the same system of accrual accounting as used in industry. Whereas previously cash-based accounting, the usual method of public-sector accounting, focused on probity in the use of funds, accrual accounting makes possible a standardised calculation of the profitability of each output, which is taken as a measure of efficiency. In one university's board meeting we witnessed an attempt to use 'profitability' as a measure of the efficiency with which the university organises its activities.

In principle, accrual accounting allows the income from every output to be matched against the 'real' cost of its production, including the depreciated value of assets, use of space, staff costs, and materials. This raises serious questions about which university activities can be converted into outputs, and which cannot – like, for example, thinking, discussing ideas informally with local and international colleagues, and generating ideas for critiquing the present and developing alternative futures. As Mahon (2009) has made clear, it is a political decision to focus on some things and leave other things – especially public benefits of research – out of the reckoning. If academics follow government and institutional incentives to focus on 'what counts' (Wright 2011), there seems to be a danger that this system will squeeze out activities that cannot be recorded or measured as outputs or that do not yield 'points' in the competitive funding algorithm. At one point it seemed that universities would try and record the detailed use of resources at departmental and faculty levels so as to give the central administration access to detailed and comparable information and enable them to provide the governing board with standardised accounts. For example, Copenhagen University set up a project called KU 2005, which required department administrators to allocate each transaction to a standardised system of codes in a new computerised system. One expected outcome of KU 2005 was to transfer the effort previously put into local administration of budgets and expenditure into a centralised system designed to provide administrators and the governing board with the kind of information needed for them to make strategic decisions (Øbing 2004: 5). Such an accounting system would also give the Ministry the capacity to compare the unit cost of each university's activities, for example, how much it costs to produce a PhD student or a patent, and to decide at what level to base future performance payments (taximeter tariffs) to induce further efficiencies. These accounting and reporting systems could also make the profitability of each university transparent and comparable to firms that may wish to compete for research and teaching contracts in future (along the lines envisioned by Ministry of Finance (2003: 42–43)). However, after the Minister made a brief call for privatising one of Denmark's universities (Ejsing 2010), the potential for using this funding and accounting system as a basis for comparing the efficiency and profitability of universities and for assessing the viability of competition from private providers has lain dormant (Wright 2012).

The internal organisation of most universities has changed in order to meet the demands and expectations of this new steering system. The new leaders appointed in response to the 2003 law are deploying a range of management techniques, in different combinations in each university. The overall effect is to extend Figure 1C into the internal organisation of universities. The responsibility for meeting government policy passes down a line of contracts, from government to ministry, from ministry to university board, thence to rector, dean of faculty and department leader. Each leader is upwardly accountable for performance and efficiency. Responsibility and accountability for meeting the outputs necessary to fulfil the development contract – and thereby achieve government policy – are outsourced down this chain of contracts. Ultimately the department leader can require each research group or even individual to enter into an action plan stating their expected outputs over the next period, against which their performance can be judged, for example by annual 'individual audits'. The University Law, which even before 2003 empowered department leaders to direct employees on the tasks they are to undertake, now reinforces the power of department leaders to get employees to perform in accordance with the performance outputs in the chain of contracts.

From the perspective of central government documents, this model of a continuous chain of contracts seems neat and all tied up: it outsources service production, and accountability for ever-more efficient use of resources, at the same time as it outsources responsibility for the government's achieving its policy aims all the way down the line to the individual academic. But each institution, leader and individual 'freely' enters those contracts, that is, all they forfeit, if they decline, is their funding or their position. Formal lines of accountability run only upwards through this model. In 2011 the university law was changed so as to specifically require leaders to involve academics, students and administrative staff in important decisions, but the only remaining forum in which academics have a statutory right to require leaders to respond to questions is the employer-employee liaison committee (*samarbejdsudvalg*). Students, academics, department leaders, deans, rectors and governing board members are all free in their own sphere to try and find room for manoeuvre – whether that be through quiet acceptance, negotiation, hard bargaining or protest. They are free to try and also operate according to other notions of academic freedom and collegiality. But are the conditions in which they try to exercise this freedom – this combination of independence and control – more reminiscent of the Danish self-owning peasant, or the continually in-debted share cropper?

Conclusion

The reforms set out in the Danish University Law of 2003 rely on the concept of the self-owning institution. According to the law this new status requires universities to appoint governing boards, remove previous democratic decision-making forums and replace them with top-down appointed leaders for the university, the faculty and the department. Preceding the passage of the law, there had been a number of other isolated reforms – development contracts between the university and the government, taximeter payments for teaching, annual appraisal meetings for all staff. These existing reforms were brought into a new relation with each other and acquired a new meaning as they slotted into place in a model of outsourcing contracts that, in its 'cleanest' forms ran from the Minister down to the individual academic, with a system of accountability for meeting outputs, and therefore achieving government policy, running back up from the individual to the Minister. In this model, contracts were to be understood as an expression of the freedom of each party. But that freedom is modified by the funding system, in which universities have very few independent assets and are heavily dependent on the state's short-term payments for outputs. As Graebner (2011) has argued, debt is the purposeful creation of political dependency, and the combination of making universities responsible for their own solvency and then tightly controlling their liquidity gives the state a very strong instrument for steering self-owning institutions.

The model started out under a Liberal minister as a version of free-market autonomy – an international discourse about giving universities independence from the state so that they are free to operate in the global knowledge economy according to the profit motive. The Social Democrats reintroduced into this model strong elements of the 'modernising government' version of autonomy, with a new combination of independence and state control. An argument derived from Polanyi (1944) would suggest that a free-market version would undermine the social relations on which civic life, including universities, depends and that social action is always needed to modify the worst excesses of the market. However, by taking universities out of the state hierarchy and making them self-owning institutions, the government is not responsible for protecting the independence and freedom of universities. The 2003 Danish University Law gives universities a responsibility to be open to their surrounding society, and this means not just that industry and civil society have the right to try and influence the work of universities, but also government ministers, as stakeholders, have the right directly to lobby the governing boards and rectors to include research that meets their political interests in their development contracts. Maybe if universities, or departments, or individual academics made contracts with as diverse a range of social stake-holders as possible, so as to reduce dependence on the government's contract, on which its steering mechanism relies, this would provide more room for manoeuvre? Meanwhile, the visit of the Minister of Education to inform the Danish University of Education what they should put in their development contract was no scandal at all: the Minister was acting according to the new ethics of university autonomy. As Scott has remarked,[8] the Danish model combines the worst of both the free trade and the modernising state models of autonomy: universities, their leaders and academics are given freedom in the sense of individual responsibility for their own economic survival, whilst the sector comes under heavy political control. This is called 'setting universities free'. Yet the controls are not, and never were those of slavery, just as they do not entail the independence of the iconic self-owning Danish peasants with their own assets: as Deleuze (1995: 181) has pointed out, and like third world asset-less sharecroppers have long understood, it is the freedom to try and manoeuvre within constraints imposed by a system of continual indebtedness.

Acknowledgements

Earlier versions of this chapter were given to the conference of C-SAP, the U.K. Higher Education Academy's Centre for Learning and Teaching in Sociology, Anthropology and Politics (Birmingham, November 2005), the meeting of Nordic Academic Unions, Stykkisholmur, Iceland (8 June 2006), the conference of the Trans-Atlantic Forum on the Future of Universities (Copenhagen 27–30 June 2006) and the ESRC-funded seminar, Geographies of Knowledge, Geometries of Power, Wales, 10–12 July 2006. We are grateful to Rebecca Boden and Penny Ciancanelli for explaining different systems of accounting and their implications. We received useful and stimulating comments on the draft article from Davydd Greenwood, Cornell University, Alan Scott, Innsbruck University and David Mills, Oxford University.

◆

Susan Wright is Professor of Educational Anthropology at the Danish School of Education, University of Århus. Her research focuses on transformations in processes of governance. With Cris Shore, she pioneered the anthropology of policy. She has studied of processes of university reform in Britain and Denmark and is now leading an EU project, comparing 'Universities in the Knowledge Economy' (UNIKE) in Europe and the Asia-Pacific Rim. She is co-editor of Learning and Teaching: International Journal of Higher Education in the Social Science.

Jakob Williams Ørberg is a Post.Doc. Fellow at the Danish School of Education, Aarhus University. He did his doctoral work on engineering students as the heroes of the Indian knowledge economy. His current research concerns the 'shadow education' preparatory courses for entry into top engineering schools in India. Previously he has been Research Assistant to the project 'New Management, New Identities? Danish University Reform in an International Context', based at the Danish School of Education, University of Aarhus. He has also worked as Head of Section in the Danish Ministry of Science, Technology and Innovation.

Notes

This chapter originally appeared in *Learning and Teaching: The International Journal of Higher Education in the Social Sciences* Spring 2008, 1(1): 27–57.

1. The 2003 university law defined the university sector as those institutions that referred to the Ministry of Science, Technology and Innovation. They included the five multidisciplinary universities, two business schools and five institutions specialising in technology, IT, pharmacy, agriculture and education.
2. The research was part of a project called 'New Management, New Identities? Danish University Reform in an International Context' (2004–2009), funded by the Danish Research Council. This chapter draws on documentary research by

Jakob Williams Ørberg, jointly conducted interviews and participation at university meetings, and Susan Wright's comparative work on the reform of universities in other Scandinavian countries and the U.K. Further information is available at http://edu.au.dk/en/research/research-areas/epoke/reseach-projects/archive/.

3. There are of course notorious breaches when, for example, governments have decided to close departments they did not favour politically.

4. Autonomy (*nomos* meaning law) implies each person governing themselves, as against autocracy (*cracy* meaning power) which means the absolute government of one person over all.

5. In referring to Danish political parties we are using the English translations preferred by the parties themselves on their homepages.

6. The word 'statutes' is a translation of the Danish *vedtægter* and not *statutter*, which was the term used in relation to universities up until 2003. The use of *vedtægter* corresponds to the language used in private corporations. In the proposal for the law that set out the framework for the self-owning Technical University of Denmark (DTU), the science ministry found it necessary to correct the language used by administrators at DTU and underline that the word *statutter* is no longer appropriate (Folketinget 2000: 53–54).

7. The Netherlands advertised such an 'open system experiment' whereby providers that were not currently part of their publicly funded system of higher education were eligible to tender for bachelor and master level programmes (THES 21 July 2006).

8. Alan Scott, personal communication, 27 July 2006.

References

Bologna Process (2003) *Realising the European Higher Education Area*, Communique of the Conference of Ministers responsible for Higher Education, Berlin, 19 September.

Deleuze, G. (1995) 'Postscript on control societies', in G. Deleuze (ed.) *Negotiations 1972–1990*, New York: Columbia University Press.

Ejsing, J. (2010) 'Regeringen vil privatisere universiteterne', *Berlingske*, 12 January 2010 < http://www.b.dk/politik/regeringen-vil-privatisere-universiteterne > (accessed 16 August 2013).

European University Association (2003) *Trends 2003: Progress towards the European Higher Education Area*, July.

Farrant, J. (1987) 'Central control of the university sector', in T. Becher (ed.) *British Higher Education*, London: Allen and Unwin.

Folketinget (Parliament) (2000) *Forslag til Lov om Danmarks Tekniske Universitets (DTU) overgang til selveje* [Proposal for Law about the Technical University of Denmark's Transition to Self-ownership], Copenhagen: The Danish Parliament.

Folketinget (Parliament) (2002) *General Notes to the Draft Bill on Universities* [The University Act] < http://www.videnskabsministeriet.dk/cgi-bin/theme-list.cgi?theme_id = 138230 > (accessed 8 November 2005).

Folketinget (Parliament) (2003) *Act on Universities,* Act no 403 of 28 May 2003. < http://www.videnskabsministeriet.dk/cgi-bin/theme-list.cgi?theme_id = 138230 > (accessed 8 November 2005).

Forskerforum (2005) 'DPU: Bertil ind ad bagdøren' [Danish University of Education: Bertil (Minister of Education) in through the back door], November 189: 1.

Graebner, D. (2011) *Debt: The First 5000 Years,* New York: Melville House Publishing.

Harvey, D. (2004) 'Neo-Liberalism and the Restoration of Class Power', Paper presented at University of Oslo Centre for Development and the Environment seminar *Humanism for the 21st Century: Perspectives East and West,* June 4–5. < http://www.sum.uio.no/research/changing_attitudes/humanism/harv ey080604.pdf > (accessed 26 May 2007).

Koolhaas, R. (1978) *Delirious New York: A Retroactive Manifesto for Manhattan,* Oxford: Oxford University Press.

McMahon, W. (2009) *Higher Learning, Greater Good. The Private and Social Benefits of Higher Education,* Baltimore, MD: John Hopkins University Press.

Ministry of Education (1997) *Selvejende undervisningsinstitutioner* [Self-owning Educational Institutions], Copenhagen: Danish Ministry of Education.

Ministry of Finance (1996) *Budgetredegørelse 96. Tillæg: Styringsformer i den offentlige sektor* [Budget Memorandum 1996: Methods for Management in the Public Sector], Copenhagen: Ministry of Finance.

Ministry of Finance (1998) *Fonde med offentlig interesse* [Trusts vested with public interest], Copenhagen: Ministry of Finance.

Ministry of Finance (2003) *Omkostninger og effektivitet i staten – Rapport fra udvalget om omkostningsbaserede budgetog regnskabsprincipper* [Cost and Efficiency in the State – Report from the Committee Concerning Cost Based Budgeting and Accounting Principles], Copenhagen: Ministry of Finance.

Ministry of Science, Technology and Innovation (2006) 'Aktstykke 148' (Finance Committee Document number 148).

Øbing, L. (2004) KU2005 og medarbejderne. *Københavns Universitet: Økonomireformprojekt KU2005* [*University of Copenhagen: Financial reform project KU2005*], Copenhagen: University of Copenhagen.

Ohnuki-Tierney, E. (2004) 'Betrayal by idealism and aesthetics: Special Attack Force (kamikaze) pilots and their intellectual trajectories', *Anthropology Today* 20(2): 15–21.

Ørberg, J. W. (2006a) 'Setting universities free? – the background to the self-ownership of Danish universities', *Working Papers on University Reform 1,* Copenhagen: Danish University of Education.

Ørberg, J. W. (2006b) 'Trust in universities – parliamentary debates over the 2003 university law', *Working Papers on University Reform 2,* Copenhagen: Danish University of Education.

Osborne, D. and Gaebler, T. (1992) *Reinventing Government: How the Entrepreneurial Spirit is Transforming the Public Sector,* New York: Plume.

Østergaard, H. H. H. (1998) 'Resume´ af "At tjene og forme den nye tid – Finansministeriet 1848–1998" ' [Summary of 'To serve and shape the future — Ministry of Finance 1848 to 1998'], Copenhagen: Ministry of Finance.

Polanyi, K. (1944) *The Great Transformation: The Political and Economic Origins of Our Time*, Boston: Beacon Press.

Scott, A. (1997) 'Between autonomy and responsibility: Max Weber on scholars, academics and intellectuals', in J. Jennings and A. Kemp-Welch (eds) *Intellectuals in Politics: From the Dreyfus Affair to Salmon Rushdie*, London: Routledge.

Shore, C. and Wright, S. (2000) 'Coercive accountability: the rise of audit culture in higher education', in M. Strathern (ed.) *Audit Cultures: Anthropological Studies in Accountability, Ethics and the Academy*, (EASA Series), London: Routledge.

Shore, C. and Wright, S. (2004) 'Whose accountability? Governmentality and the auditing of universities', *Parallax* 10(2): 100–116.

Tapper, E. R. and Salter, B. G. (1995) 'The changing idea of university autonomy', *Studies in Higher Education* 20(1): 59–71.

THES (Times Higher Education Supplement) (2006) 'Provisional grants scheme for open system experiments of the Ministry of Education, Culture and Science in the Netherlands' (advertisement) 21 July.

Wright, S. (2004) 'Markets, corporations, consumers? New landscapes in higher education', *LATISS – Learning and Teaching in the Social Sciences* 1(2): 71–93.

Wright, S. (2005) 'Processes of social transformation: An anthropology of English higher education policy', in J. Krejsler, N. Kryger and J. Milner (eds) *Pædagogisk Antropologi – et Fag I Tilblivelse*, København: Danmarks Pædagogiske Universitets Forlag.

Wright, S. (2011) 'Viden der tæller' [Knowledge that Counts] in K. M. Bovbjerg (ed.) *Motivation og mismod*, [Motivation and Despondency] Århus Universitetsforlag.

Wright, S. (2012) 'Danske universiteter – virksomheder i statens koncern?' [Danish universities – companies in the corporation of the state?] in J. Faye and D. Budtz Pedersen (eds) *Hvordan Styres Videnssamfundet?* [How to Govern a Knowledge Society?] Copenhagen: Samfundslitteratur.

Wright, S. (2014) 'Knowledge that Counts: Points Systems and the Governance of Danish Universities' in D. Smith and A. Griffith (eds) *Under New Public Management: Institutional Ethnographies of Changing Front-line Work*. Toronto: University of Toronto Press.

Afterword

DAVYDD J. GREENWOOD

———————————————————————————————◆◆◆

The reader of these chapters has already been rewarded with a nationally, topically and analytically diverse set of essays on the current state of higher education. The aims of this volume are not just to analyse current trends in the organisation, governance and priorities of universities, but to go beyond critique and explore ways to develop collective critical awareness and optimally action, especially through teaching. There is diversity of material and approaches in the chapters here, much to agree with, and some things to question. I will use the space here to highlight those threads that seem particularly important for the future direction of this kind of work on higher education. I will organise this 'afterword' in a series of points about the analytical concepts that, as the chapters in this book demonstrate, are crucial to clarify for an effective critique. Towards the end I will turn my attention to the ways the authors have used their critique in their teaching and point to the next steps that are needed to develop collective action for change in higher education.

Clarification of crucial concepts

Institutional diversity

A central theme emerging from this collection is the importance of attending to the complexity, diversity and historicity of higher education institutions and systems. An advantage and also a limitation of this collection is that, as the introduction makes clear, the volume largely refers to public universities. It does so while speaking about higher education as a whole. This does not invalidate the analyses but in future, we must distinguish higher education institutional types and analyse them in their context: e.g. public universities, private universities, research universities, primarily teaching universities, public colleges, private colleges, denominational colleges, community colleges, technical schools, for-profit universities and colleges, etc. There are some overarching similarities but there are also crucial differences. This matters as one-size-fits-all reforms certainly will not work for them all. To be most useful, ethnographic work should attend to differences among the types of institutions, their unique features and their problems.

Institutional complexity

The complex multiplicity of regimes, overlapping systems and historical sediments of earlier regimes are well captured in many of the chapters. The neoliberal juggernaut, as powerful as it is, does not erase the Gramscian 'fragments' or 'traces' of all the previous systems, the messy and confusing overlaps and tensions among all the successive attempts to organize and reorganize universities are present in most institutions simultaneously. Understanding this contested internal terrain is key to understanding the change processes currently taking place.

Historicity

Nor were prior regimes less controversial. The history of Taylorism, in industry and in academia, shows it to be filled with tensions and contradictions between craft work, technical command and control management, worker individualization versus labour solidarity and soldiering rather than working. So the current multiplicity and complexity is not a new situation for our institutions. Just as the scientific managers under Taylorism tried to banish irrationality from the system with very mixed results, the current neoliberal leaders of higher education are doing the same. The past was not simpler or more homogeneous. Nevertheless, I do agree that the neoliberals have captured the state educational policy apparatus to an extraordinary degree now. They have the backing of international, multilateral organizations that gives them a kind of power and political legitimacy that Taylorists, even in their heyday, never achieved.

But even the power of the neoliberals is not absolute and their 'paint-by-the-numbers' approach to regulating universities cannot overcome the complexity of the world they are trying to regulate. Just as Taylorism tried to migrate from industrial manufacturing to stock companies, service organizations and the financial industry by imposing a hierarchical authoritarian commodity production model on them all with poor results, so neoliberalism in higher education tries to remake universities in the image of the simple rational choice model that drives it. The model simply does not work now, did not work in the past and no amount of tweaking will make it work in the future. The recurrent manufacturing and financial crises we are experiencing as a result of Tayloristic and neoliberal policies in the private and public sectors are equally visible in higher education. The model does, however, lay waste to the social fabric of higher education.

Multiplicity

This complexity and multiplicity matters for the authors' projects because it links to understanding universities as diverse fields of relations and choices. The tensions among the parts create significant opportunities for action, resistance and reform. One of the striking features of the chapters is their awareness of this multiplicity. They share an emergent notion that emphasizing the multiplicity of agendas ethnographically provides a new starting point for pro-social change processes. There are many different points of entry, many dilemmas and diverse stakeholders who move in a wide variety of directions. I will return to this point about the power of ethnography at the end.

Corporatisation

The chapters all deal with 'corporatisation' in one way or another but the meanings and analytical perspectives applied to this concept are diverse and divergent. Looking ahead, there is a significant need to complicate and map the concepts of corporatisation in our work, following the lead of Wright and Ørberg, Shore, Clarke and Shear and Zontine. Overall, these authors treat corporatization with greater nuance than is routinely found elsewhere and this matters both analytically and politically; but there is still more to do.

To move ahead with this kind of analysis, we need to press hard to clarify what we mean by such concepts as corporate, business-like, managerialist, market-like, consumerist and other terms now in wide use. Relatively few anthropologists have had much experience working in contemporary manufacturing and service businesses, stock corporations and in public sector organizations because anthropology, unfortunately, accepted being exiled to the non-Western world for many decades in a neat division of labour with sociology, political science, economics and history. Without the personal experience of the diversity and complexity within and among manufacturing and service organizations, it is easy to homogenize them with vague references to 'corporate' and 'business' behaviour and organizational routines. Some corporations are strongly Tayloristic and commodity driven but many others are not. Some are managed as matrix organizations with fluid relations among the employees in different areas and the emergence and disappearance of project teams. Corporations that make things are not the same as corporations that provide services. Those that provide financial services, and those that are owned by stockholders, as we have learned through global disaster, are different from all others regarding their rationalities, pay structures and sense of right and wrong. Furthermore, neoliberalism is not coterminous with managerialism. Managerialism, even in service organizations long antedates the current neoliberal era. Without definition and good ethnographic backup, these concepts become moral terms in a dichotomy between good and evil that can undermine both ethnography and analysis.

Avoiding anachronisms

Analyses always rely on comparisons, either synchronic or diachronic and sometimes both. In the case of research on higher education reform, analytical work is routinely cast against either an explicit or implicit historical picture that highlights what the analyst believes is going on in the present. Since these explicit and implicit historical references cannot be eliminated, studies of higher education need to take on the past in an ethnographic spirit. Various contributors note that the present is composed of a ragtag combination of elements deriving from past reforms and I certainly agree. Several authors also caution against overly romantic views of the academic past, seeing them as useless in addressing current problems. I also agree.

However, in this larger field of inquiry, I believe we need more explicit and systematic attention to the history of higher education institutions to set the ethnographic context appropriately. Historical perspectives have a major impact on the analysis of contemporary data. For example, as a long-term veteran of university life (44 years as a professor) I clearly remember the competitive, cutthroat behaviour of colleagues climbing the career ladder in the 1970s and raids on other departments to get their best faculty. We were competitive and anything but solidary. But the competition did have a different flavour, emphasizing competition among peers in a discipline and competition with each other in the department. Competition is not new; larger national and global ranking systems and the implication of deans and university leaders in the imposition of the rules and values to be competed over is. Proceeding in a more contextual and historically specific way, allows us to understand better how neoliberal policies affect us than if we imagine that competition was not present before neoliberalism arrived.

The history of higher education in the 19th and 20th centuries is directly relevant. I will give examples from the case I know best: the U.S.A. The creation of doctoral programs in the social sciences and history in the U.S.A., supposedly a direct import from the German research university model, actually was parachuted in on top of an Oxbridge-inspired collegiate model to create a new type of hybrid institution. And it also unleashed competition to create PhD fields, staff them and attract faculty, funds, facilities and students to them by proliferating academic silos in what Christopher Newfield rightly observed was an organizational model that directly imitated the structure of Henry Ford's Tayloristic factories (Newfield 2004). So Taylorism, competition and managerialism are not new. However, the kind of paint-by-numbers managerialism and the policy environment these competitive forces are deployed in now does seem to be new. What is needed is a careful empirical analysis of the changing conditions and execution of neoliberal management because it helps reveal which options are taken and which are suppressed in these pseudo-efforts to rationalize the world of higher education.

Discipline and control

Some scholars write as if such issues as censoring and controlling academic teaching and research, gentrification and privileging of elites are problems uniquely associated with neoliberalism. It is worth remembering that the American Association of University Professors was founded by the likes of John Dewey and Arthur Lovejoy in response to ideological purges of faculty whose freedom of speech had been abused by their universities. In the U.S.A., during the 'Red Scare', hundreds of faculty members were purged and again during the events of the 1960s surrounding the Vietnam War. More subtly, the social sciences were strongly pressured to turn toward analysis and methodology and away from issues of social reform. The split between 'academic' and 'applied' work was used as a method to control the engagement of academic research and speech with conflict-producing public issues (see, for example, Furner 1975; Ross 1991; Madoo Lengermann and Niebrugge-Brantley 1998). Disciplining and domesticating professors is not new. A key ethnographic challenge is to understand how the current regimes of discipline and domestication are different from prior ones and where the weaknesses and vulnerabilities can be found to enable confrontation with these current regimes. This kind of intentional ethnographic work relies on a solid historical base.

Anthropology of policy

Wright, Ørberg and Shore are very much at the centre of developing an anthropology of policy in general, in addition to having a particular focus on higher education (Shore and Wright 1997; Shore, Wright and Peró 2011). This work is vital to all of us and adds dimensions to policy analyses and policy environments that had grown stale and ineffectual. A number of points about policy in this book deserve emphasis.

Though it is not a central feature of these chapters, I am struck by the degree to which the institutional and national policy scenarios described are based on a sense that national policy is still possible despite the recognition that we are now operating in an increasingly global system with highly mobile students and faculty and a variety of binding international agreements. The processes of conciliating the campus, national and global levels of policy change and implementation make their appearance in these chapters and need further study and problematization. Is national policy even possible? Can global policies be context-specific enough to produce anything other than disasters? Studying these issues can help us envision possibilities for effecting local change by selectively using forces in the larger system to pressure local actors in particular ways. As Boden and Wright (2010) have done, it is possible to use the claims the EU and national governments make about accountability to show ethnographically that they are not doing what they say and to use their own ideological cover to hold them 'accountable'.

Public good

It is not news that the political left and political right in the U.S.A. and Europe have become harder to distinguish than Tweedle Dee and Tweedle Dum but there is more to be done with the impact of this fundamental change on most educational systems. When the differences between a political left and right were sharper, policy alternatives were more pronounced. The left could be counted on, at least modestly, to defend the welfare state and concepts like the public good (including social security systems, health care and education) as a way of maintaining their political constituency. Now that the new left has become as neoliberal as the right, the defence of the 'public good' is not part of any major party's repertoire. Looking at education in the U.S.A., we have seen a change from a Conservative Republican like George W. Bush to a supposedly Liberal Democrat, Barack Obama, occur without the slightest change in the neoliberal designs for public primary, secondary, or tertiary education.

So a left/right analysis gets us nowhere in thinking about higher education policy and we have to find new allies in the defence of the public good. We also need to understand how a concept that was venerated and protected for so long, the public good, could have been eclipsed so dramatically, especially when this change in perspective was completely unsupported by economic analysis. Indeed, serious economic analyses show that public goods are an essential element in a healthy economic system and are a major ingredient and product of higher education (McMahon 2009).

Market

Seen ethnographically in terms of institutional logic, universities cannot operate without public goods of various sorts. Tax exemptions already define universities partly as a public good subsidized by the taxpayers in the interest of society at large. At the institutional level, the composition of disciplines – and specialties within them – cannot be driven solely by the market for their services. Were this to be the case, there would be no classics departments, no art history, no philosophy and probably no theoretical physics or chemistry either. There would be no 'pure' research. Universities would only engaged in 'fee-for-service' research on short time horizons as many of the most neoliberal policymakers recommend.

It is ethnographically obvious, if we choose to spend the time to demonstrate it, that to survive and thrive, universities rely on many elements that do not pay their own way and that must rely on social subsidies (Greenwood 2013). To pretend that these public goods can be done away with and be replaced with student fees and private sector contracts is not just bad academics; it is a fool's economics as well. Given that, I miss more emphasis on this key issue in the chapters and I see it as a rich and promising topic for future ethnographic work.

'Steering' and the 'referee state'

Susan Wright and Jakob Ørberg have led the way in their studies of the clever way the Danish authorities legitimated their academic coup d'état by claiming they have made the universities self-owning and that their governmental role is as managers who are only 'steering' these autonomous institutions. In addition to being astonished by the brash creativity of such a perverse falsehood, Wright and colleagues show us we can learn more about the current scene by analysing these practices than we get from just denominating them neoliberal (Wright and Ørberg 2009; 2012).

This governmental sleight-of-hand, viewed ethnographically, recreates the government as the referee/judge of performance rather than as the very mechanism charged with achieving that performance. It also separates the work of being a professor and a student completely from the work of those who set the policies and enforce the rules and who are not accountable to the professors and students. In effect, this legitimates absentee management by those who do not, in fact, know what the work of the university is or how it is done and who therefore cannot provide meaningful support for that work. Like tax farmers, patent 'trolls' and absentee landlords, this steering system reconceives the state as the referee, the arbiter of quality with no rational justification for the state's ability to do so. Indeed, most historical examples would suggest that national governments are unable to perform these functions with any degree of competence at all.

It is useful to link this back to the need to complicate the idea that university policy is being corporatized. Among the most effective and successful corporations at present are those that minimize hierarchy, decrease administrative overheads and promote collaborative creativity. By contrast, the referee state and their minions at each university are much more like Fredrick Winslow Taylor's efficiency engineers with their stopwatches who do not lift a finger to help and could not do the jobs they observe and pretend to judge. As was learned from generations of research on Taylorism, making the rules without knowing how to do the work is a recipe for disaster. Many problems created by the Bologna Process reforms make this ethnographically clear.

Education

This sleight of hand has another effect that deserves more ethnographic attention. The referee state is largely silent on what a higher education is. Rather it takes intuitive homilistic definitions of education for granted and often conflates being educated with passing a state-mandated test and being good at research with publishing x number of articles or winning x number of grants. The referee state actually shuts down the discussion of what education is and should be at the very time most of us recognize that what we teach and research must be revised to fit current conditions better. After all, if the state is spending vast resources holding universities to account, the last thing they want to do is to change what universities are held accountable for. Thus, making the meaning of education undiscussable is another feature of the audit culture.

Audit and debt

A related feature of the audit culture linked to the above considerations is the role of debt as justifying the state's auditing operations. Audits of various sorts have long been used and are not inherently neoliberal. However, audit has taken a new turn under current conditions, as can be seen from many of the chapters. To justify the state's position as the referee of quality without the state being able to claim to be the 'expert' in education requires it to find another justification for its interventions. That justification is found in the fictitious creation of a debt that public universities cannot repay. Never mind that public universities were built with tax money and were public goods. The state now claims to own/manage them on behalf of the public while cutting state allocations to support them and forcing students to pay ever-higher fees to attend them. In effect, under the cover of debt, the state has expropriated the public universities.

This operation is precisely analogous to the way David Graeber (2011) and Ellen Brown (2012) frame the use of debt as a weapon of political subordination by the IMF, World Bank and others in the national and international arena. By putting universities in perpetual debt, universities are made wards of the state that can be ordered around at will (Samuels 2013).

Meritocracy and the creation of the neoliberal actor

Meritocracy is often mentioned in these chapters and it is pervasive in university settings though not limited to them. The claim that the neoliberal turn emphasizes the production of meritocratic individuals who complete and judge themselves according to the externally imposed standards of the referee state is strong and well documented. There is no question about the psychic violence that this kind of system causes, as Walter Kirn so poignantly documents (2009).

Still, ethnographically, we need to work more with the notions of meritocracy and fill out the picture more completely. We can see how students and faculty are constituted as meritocratic actors by the current systems but there is much less ethnography about university leaders as meritocratic subjects (except for Tuchman 2011 and Ginsburg 2011). I am not aware of a synthetic treatment of students, faculty, managers, staff and policymakers all as meritocratic actors operating in the same system. If we were to follow this ethnographically, the picture of an arena of discordant, competitive and probably somewhat sociopathic individuals would emerge, all pursuing their advantage at the expense of the others. If there is a scene in which the idiosyncrasies and dangers of neoliberalism as Karl Polanyi's 'stark utopia' is clear, it is probably in this kind of university environment. Everyone is climbing over everyone else, each on ladders managed for them by the referee state. Of course, students, faculty, university administrators and policymakers were individualistic, competitive and selfish before neoliberalism. The issue is not that their behaviours are new but that they are now so unilaterally encouraged.

Beyond critique to collective action

One of the most rewarding results of reading this collection is seeing in it the gradual emergence of a strategy of resistance to neoliberal reforms. There are many echoes in the chapters of the problems of collective action under current conditions and the difficulty of moving from critical analysis to action. It feels as if we are victims of a mammoth prisoner's dilemma.

Many of the chapters focus on the value of critical analysis and awareness in understanding the regime we are under and what is wrong with it. But they also recognize that critical awareness not accompanied by a strategy for change is not a satisfactory result either. This is the age-old problem of social action under oppressive systems and it would be unrealistic to expect the present volume to solve it. Many of the authors acknowledge the problem clearly and provide ethnographic examples and make it clear that these have emerged, not just from research, but as part of a teaching process in the classroom. They have used ethnography as a means of deepening students' and faculty's critical self-awareness (see, for example, Hyatt's chapter).

A more robust agenda begins to emerge from these pages. A number of chapters emphasize the 'fragments' and 'traces', the multiplicity of contradictory elements that make up our institutions. They see working with them in various ways as a possible road to opening up a more fundamental change process. This is valuable because of the fragility of totalizing systems like neoliberalism. Like all totalitarian doctrines, neoliberalism admits no exceptions. Therefore, it is threatened by any deviation from its dictates. However, unlike fascism and other dictatorial regimes, neoliberalism claims the legitimacy of economic rationality, rather than the divine right of kings or the military power of the man on horseback.

If we demonstrate persuasively with ethnographic detail the economic irrationality of how neoliberal policies work in practice and if we publicize this appropriately, we do put their legitimacy into question. Having identified these cracks in the neoliberal edifice, we ethnographers can follow Clarke, Shear and Zontine, Shore, Wright and Ørberg and conduct 'purposeful ethnography' that clearly documents and reveals the sham economic and administrative rationality of the system. That is necessary and enlightening but clearly still insufficient to promote the needed reforms in higher education.

Shear and Zontine and Lyon-Callo call attention to the dilemmas of analyses that reveal the negative dynamics in these systems, many of which are known to the participants from personal experience but that result in a state of inaction or anomie in the face of what seem to be overwhelming forces. Their identification of negative or inactive responses to critique needs to be emphasized because critical social research on higher education abounds and the neoliberal juggernaut continues to roll on.

At the risk of offering an overly personal view of some steps out of the dilemmas of critical analysis without social action, I would like to suggest we alter the research model in the direction of action research. Action research is research involving professional researchers in collaboration with the relevant stakeholders in a community or organization who together set the problems to be examined, develop preliminary explanations, jointly collect and analyse the data and collaboratively put the results into action. In this case, the relevant stakeholders are not just students (as in many chapters of this book) but also other faculty, administrators, support staff and, in many institutions, public sector and private sector parties affected by the same problems. Rather than having critical research on higher education be the possession of the professional researchers, it becomes a joint project of the stakeholders as in the case of Hyatt's and Shear and Zontine's projects. Operating this way places combined research and teaching at the centre of the reform activity and calls on the knowledge, experience, frustrations and desires of all categories of stakeholders to propose viable improvements in the institutions. This approach has been described in detail in Greenwood (2007; 2012), Greenwood and Levin (2001; 2005; 2007; 2008; 2011) and put into practice in the University of Mondragón (Wright, Greenwood and Boden 2012).

While this might seem an odd step, it actually has a respectable precedent in higher education in the original design of the Humboldtian university where the central principles were the freedom to teach and freedom to learn, and the professors and the students had to negotiate what they were going to do together to meet their mutual needs. While this noble idea seems to have been little practiced, it was a key basis for a broad idea of academic freedom for both faculty and students. Students and faculty as collaborators in institutional reform have a better chance than either on their own and collaborative research and action is both research and pedagogy combined.

But what about administrators? Certainly many administrators would not welcome the development of collaborative stakeholder groups of students and faculty and could easily view this as a threat. But my own experience tells me that there are also many unhappy and frustrated administrators who feel as oppressed by these systems as do students and faculty. And many staff are even more frustrated and worried about their futures. So perhaps a coalition of the willing could emerge under the banner of an action research project to improve the quality and organization of working life for all stakeholders.

Undoubtedly certain faculty and administrators heavily favoured by the current neo-liberal system would do all they could to block such actions. But as Paolo Freire argued years ago, the first job is to liberate the oppressed and the second is to liberate the oppressors as well (Freire 1970). Faced with a broad coalition of stakeholders from all parts of the institution, the power of these individuals, like all authoritarian power turns out to be more limited than it appears.

One thing I have learned in two decades of research on higher education is that a very significant percentage of the faculty, students, staff and administrators are frustrated, feel blocked in their efforts and wish the world were otherwise. If we cannot use what we have already learned about what is wrong with higher education to create the basis for a genuinely collaborative response to these problems, then our analyses are for naught. If we cannot take the minimum steps to recognize one another as legitimate stakeholders all of whose interests matter, then our jeremiads are just so much noise.

All in all, this collection is rich in ethnographic data, multi-dimensional analysis and the practice of the ethnography of hope for the future of higher education. I share this hope but do not think it will be realized until more of us put our shoulders to the purposive wheel of collaborative action research that links research, pedagogy, learning and collaborative organizational redesign to meet the legitimate interests of all stakeholders.

◆

Davydd J. Greenwood is the Goldwin Smith Professor of Anthropology Emeritus (Cornell University, USA). He is a Corresponding Member of the Spanish Royal Academy of Moral and Political His work centers on action research, political economy, ethnic conflict, community and regional development, and neo-liberal reforms of higher education. His ethnographic work has focused on the Spanish Basque Country, Spain's La Mancha region, and higher education institutions. Greenwood is the author/co-author of 9 books and scores of articles. Since the early 1980's he has focused on the relationships between action research and higher education reform, publishing extensively on this subject. He currently participates in an international network to create democratically-organized public universities. He is the co-author with Morten Levin of the book, Creating a New Public University and Reviving Democracy: Action Research in Higher Education (Berghahn, 2016)

References

Boden, Rebecca and Wright, Susan (2010) *Follow the Money: An interim report on Danish University funding prepared for Dansk Magisterforening*, Copenhagen, < http://www.dm.dk/OmDM/Medlemskab/Publikationer/ ~ /media/DM_dok umenter/Rapporter/FollowTheMoney.ashx > (accessed on 14 November 2014).

Brown, Ellen (2012) *The Web of Debt; The Shocking Truth about Our Money System and How We Can Break Free.* 5th ed. rev. Baton Rouge, LA: Third Millennium Press.

Freire, Paolo (1970) *Pedagogy of the Oppressed,* (trans.) Donaldo Macedo. New York: Continuum.

Furner, Mary (1975) *From Advocacy to Objectivity.* Lexington: University of Kentucky Press.

Ginsburg, Benjamin (2011) *The Fall of the Faculty: The Rise of the All Administrative University and Why It Matters.* Oxford: Oxford University Press.

Graeber, David (2011) *Debt: The First 5000 Years.* Brooklyn, NY: Melville House.

Greenwood, Davydd (2007) 'Teaching/Learning Action Research Requires Fundamental Reforms in Public Higher Education' in Morten Levin and Ann Martin (eds), The Praxis of Education Action Researchers, theme issue, *Action Research* 5: 249–264.

Greenwood, Davydd (2012) 'Doing and Learning Action Research in the Neo-liberal World of Contemporary Higher Education' *Action Research* 10 (2): 115–132.

Greenwood, Davydd (2013) 'Organizational Anthropology: An Analysis of American Anthropology and the Organization of Higher Education in the United

States' in D. Douglas Caulkins and Ann Jordan (eds), *A Companion to Organizational Anthropology*. Chichester: Wiley-Blackwell, pp. 27–55.

Greenwood, Davydd and Levin, Morten (2001) 'Pragmatic Action Research and the Struggle to Transform Universities into Learning Communities' in Peter Reason and Hilary Bradbury (eds) *Handbook of Action Research*, London: Sage Publications, pp. 103–113.

Greenwood, Davydd and Levin, Morten (2005) 'Reform of the Social Sciences, and of Universities Through Action Research' in Norman Denzin and Yvonna Lincoln (eds) *Handbook of Qualitative Research*, 3rd ed. Thousand Oaks: Sage Publications, 43–64.

Greenwood, Davydd and Levin, Morten (2007) 'The Future of Universities: Action Research and the Transformation of Higher Education' in Peter Reason and Hilary Bradbury (eds) *Handbook of Action Research*. 2nd ed. Los Angeles: Sage Publications, 211–226.

Greenwood, Davydd and Levin, Morten (2008) 'The Reformed Social Sciences to Reform the University: Mission Impossible?' *Learning and Teaching: International Journal of Higher Education in the Social Sciences* 1(1): 89–112.

Greenwood, Davydd and Levin, Morten (2011) 'Revitalizing Universities by Reinventing the Social Sciences' in Norman Denzin and Yvonna Lincoln (eds) *Handbook of Qualitative Inquiry*, 4th ed. Thousand Oaks, CA: Sage Publications, 27–42.

Kirn, Walter (2009) *Lost in the Meritocracy: The Overeducation of an Underachiever.* New York: Doubleday.

Madoo Lengermann, Patricia and Niebrugge-Brantley, Jill (1998) *The Women Founders.* Boston, MA: McGraw-Hill.

McMahon, Walter (2009) *Higher Learning, Greater Good: The Private and Social Benefits of Higher Education.* Baltimore, MD: Johns Hopkins.

Newfield, Christopher (2004) *Ivy and Industry: Business and the Making of the American University, 1880-1980.* Durham, NC: Duke University Press.

Ross, Dorothy (1991) *The Origin of American Social Science.* Cambridge: Cambridge University Press.

Samuels, Robert (2013) *Why Public Higher Education Should Be Free. How to Decrease the Cost and Improve the Quality at American Universities.* New Brunswick, NJ: Rutgers University Press.

Shore, Cris and Wright, Susan (eds) (1997) *Anthropology of Policy: Critical Perspectives on Governance and Power.* EASA Series, London: Routledge.

Shore, Cris, Wright, Susan and Peró, Davide (eds) (2011) *Policy Worlds: Anthropology and the Anatomy of Contemporary Power.* EASA Series. Oxford: Berghahn Books.

Tuchman, Gaye (2011) *Wannabe U: Inside the Corporate University.* Chicago: University of Chicago Press.

Wright, Susan and Ørberg, Jakob Williams (2009) 'Prometheus (on the) Rebound? Freedom and the Danish Steering System' in Jeroen Huisman (ed.) *International Perspectives on the Governance of Higher Education,* London: Routledge, 69–87.

Index